THE PHARMACEUTICAL INDUSTRY: ACCESS AND OUTLOOK

THE PHARMACEUTICAL INDUSTRY: ACCESS AND OUTLOOK

ETHAN N. PARVIS (EDITOR)

Nova Science Publishers, Inc.
New York

Senior Editors: Susan Boriotti and Donna Dennis
Coordinating Editor: Tatiana Shohov
Office Manager: Annette Hellinger
Graphics: Wanda Serrano
Editorial Production: Jennifer Vogt, Matthew Kozlowski,
Jonathan Rose and Maya Columbus
Circulation: Ave Maria Gonzalez, Indah Becker, Raymond Davis,
Vladimir Klestov and Jonathan Roque
Communications and Acquisitions: Serge P. Shohov
Marketing: Cathy DeGregory

Library of Congress Cataloging-in-Publication Data

The pharmaceutical industry: access and outlook / [edited by] Ethan N. Parvis.
p.cm.
Includes index.
ISBN 1-59033-199-0.
1. Pharmaceutical industry—United States. 2. Pharmaceutical industry—Government policy—United States. 3. Drugs—United States—Marketing. I. Parvis, Ethan N.

RS192 .P462 2002
615'.19'0973—dc21

2001059624

227 Main Street, Suite 100
Huntington, New York 11743
Tele. 631-424-NOVA (6682) Fax 631-425-5933
E Mail: Novascience@earthlink.net
www.novapublishers.com

Printed in the United States of America

CONTENTS

PREFACE

Politicians consistently wage high-profile battles over prescription drugs and the companies that make them. The dilemma is balancing the pharmaceutical industry's need to make a profit with the public's need for affordable medical care. This book presents analyses of the federal government's regulation of the drug industry and the arguments over the prices of prescription drugs.

Chapter 1

DRUG REGULATION: HISTORICAL OVERVIEW AND CURRENT REFORM PROPOSALS

Blanchard Randall

This report is a brief review of the events and legislation that led to the current standards for drug approval in the United States. Offered within a historical context, the report describes the evolution of current standards of drug safety and efficacy and the fundamental principles that have governed the Food and Drug Administration's (FDA) regulatory policy for almost three decades. The agency's current mechanism for approving new drugs is discussed along with a brief description of recent regulatory actions implemented to expedite access to new treatments for serious and life-threatening diseases. Recent FDA policy changes concerning drug testing for women and children are addressed as well as an update on the Prescription Drug User Fee Act passed by Congress in 1992. In the context of the 104th Congress, the report concludes with an overview of some of the recent proposals made to change FDA's regulatory policies regarding the drug approval process.

BRIEF REGULATORY HISTORY

The regulation of medicinals and therapeutic remedies in the United States has evolved slowly since colonial times. Even though early drug manufacturing and distribution were relatively unsophisticated, they were regulated, nonetheless, through a patchwork of State and local laws enacted primarily to establish standards of weight and measure and to govern domestic commerce and export transactions. Primarily derived or concocted from natural substances, medications were reconstituted, packaged, and sold to the general public through apothecaries and physicians, or in some cases, the "infamous" patent medicine salesmen.

Accounts of drug marketing practices during the 18th and 19th centuries are rife with descriptions of "cure-alls" being offered with little or no concern for product quality or labeling accuracy. Lacking regulatory standards, makers of so-called "patent drugs" marketed them with impunity until the public, having grown suspicious of fraudulent claims and product purity, eventually persuaded Congress to enact the Pure Food and Drugs Act of 1906.[1]

The 1906 Act's passage established the first comprehensive federal law prohibiting the introduction of adulterated and misbranded drugs (and foods) into interstate commerce and gave Federal officials the authority to take actions against violative products.[2] The 1906 Act, however, contained no provisions for any sort of pre-market approval before a drug could be offered for sale.

Although the new law had a positive effect on drug content and labeling disclosure, reformers quickly voiced their concern about deficiencies they felt existed under the 1906 act. Although content disclosure improved, there was still growing concern that the legislation had little or not impact on the level of fraudulent promotional claims that continued unabated in commercial advertising. For all practical purposes, most consumers were unaware that drug sellers' myriad health claims were still supported by very little scientifically derived evidence.

Despite attempts to amend the 1906 Act, it was not until the early 1930s that public concern about food and drug reform was sufficient to sustain renewed congressional interest. Unfortunately, the tragic 1937 "elixir of sulfanilamide" incident became the catalyst for enacting the next major food and drug law. More than a hundred patients died from consuming a product they thought was simply a reformulated antibiotic.[3] In response, Congress quickly passed the Federal Food, Drug and Cosmetic Act of 1938 (FDCA).[4] Among other provisions, the 1938 Act required for the first time that drugs be tested for safety before they could be sold.[5] It also required drug packages to be labeled with adequate warnings and directions for use by the lay public. Drugs available only by a physician's prescription were exempt from this requirement that they be labeled with "adequate directions for use."

During the next three decades, Congress adopted several amendments related to drugs to the 1938 legislation that had a significant impact on the current system for approving and marketing new products. One amendment was necessitated by an incongruity of the 1938 drug law, which unintentionally had blurred the distinction between drugs needed a physician's prescription and those that did not. The Durham-Humphrey Amendment of 1951[6] resolved this ambiguity by separating drugs into two different categories: prescription and nonprescription.

During the late 1950s and early 1960s, another tragic drug-related event captured worldwide attention. The drug "thalidomide" rapidly became a household word as the public became aware of the thousands of birth defects occurring in infants born to women who had

[1] Pub. L. 384, 34 Stat. 768 (1906).

[2] Food and drug regulator functions, including investigations, product quality testing and seizures, have been conducted by different government agencies since the late 1870s. Initial efforts were carried out by the Division of Chemistry, U.S. Dept. of Agriculture (USDA). This Division became the Bureau of Chemistry in the late 1880s and was then reorganized in 1927 to form the Food, Drug, and Insecticide Administration. The agency's name was changed to the Food and Drug Administration in 1931, and its functions later transferred from USDA to the Federal Security Agency (FSA) in 1940. FSA evolved into the U.S. Department of Health, Education, and Welfare in 1953, which, in turn, became the U.S. Department of Health and Human Services (DHHS) in 1980.

[3] The "elixir of sulfanilamide" incident occurred when a chemist attempted to create a liquid dose of the antibiotic sulfanilamide. Needing a solvent to suspend the drug in solution, the chemist chose diethylene glycol because of its appearance, flavor and fragrance. Although it had never been tested in humans, it later was learned that diethylene glycol caused kidney failure.

[4] Pub. L. No. 717, 52 Stat. 1040 (1938).

[5] The 1938 Act essentially repealed the Act of 1906.

used the drug during their pregnancies to alleviate morning sickness.[7] Though thalidomide never was approved in the United States,[8] the incident became one of the major events that precipitated enactment of the 1962 Kefauver-Harris Amendments.[9] The new measures further tightened the safety requirements for testing new prescription drugs, and added the requirement that manufacturers provide evidence that their products were effective – as well as safe – before FDA would grant approval.

DRUG SAFETY AND EFFICACY STANDARDS

The statutory requirement of the Federal Food, Drug, and Cosmetic Act (FDCA) that drugs be proven "safe" and "effective" before they are marketed has not changed since 1962. The following excerpts from FDCA emphasize Congress' intention of requiring drug companies to provide evidence that their products are safe, effective, and properly labeled. Section 201(g)(1) of the Act defines a "drug" as follows:

> (A) articles recognized in the official United States Pharmacopoeia, official Homeopathic Pharmacopoeia, of official National Formulary, or any supplement to any of them; and (B) articles intended for the use in diagnosis, cure, mitigation, treatment, or prevention of disease in man or other animals; and (C) articles (other than food) intended to affect the structure or any function of the body of man or other animals; and (D) articles intended for use as a component of any articles specified in clause (A), (B), or (C).

Congress never specified in FDCA the definition of a "safe" drug, nor for that matter, for FDA should determine that a drug's safety has been sufficiently established.[10] Section 505(d) of the Act, however, specifies that the Secretary of DHHS shall not approve a new drug unless a manufacturer's evidence of safety has been suitably demonstrated by:

> . . . adequate tests by all methods reasonable applicable to show whether or not such a drug is safe for use under the conditions prescribed, recommended, or suggested in the proposed labeling thereof.

To satisfy "effectiveness" standards, Section 505(d) also states that FDA shall not approve a new drug if, based on clinical evidence submitted to the agency there is:

> . . . a lack of substantial evidence that the drug will have the effect it purports or is represented to have under the conditions of use prescribed, recommended, or suggested in the proposed labeling thereof.

---

[6] Pub. L. NO. 82-215, 65 Stat. 648 (1951).

[7] Grigg, William. The Thalidomide Tragedy – 25 Years Ago. FDA Consumer, v. 21, no. 1, Feb. 1987, p. 17.

[8] Thalidomide had been supplied by the manufacturer to some U. S. doctors to conduct clinical trials. The drug had been approved in some foreign countries and small amounts were brought into the United States by some patients who obtained it abroad. An application to market the product in the United States was under review by the FDA, but the agency never granted final approval.

[9] Pub. L. No. 87-781, 76 Stat. 780 (1962).

[10] Hutt, Peter Barton and Richard A. Merrill. Food and Drug Law. Cases and Materials. 2d Ed. Westbury, New York, The Foundation Press, Inc., 1991, p. 622.

Safety and effectiveness must be confirmed by "substantial evidence" derived from well-controlled clinical trials. Section 505(d) of the FDCA defines "substantial evidence" as evidence . . .

> . . . consisting of adequate and well-controlled investigations, including clinical investigations, by experts qualified by scientific training and experience to evaluate the effectiveness of the drug involved, on the basis of which it could fairly and reasonably be concluded by such experts that the drug will have the effect it purports or is represented to have under the conditions of use prescribed, recommended, or suggested in the labeling or proposed labeling thereof.

DRUG LABELING AND PROMOTION

Among the earliest efforts to achieve integrity in drug marketing to American consumers were laws requiring that product labeling be truthful and not misleading. Since 1962, FDA has promulgated regulations extending the FDCA's prohibition against false and misleading labeling to cover advertising and other promotional materials.[11] The following segments from FDCA characterize some of the working principles on which drug labeling is based. This section does not include all of the Act's references to drug labeling, nor does it attempt to explain their legal subtleties.[12, 13]

Section 201(k) of the Act states in part that . . . "the term 'label' means a display of written, printed, or graphic matter upon the immediate containing of any article . . ."

Section 201(m) more specifically declares that . . . "the term "labeling" means all labels and other written, printed, or graphic matter (1) upon any article or any of its containers or wrappers, or (2) accompanying such article."

Section 502(a) of the Act provides that a drug . . . "shall be deemed to be misbranded – (a) If its labeling is false or misleading in any particular."

Section 502(f) states that a drug will be misbranded . . . "unless its labeling bears (1) adequate directions for use; and (2) such adequate warnings against use in those pathological conditions or by children where its use may be dangerous to health or against unsafe dosage or by methods or duration of administration or application, in such manner and form, as are necessary for the protection of users . . ."

Congress gave FDA authority to regulate prescription drug advertising in 1962. From the agency's perspective, product advertising and labeling are virtually the same. A drug company only can promote those therapeutic uses that have been approved, and are accurately represented on the product's label. In other words, it may not promote so-call "off-label" uses until they have been approved by the agency.[14] FDA states that it does not have the authority

---

[11] Kessler, David A., and Wayne L. Pines. The Federal Regulation of Prescription Drug Advertising and Promotion. *Journal of the American Medical Association*, v. 264, no. 18, Nov. 14, 1990. P. 2409.

[12] For example, both prescription and over-the-counter (OTC) drugs must be labeled in a manner that is not false or misleading. However, form a regulatory perspective, each category must comply with its own, substantially different, labeling requirements. OTC labeling is designed and worded to be understood by consumers while prescription labeling is targeted to physicians.

[13] See also 21 C.F>R. 202 (1994). Prescription Drug Advertising.

[14] "Off-label" is the term often used to describe the practice of using or promotion a drug for a medical treatment not indicated or addressed in the product's official FDA approved labeling. It is not illegal for physicians to prescribe or use a drug for off-label purposes. However, because the safety and efficacy of such uses often is

to require pre-clearance of pharmaceutical advertising, but the agency can take legal action if a drug company makes unsubstantiated (i.e., false and misleading) therapeutic claims for its product.[15]

In 1990, FDA Commissioner David Kessler stated that, "[A] fundamental provision of the Act is that drug labeling not be false or misleading in any particular or fail to reveal any material fact."[16] This dictum is significant from two perspectives. First, accurate and truthful labeling allows consumers to make informed choices. Secondly, labeling standards provide FDA with a regulatory instrument to enforce the "misbranding" provisions of the Act.

For some time, drug manufacturers have argued that they should be permitted to use a variety of communication methods to convey medical information about newly discovered therapeutic benefits of already FDA-approved products, even if those uses have not yet been validated through conventional clinical trials. FDA and some consumer groups maintain that the public interest is not well-served by allowing companies to use subtle methods to "promote" uses that either are not included in a product's approved labeling, or are of unproven safety and effectiveness. The drug industry counter argues that the dissemination of new medical information "outpaces" efforts to file new labeling changes with the FDA. The industry also claims that the agency's regulatory action against certain promotional activities infringes upon free speech.

Since 1992, FDA has been seeking to formulate a policy compromise that would establish conditions under which the dissemination of educational and scientific information might be acceptable without causing them to be regulated as advertising or promotional activities. On December 6, 1995, FDA published draft guidelines that would permit companies to disseminate, under certain circumstances, reprints of peer-reviewed journal articles that describe uses that are inconsistent with the product's FDA-approved labeling.[17] In addition, the draft guidelines would permit manufacturers to distribute independently produced textbooks that contain information on unapproved uses if the text does not focus on a company's specific product.

DRUG DEVELOPMENT: PRECLINICAL TESTING

The development of a new drug usually beings in the pharmaceutical company's laboratory where scientists initially seek to determine how a new compound might be used to prevent, treat, or conceivably cure a disease or medical condition. An understanding of the disease's cause or process is important because it enables researchers to pursue steps in the process (e.g., cellular or molecular abnormalities associated with the disease) with which the new chemical may be able to interfere. When a compound is found to be promising, the manufacturer files a patent application, an important early step in an intensely competitive industry. At this point the chemical already is being evaluated in a variety of testing modes

unsubstantiated, health agencies (including FDA) usually consider such use to be experimental. "Extra-label" is a phrase sometimes used to express the same concept.

[15] Kessler, David A., et. Al. Therapeutic-Class Wars – Drug Promotion in a Competitive Marketplace. *The New England Journal of Medicine*, v. 331, Nov. 17, 1994, p. 1350.

[16] Kessler and Pines. The Federal Regulation of Prescription Drug Advertising and Promotion. p. 2410.

[17] U.S. Dept. of Health and Human Services. Advertising and Promotion; Draft Guidelines. Federal Register, v. 60, no. 234, Dec. 6, 1995, p. 62471.

including test tubes, culture cells, and appropriate animal models, as information and data are gathered about its effect and impact on disease.

Federal law and regulations require careful drug testing in laboratory animals – referred to as "preclinical" evaluations – before FDA will permit human "clinical" trials to begin. Such studies provide basic information about how a drug is metabolized, its toxicity, and in some instances, possible dosage levels. The drug's effect in the animal model is examined in detail, including the amount of the drug that is absorbed into the bloodstream and the what at which it is metabolized (broken down) and eventually eliminated or excreted. The drug also is evaluated for its carcinogenic, mutagenic, and its teratogenic (abnormal fetal development) potential.

At this stage, the majority of compounds studied are not found worthy of further investigation. For those that do warrant further research, the results of laboratory and animal studies help define a detailed plan for eventual testing in humans. Before human testing can begin, a drug's sponsor must file an Investigational New Drug (IND) application with the FDA.[18] In filing an IND, the manufacturer submits its animal data, explains the drug's intended purpose, and provides a full description of the clinical trial protocols intended to further demonstrate the drug's safety and effectiveness. The number of patients, route of drug administration (whether oral or intravenous), and doing levels in the proposed trials must be included in the application. The names and qualifications of the clinical investigators, site of the studies, and chemical and manufacturing information also are provided. If after 30 days FDA has no objection to the protocol, testing can begin.

Sponsors of the drug arrange with physicians and hospitals to conduct the studies. Institutions conducting clinical trials must have Institutional Review Boards (IRBs) made up of a minimum of five individuals with varying backgrounds (e.g., medical ethicists, clergy, and physicians) that evaluate the ethical aspects of the proposed studies. Before the trial begins, IRB members must assure that informed consent obtained from study participants complies with requirements in the protection of Human Subjects regulations.[19]

DRUG DEVELOPMENT: CLINICAL TRIALS

Clinical trials usually are conducted in three phases. Phase I studies are directed at determining the drug's safety and metabolism in humans. In this phase, the drug is administered to fewer than 100 healthy volunteers, usually around 50. Information that can be used in establishing a dosing regimen is obtained; that is, the amount of the drug and frequency of administration to the patient. Phase I trials ascertain whether a drug presents safety problems that might make further testing impossible. If no serious complications arise, the drug goes on to phase II.

Most, but not all, phase II trials are randomized, controlled studies in which a group of patients receiving the drug, a "treatment group," is matched with a "control group" that is similar in age, sex, and disease characteristics. The control group may receive a placebo rather than the drug being tested. Phase II trials are designed to provide information about the

---

[18] In FDA/drug industry parlance the acronym IND refers to Investigational New Drug application. IND denotes the drug testing phase and drug manufacturers or sponsors must have a valid IND before they can begin clinical (human) testing.

[19] 45 C.F.R. 46.

drug's safety at therapeutic levels and to determine its effectiveness. A number of different kinds of controls may be used, depending on the study design chosen, knowledge of the illness or condition to be treated, and available alternative courses of therapy. Phase II studies frequently involve from 50 to 200 patients.

Phase II studies may include both controlled and uncontrolled trials, involving as many as several thousand patients. These studies are intended to gather additional information on safety and effectiveness that it needed to determine the overall benefit-to-risk ratio of the drug and provide the basis for physician labeling, including information on side effects, patients who should not use the drug, and possible drug interactions.

If Phase III studies demonstrate that the drug is effective at levels that do not pose unreasonable risks, the drug sponsor (manufacturer) files a New Drug Application (NDA) with FDA seeking approval to market the drug. The NDA must contain all the information – or data – the sponsor has gathered throughout the entire testing process. Numerous volumes will be submitted including information about the chemical structure of the drug, animal, and laboratory studies, as well as the results of all human testing.[20] Copes of the drug's labeling content are a significant component of an NDA that must be reviewed and approved by the agency. Manufacturers also are required to provide production details and samples of the finished product. For every 20 drugs tested in clinical trials, only one or two survive all three phases of testing; of those, around 75 percent eventually are approved for marketing by FDA.

FDA Amends Drug Testing Policy for Women and Children

Recently, there has been growing interest in allowing – and even encouraging – drug testing in patient population that have, for the most part, been neglected in the past, especially women and children. Historically, children have not been used in trials until the drug has been tested in adults. Today, it is argued that without pediatric studies, drug labels cannot provide professional guidance about dosage and side effects or the appropriate circumstances under which children should (or should not) be administered a given drug. In 1994, FDA issued a final rule specifying content and format labeling governing prescription drugs for pediatric use.[21] The new regulation encourage drug manufacturers to develop pediatric information through clinical trials or allow them to extrapolate findings from adult studies.

In 1993, FDA issued guidelines strongly urging drug companies to consider gender differences when selecting patient groups to conduct clinical trials.[22] The guidelines encourage manufacturers to be aware of factors such as menstrual cycles, menopause, and the concomitant use of hormonal drug products that can affect drug behavior. This new directive superseded previous FDA policy that excluded women of childbearing potential from

[20] Much of the voluminous information presented to FDA in support of a New Drug Application now is submitted via the agency's Computer-Assisted Drug Application System (CANDA). This system gives drug reviewers quick access to the raw clinical data contained in the application.

[21] U.S. Dept. of Health and Human Services. Specific Requirements on Content and Format of Labeling for Human Prescription Drugs; Revision of "Pediatric Use" Subsection in the Labeling. Federal Register, v. 59, no. 238, Dec. 13, 1994. p. 64240.

[22] U.S. Dept. of Health and Human Services. Guidelines for the Study and Evaluation of Gender Differences in the Clinical Evaluation of Drugs. Federal Register, v. 58, no. 139, July 22, 1993. p. 39406.

participating in most clinical trials. The agency's position is that institutional review boards and women participants themselves should decide whether participation is appropriate.[23]

Food and Drug Administration Review

Although a new drug's review begins when the manufacturer submits an IND, the actual review for marketing approval commences with filing of the product's NDA.[24] Depending on the NDA's size and complexity, FDA reviewers may take months or years to evaluate every aspect of the application, analyzing the clinical trial data, reviewing the drug's pharmacology, and examining how the finished product is manufactured and processed. FDA also will perform laboratory analysis on samples of the drug and review the finished product's labeling to determine whether it factually states what is medically known about the drug and accurately reflects the manufacturer's intended therapeutic claims.

During the course of the review, FDA officials may meet with the manufacturer to discuss any possible deficiencies in the application. If the agency has serious questions concerning a new drug's safety and /or efficacy data, it may insist that the manufacturer conduct additional studies or analysis. Even questions involving minor discrepancies must be resolved to FDA's satisfaction before final approval is granted. By law, FDA has 180 days either to approve or to disapprove a company's NDA.[25] If the review cannot be concluded in this period of time, it can be extended with mutual consent.

At the end of the review process, FDA writes the manufacturer to say that the drug is approved for marketing, is approvable if some last-minute changes are made, or is not approvable because of some unresolvable problem. In the latter situation, the sponsor can withdraw its application or request a hearing.

In today's regulatory environment, however, satisfying these requirements is a formidable undertaking. Drug manufacturers invest years and hundreds of millions of dollars to evaluate new compounds, and shepherd them through the regulatory system. Throughout the testing process, manufacturers know that assessing a drug's safety and efficacy can be rather subjective and the results open to different interpretations. During the early phases of testing, a compound may produce few side effects and appear relatively effective. However, as testing proceeds under fairly strict "controlled-randomized-blinded" clinical conditions, the drug may demonstrate little or no therapeutic effect and/or have serious side effects.[26] In other

---

[23] U.S. Library of Congress. Congressional Research Service. Women's Health Research. Report No. 94-495, by Irene Stith-Coleman and Judith A. Johnson. Washington, 1994. p. 10.

[24] NDA refers to New Drug Application. Drug manufacturers must have an FDA-approved NDA in order to market a drug in the United States. Section 5050(a) of the Food, Drug, and Cosmetics Act states that "no person shall introduce or deliver for introduction into interstate commerce any new drug, unless an approval of an application filed pursuant to subjection (b) is effective with respect to such drug." Subsection (b) refers to the NDA and the investigative reports it must contain.

[25] Sec. 505(j)(4)(A) of the Federal Food, Drug, and Cosmetic Act requires that FDA act on a new drug application (NDA) within 180 days – or seek a time extension by mutual consent. Few drugs, if any ever are approved within six months.

[26] The term "controlled-randomized" refers to clinical trials in which a group of patients receiving the drug, a "treatment group," is matched with a "control group" with similar age, sex, and disease state characteristics. The control group does not receive the drug being tested. "Blinded" means that neither the principal investigator nor the patients know which group actually is receiving the drug being tested.

words, in preliminary testing, a drug may look relatively effective in a percentage of the patients, yet in expanded trials may prove to be so toxic that it presents an unacceptable risk.

As an endnote, it should be reiterated that FDA's review process places emphasis on a drug's benefit-to-risk ration. No drug is absolutely safe, and every product can have undesirable side effects. The criteria necessary to meet safety and effectiveness requirements are not identical for every product. Society probably is willing to accept greater risks for drugs that treat life-threatening conditions or for which there is no other alternative therapy available.

FDA Intiative to Expedite Drug Approval

To respond to charges that its regulations and drug testing requirements were excessive and stifled innovation, FDA began planning a series of initiative sin the early 1980s to improve agency efficiency and effectuate regulatory reform of the drug approval process.[27] These efforts culminated in a rulemaking referred to as the IND/NDA Rewrite. The first phase – referred to as the NDA Rewrite[28] – was completed in 1985; the second phase – the IND Rewrite[29] – was completed two years later. Among the goals of the IND/NDA Rewrite was to foster better planning and improved communication between FDA and pharmaceutical companies in an effort to reduce some of the more confrontational issues involved in the overall approval process.

In brief, this rulemaking intensified pre- and post-marketing adverse drug reporting; allowed the submission of pharmacological and statistical data summaries; and, for the first time, allowed drug makers to file new drug applications who safety and efficacy data were derived from studies outside the United States. These revisions were noteworthy from the standpoint that they signaled FDA's willingness to work more closely with the pharmaceutical industry, and established a framework upon which the agency could introduce further changes affecting drug regulatory policy.

By the late 1980s as the AIDS crisis escalated, AIDS activists charged FDA with what they saw as exemplifying government apathy toward people suffering from life-threatening diseases. They also accused the agency of being uncompromising in not allowing terminally ill patients access to unapproved therapies that they believed at least could improve their quality of life and chances for survival.

FDA argued that such criticisms were unjustified because most of the treatments AIDS activists claimed were beneficial had not yet been subjected to scientific evaluation of their safety and effectiveness. They agency further pointed out that under its existent "compassionate IND" program[30] patients have been allowed access to unapproved,

---

[27] The IND/DNA Rewrite proposal emerged from the collective efforts of the following: recommendations from the congressionally sponsored Commission on the Federal Drug Approval Process, the mandate of President Reagan's executive Order 12291, which directed all Federal agencies to scrutinize their existing regulations, the President's Task Force on Regulatory Relief, and the [FDA] Commissioner's Task Force for the Review and Improvement of the Drug Approval Process.

[28] U.S. Dept. of Health and Human Services. New Drug and Antibiotic Regulations. Federal Register, v. 50, no. 36, Feb. 22, 1985. p. 7452.

[29] U.S. Dept. of Health and Human Services. New Drug and Antibiotic Regulations. Federal Register, v. 52, no. 53, Mar. 19, 1987. p. 8798.

[30] Even before "Compassionate IND's" were codified, FDA maintains that it always had a policy of allowing investigational new drugs to be used in emergency life-threatening situations.

investigational therapies on a provisional basis. FDA also has permitted cancer patients access to experimental therapies under a program administered in cooperation with the National Cancer Institute of the National Institutes of Health.

Influenced by political and social pressures, FDA changed its regulations in 1987 to allow promising investigational new drugs be made available to treat desperately ill persons with AIDS and other immediately life-threatening diseases.[31] The agency, through the rulemaking process, was able to transform its informal "compassionate IND" policy into a codified set of "treatment IND" rules to enhance patients' access to experimental drugs. Despite FDA's efforts to make it easier to gain access to experimental drugs. Despite FDA's efforts to make it easier to gain access to experimental therapies, AIDS activists remained skeptical of the new policy changes, and characterized the agency's "compassionate use" policy as being of little value in serving the needs of most AIDS patients.[32]

In 1988, FDA responded to recommendations of a taskforce on regulatory relief by issuing interim regulatory procedures to expedite the development, evaluation, and marketing of new therapies to treat life-threatening and severely debilitating illnesses.[33] In effect, these interim rules and procedures were established to cover the breadth of the entire U.S. drug development and approval process from preclinical trials to postmarketing surveillance.

In April 1992, the Public Health Service published its final policy statement making promising investigational drugs for AIDS and other HIV-related diseases more widely available under what became known as a "parallel track" mechanism.[34] This strategy was directed at making investigational drugs available for treatment purposes at the same time that their clinical trials are being conducted. Later that same year, FDA issued "accelerated approval" regulations explicating the agency's intention to speed the approval process for certain new drugs and biological products for serious or life-threatening illnesses.[35] The new rules not only created a "fast track" for approving AIDS drugs, but also established that when a drug's approval is based on so-called "surrogate endpoints,"[36] the manufacturer will be required to conduct additional clinical studies necessary to verify any unresolved questions concerning the drug's clinical benefit.

Though it appears that most of the policy changes to accelerate the approval process have resulted in beneficial gains for both consumers and drug makers, the modifications have had inevitable drawbacks. Certain AIDS advocacy groups, who five years ago ardently protested

---

[31] U.S. Dept. of Health and Human Services. Food and Drug Administration. Investigational New Drug, Antibiotic, and Biological Drug Product Regulations; Treatment Use and Sale. Federal Register, v. 52, no. 99, May 22, 1987. p. 19466.

[32] Kolata, Gina. The Philosophy of the New FDA Is mostly a Matter of Packaging. New York Times – Sunday, May 19, 1992. Sect. 4, p. 4.

[33] U.S. Dept. of Health and Human Services. Food and Drug Admin. Investigational New Drug Antibiotic and Biological Drug Product Regulations; Procedures for Drugs Intended to Treat Life-Threatening and Severely Debilitating Illness, Interim Rule. Federal Register, v. 53, no. 204, Oct. 21, 1988. p. 41516.

[34] U.S. Dept. of Health and Human Services. Expanded Availability of Investigational New Drugs Through a Parallel Track Mechanism for People with AIDS and Other HIV-Related Diseases; Notice Final Policy Statement. Federal Register, v. 57, no. 239, Dec. 11, 1992. p. 58942.

[35] U.S. Dept. of Health and Human Services. New Drug, Antibiotic, and Biological Drug Product Regulations; Accelerated Approval; Final Rule. Federal Register, v. 57, no. 239, Dec. 11, 1992. p. 58942.

[36] In the "accelerated approval" rule (Federal Register, Apr. 15, 1992, p. 13235), FDA defined "surrogate endpoint" as a "laboratory measurement or physical sign that is used in therapeutic trials as a substitute for a clinically meaningful endpoint that is a direct measure of how a patient feels, functions, or survives and that is expected to predict the effect of the same therapy." The agency used elevated cholesterol and hypertension as two examples of surrogate endpoints because of their relationship as risk factors for coronary and cerebral artery disease.

against FDA's slow and deliberate review process, recently have challenged the wisdom of speeding up the regulatory system if that action unwittingly results in the approval of toxic or ineffective treatments. Some health care community professionals have questioned whether FDA may have gone too far in lowering its approval criteria, and is ignoring its own mandate of requiring makers of "fast tracked" drugs to conduct postmarketing safety and efficacy studies.[37]

Evaluating the benefits derived from these reform measures can be problematic when FDA and the pharmaceutical industry emphasize different statistical outcomes in assessing improvement or decline. For example, in 1995 the agency announced that it had approved 85 new drug and licensed biological products during the previous year.[38] The median review time for the 62 new drug approvals and the 23 approved vaccines and biological products was 19 and 12.2 months, respectively. Of the approved drugs and biologics, 22 were new molecular entities (NMEs) or products containing an active substance that had never before been marketed in the United States.

FDA reported median drug approval time as follows: a 21 percent shorter review time for 62 new drug approvals; 12.2 months in 1994 versus 23.4 months in 1993 for vaccines and other biological products; and 17.5 months in 1994 versus 23 months the year before for 22 NMEs. FDA also claimed it had been made "significant reductions" in the 1994 approval times for drugs and biologics.

In contrast, the Pharmaceutical Research and Manufacturers of America (PhRMA) disregarded FDA's approval time reductions, and instead emphasized that the agency had approved fewer pharmaceutical products during that same time period.[39] Such contrasting portrayals are not unusual, but it is important to note that these data represent changes measured during a single year, and a fuller evaluation of regulatory improvements necessarily requires longer-term results.

CONGRESS ENACTS PRESCRIPTION DRUG USER-FEES

In an effort to enhance FDA's drug review capabilities, Congress enacted the Prescription Drug User Fee Act (PDUFA) in 1992.[40] The Act established a mechanism that allowed FDA to assess drug companies "user fees." The fees are to offset some of the regulatory costs associated with drug application review and product registrations. The idea is not entirely new. For decades, FDA has charged user fees for color additive and insulin certifications.[41]

The concept of charging drug manufacturers fees to have their applications reviewed actually dates back to the Reagan Administration, which included budgetary requests for drug user fees in its annual budget proposals to Congress. Throughout the 1980s, drug makers and the majority in Congress opposed the idea based on their concern that the Administration would substitute revenue gained from user fees for full FDA appropriations. In addition,

[37] Brown, David. Speedy Release of AIDS Drugs Challenged on Lack of Follow-Through. Washington Post, Sept. 11, 1994. p. A1.

[38] U.S. Dept. of health and Human Services. FDA's 1994 Medication Approvals. Food and Drug Admin. Talk Paper. T95-2, Jan. 17, 1995. 4 p.

[39] Pharmaceutical Research and Manufacturers of America. FDA Approves Fewer Pharmaceutical Products in 1994 With Approval of 22 New Drugs and One Biotech Medicine. Jan. 1995. 10 p.

[40] Public Law 102-571.

[41] Henkel, John. User Fees to Fund Faster Reviews. FDA Consumer Special Report, 2d. ed., Jan. 1995. p. 51.

Congress never supported the user fees proposal claiming that the Administration wanted to use them to offset a growing national budget deficit. In 1992, a compromise was reached – the PDUFA – that requires that user fee revenues be dedicated to hiring additional FDA reviewers and speeding the drug approval process.

FDA dedicates all the collected funds to activities aimed at accelerating the drug approval process (e.g., hiring additional drug reviewers). In addition, Congress broadened the agency's authority to collect user fees by enacting the Mammography Quality Standard Act (MQSA) in 1992.[42] This Act allows the agency to collect additional user fees to cover the cost of inspecting mammography facilities, and for certifying technicians and equipment. In FY 1996 FDA expects to raise an additional $6.5 million from MQSA user fees.

Congress appropriates funds annually for the administration of the drug user-fee program. To continue its implementation and hire additional review personnel, FDA's total FY 1996 user fee request for the biologics and human drugs programs is $84.7 million. The FY 1996 House concurrent budget resolution proposes increasing the level of fees charged by FDA on a number of products it regulates, and recommends raising drug user fees 40 percent.[43] The Senate FY 1996 concurrent budget resolution report acknowledges the importance of user fees, but does not make a similar recommendation for fee increases.[44]

ISSUES FOR THE 104TH CONGRESS

Since the 104th Congress convened, FDA drug approval reform has been high on the agenda of the new leadership. House Speaker Newt Gingrich and Commerce Committee chairman Thomas Bliley have publicly expressed their own reservations about FDA's drug approval policies. The U.S. pharmaceutical and biotechnology industries, recognizing opportunities for regulatory change, have made efforts to persuade Members of Congress that drug reform should be given high priority. Agency oversight hearing have been held in the House by subcommittees of the Committees on Commerce and the Government Reform and Oversight and the Labor and Human Resources Committee in the Senate. Members have questioned whether reform of the drug review process can be achieved through congressional oversight, or whether a legislative approach is needed.

In recent months, certain health policy critics have unleashed a steady stream of criticism aimed directly at FDA's drug approval process.[45, 46] Conservative advocacy groups, think tanks, and some editorial writers have characterized FDA as an antiquated bureaucracy that is too aggressive in its enforcement action, and too leisurely with its approval process. Some critics argue that this sort of regulatory environment stifles drug innovation and results in lost jobs as pharmaceutical companies relocate their research and development operations

[42] Public Law 102-539.

[43] U.S. Congress. House. Committee on the Budget. Concurrent Resolution on the Budget-Fiscal Year 1996. Report to Accompany H. Con. Res. 67. House Report No. 104-120, 104th Cong., 1st Sess. Washington, U.S. Govt. Print. Off., 1995. p. 89.

[44] U.S. Congress. Senate. Committee on the Budget. Concurrent Resolution on the Budget-Fiscal Year 1996. Report to Accompany S. Con. Res. 13. Senate Report No. 104-82, 104th Cong., 1st Sess. Washington, U.S. Govt. Print. Off., 1995. p. 142.

[45] Hilts, Philip J. FDA Becomes Target of Empowered Groups. The New York Times – Sunday, Feb. 12, 1995. p. 24.

[46] Stone, Peter H. Ganging Up on the FDA. National Journal, v. 27, no. 7, Feb. 18, 1995. p. 410.

overseas. Using examples of drugs (or medical devices) that reportedly are available in foreign countries earlier than in the United States, some of the agency's harshest critics claim that the delayed availability of some products translates into loss of patients' lives. FDA's more ardent reform proponents have suggested a number of possible remedies ranging from abolishing the agency altogether to relieving it of its primary drug review functions. Such advocates contend that many of FDA's regulatory functions could be more effectively carried out by advisory committees or other qualified groups in the private sector.

Not surprisingly, agency supporters view its regulatory track record from a vastly different perspective.[47, 48] They feel that charges of agency slowness and inefficiency are blatantly exaggerated. Some claim that FDA's critics purposely misconstrue the agency's regulatory policies in order to convince the American public – and Congress – of a need to overhaul the entire U.S. drug approval system. While conceding that the agency may be in need of modest reform, most FDA defenders still contend that it is quite sound, and more importantly, well-trusted by the public. They point out that American consumers are the beneficiaries of the world's safest and most effective drug supply. Part of their concern is that much of the negative criticism directed at the agency will inevitably be used as the impetus to introduce legislation that, in their opinion, will have the long-term effect of lowering present safety and efficacy standards. Moreover, their skepticism leads them to believe that much of the drug industries' attention to reform is motivated as much by financial self-interest as it is by improving consumer health.

Clinton Administration Initiatives

In April 1995, attempting to establish its own position on reforming the Federal government's regulatory processes, the Clinton Administration released a set of recommendations aimed at streamlining drug and medical device review.[49] Announced as part of the reinventing government initiative, the report highlighted an array of drug regulatory initiatives that could be implemented without lowering public health and safety standards. The Administration's announced proposals would:

- Allow drug and biologic companies to make certain manufacturing changes without FDA review or pre-approval, if the risks are negligible;
- Allow biotech companies to use start up "pilot" facilities instead of large manufacturing plants;
- Eliminate outdate special requirements for manufacturing insulin and antibiotics;
- Exempt from environmental assessments almost all applications for human drugs and biologics;
- Exempt nearly 140 categories of low-risk medical devices from 510(k), or premarket review;

---

[47] Carey, John, Joseph Weber, and Joan O'C. Hamilton. Is the FDA Hooked on Caution? Business Week, no. 3409, Jan. 30, 1995. p. 72.

[48] Cohn, Jeffrey P. The "Bully" Fights Back. Government Executive, Apr. 1995. p. 54.

[49] President Bill Clinton and Vice President Al Gore. Reinventing Drug & Medical Device Regulations. National Performance Review, April 1995. 35 p.

- Eliminate FDA's "reference list" program of tracking medical device firms found to have serious good manufacturing practice (GMP) violations. Instead, the agency will focus its attention on the appropriate linkage between serious GMP deficiencies and individual pending medical device applications.
- Create a pilot program for third-party device review; and
- Give drug and device manufacturers more freedom to export unapproved products to industrialized countries.

FDA Modernization Act (H.R. 1742)

Numerous bills addressing the issue of FDA drug and medical device reform have been introduced in the 104th Congress.[50] The "FDA Modernization Act of 1995" (H.R. 1742), introduced June 6th by Representative Wyden and referred to the House Committee on Commerce, would authorize FDA to grant early, conditional approval to promising life-saving drugs and devices. Conditional approval of drugs to treat life-threatening diseases would be granted on the basis of "valid scientific evidence demonstrating a reasonable assurance of safety and effectiveness."

The bill attempts to speed drug approval by requiring DHHS to use institutional review boards to review and approve early clinical investigations. The Secretary of DHHS – or the institutional review board – would be allowed to place a clinical hold on any investigation if it is determined that such action is necessary for the protection of human subjects or because the clinical investigation is being poorly supervised.

H.R. 1742 would permit the Secretary, acting through the FDA Commissioner, to establish a program under which the agency would contract with individuals or certified laboratories certain activities and responsibilities of FDA in connection with the approval of drugs and devices. These activities may include toxicology and chemistry reviews; statistical analyses; preapproval manufacturing practice inspections; and other functions of FDA relating to the review and approval of drugs and devices that can be performed adequately under contract. The legislation also addresses good manufacturing practices (GMPs) – applicable to drugs and biologics – and by specifying those circumstances under which certain manufacturing changes must receive preclearance from FDA; those that require 30-day notification; and those that need only be mentioned in annual reports.

The FDA Modernization Act introduces a novel concept that would limit FDA's present authority over drug labeling and advertising by permitting drug manufacturers to distribute "scientifically valid" information on other "off-label" uses of their products. In other words, the bill would amend FDCA to state that such terms as "advertising" and "labeling" do not include articles published in peer-reviewed scientific publications and other generally recognized materials such as textbooks, official compendia, abstracts and proceedings of scientific meetings, or information concerning decisions about drug utilization review or formulary decisions. This provision addresses an area of growing controversy between FDA and the drug industry about whether distribution of this type of information constitutes

---

[50] Most of these reform proposals also include language that would affect the regulation of medical devices as well. Since this section of the report primarily is concerned with drug approval reform, the discussion is focused more from that perspective.

dissemination of new medical knowledge or another method of promoting a product's use beyond its FDA approved indications.

Finally, H.R. 1742 would ease export requirements for unapproved drugs and devices to members of the World Trade Organization (WTO). Drug manufacturers would have to demonstrate that their products are considered acceptable by the importing country. Export to non-WTO countries would be permitted if the DHHS Secretary is given advanced notification and a brief description of the importing country's medical need for the drug.

Life Extending and Life Saving Drug Act of 1995 (H.R. 1995)

Another bill, entitled the "Life Extending and Life Saving Drug Act of 1995 (H.R. 1995), was introduced June 30, 1995 by Representative Fox and referred to the House Committee on Commerce. This legislation parallels a draft proposal previously advanced by the Pharmaceutical Research and Manufacturers of America – the leading trade association of the U.S. pharmaceutical industry. It represents a comprehensive remediation of many current regulatory policies the industry believes are obstacles to achieving a more competitive position in the world marketplace. In addition, the Act embraces many of the ideas being advocated by conservative supporters of drug reform including some new proposals for unprecedented changes in the current regulatory regime.

The bill contains several similar provisions to the "FDA Modernization Act" including changes in GMP regulations, privatization of new drug application reviews, and changes in premarket manufacturing regulations. However, H.R. 1995 does not contain language making changes in current drug labeling and promotion regulations (i.e., off-label use) as expressed in the Wyden measure.

The "Life Extending and Life Saving Drug Act" establishes a "mission statement" in FDCA characterizing the responsibilities of FDA with respect to promoting and protecting the health of the American public and encouraging the development of new drug products. Some feel that such language is necessary to legislate a higher degree of public and congressional accountability in the policy making decisions of the agency.

The measure proposes to amend the appropriate sections of FDCA in a manner that would redefine the kind and amount of drug testing data necessary to satisfy the "substantial evidence" requirement for new drug approval. This change would allow drug makers to submit "scientifically sound" data derived from only "one well-controlled clinical investigation"[51] coupled with confirmatory evidence obtained either before or after the clinical trial.

The bill also would provide for expedited FDA review of drugs approved by any of the following third-party organizations: the European Medicines Evaluation Agency, the United Kingdom Medicines Control Agency, and any competent governmental or non-governmental organization established to evaluate drug safety and effectiveness. Applications for drug

[51] The language of H.R. 1995 seeks to redefine the term "substantial evidence" to mean "evidence consisting of scientifically sound data, including data form one well-controlled clinical investigation and confirmatory evidence . . ." This contrasts with the current FDCA language the makes no reference to a specific number of investigations and states that "substantial evidence" means "evidence consisting of adequate and well-controlled investigations, including clinical investigations . . ." Historically, FDA has maintained that it has the authority to approve a new drug based on a single well-controlled clinical trial. However, for most New Drug Applications, the agency requires at least two adequate and well-controlled studies.

approval are to be reviewed and either approved or disapproved by the Secretary of DHHS within 180 days. If DHHS decides not to approve the drug – based on a showing by the Secretary that the drug either is unsafe or is ineffective – then a notice of the decision must be published in the Federal Register. If the Secretary does not publish a notice of disapproval within 180 days, then the conclusions and recommendations of a scientific review group shall be deemed the decision of the Secretary.

The foregoing brief description of the expedited approval system envisioned by provisions of H.R. 1995 is one of its more significant aspects. The bill seeks to limit review time and reverses the burden of proof by placing FDA in the position of defending its decision to disapprove an application. It would create a "default mechanism," whereby drug approval would go forward automatically unless the agency demonstrated that the drug is unsafe or is ineffective. The burden of proof on the agency to demonstrate why the product should not be marketed. Such a shift would be a significant change from the current regulatory policy and procedure.

FDA Export Reform and Enhancement Act of 1995 (H.R. 1300/S. 593)

The issue of drug export reform is addressed as part of both reform measures. H.R. 1995 would expand the export provisions of the FDCA to grant drug and device manufacturers more latitude in exporting unapproved products to foreign countries where their marketing is legal. Also, such stand-alone measures as the "FDA Export Reform and Enhancement Act of 1995" (H.R. 1300/S. 593), introduced March 22, 1995 in the House by Representative Upton and in the Senate by Senator Hatch, contain similar provisions allowing drug companies to export unapproved drugs, biologics, and medical devices. The overriding goal of all of these proposals is to expand upon the drug export provisions established by the Drug Export Amendments of 1986.[52]

On August 2, 1995, the Senate Committee on Labor and Human Resources held a mark-up on S. 593. An amendment in the nature of a substitute was adopted that would permit products to be exported to all members of the European Union and European Economic Area as well as to Australia, Canada, Israel, Japan, New Zealand, and Switzerland. The adopted measure was ordered favorably reported to the full Senate.

Access to Medical Treatment Act (H.R. 2019/S. 1035)

Sometimes overlooked in the context of drug reform are two other bills. The "Access to Medical Treatment Act" (H.R. 2019/S. 1035), was introduced on July 13, 1995 in the House by Representative DeFazio, and in the Senate on July 14 by Minority Leader Daschle. These proposals take a different approach by allowing individuals the right to be treated by health care practitioners with any medical treatment – including foods, drugs, and devices – the

[52] For years it was illegal for drug manufacturers to export products (other than investigational drugs) that were not approved for sale in the United States. In 1986, President Reagan signed into law a comprehensive health bill (P.L. 99-660) that included the "Drug Export Amendments Act of 1986." The new law allowed unapproved new drugs to be exported to 21listed countries as long as manufacturers – and their products – met other criteria specified in the statute.

individual may desire. Patients would be required to give informed consent, and treatment providers would have to provide the patient of a written statement declaring the following:

> "WARNING: This food, drug or device has not been declared to be safe and effective by the Federal Government and any individual who uses such food, drug or device does so at his or her own risk."

Supporters of the Access to Medical Treatment Act claim that legislation is intended to complement, rather than undermine, FDA's regulatory authority. Critics are not so sanguine. They believe the bill would legitimize unproven therapies often proselytized by alternative medicine advocates.

Improved Dissemination of Drug and Device Information (S. 1197)

The Improved Dissemination of Drug and Device Information (S. 1197) was introduced by Senator Mack on August 11, 1995 to address the issue of "off-label" promotion of drugs, biologics, and medical devices – see section on drug labeling and promotion. The bill would amend the FDCA to permit individuals to distribute "unabridged" versions of peer-reviewed articles from scientific or medical journals as long as the "information has been approved by a continuing medical education accrediting agency that is independent of the pharmaceutical industry as part of a scientific of medical education program approved by such agency."

The text of S. 1197 states that "in order to afford a full and fair evaluation" of the information permitted to be distributed under the bill, persons providing such information must include a statement disclosing: that the material contains information on uses not approved by the FDA, that the information is being provided at the expense of the sponsor of the drug, and that the authors of the information are employees of or consultants of the drug's sponsor. The information also must contain the official FDA-approved labeling for the drug or biological product.

In addition, the legislation would permit the dissemination of information relating to a use "recognized under Federal law for purposes of third-party coverage or reimbursement, and – (i) the text of the information has been approved by an organization referred to in such Federal law; or (ii) the information is part of a disease management program or treatment guideline with respect to such use."

FDA Performance and Accountability Act of 1995 (S. 1477)

On December 13, 1995, Senator Kassebaum introduced the FDA Performance and Accountability Act (S. 1477), a bill to amend the FDCA and the Public Health Service Act to improve the regulation of food, drugs, medical devices, and biological products. The bill is the synthesis of a draft proposal circulated in 1995 by the Senate Labor and Human Resources Committee to representatives of the U.S. health care industry and Members of Congress. In many respects, the Act would consolidate portions of reform proposals already introduced and would expand on some of the agency's own regulatory reform efforts. The proposal would require significant modifications in the way FDA performs many of its current functions. In addition, the legislation seeks to transform FDA's management philosophy by making the agency more accountable and proactive in its mandate to protect consumers from unsafe products. The bill's nine titles are briefly summarized as follows:

- **Title I – Mission and Accountability**. Creates a new statutory mission statement and requirements for performance standards and review. Requires the Secretary to establish an information system to track the status of petitions and applications. The title requires the Secretary to establish a procedure governing the development and use of all policy statements; provides for enhanced use of advisory committees; and requires FDA to establish a new system of appeals within the agency.
- **Title II – Expedited Access To Products For Seriously Ill Patients.** This title would codify many of FDA's current regulations covering access to investigational therapies for life-threatening conditions such as treatment INDs and parallel track clinical trials. Any person who meets certain criteria could request an experimental drug or device from a manufacturer or distributor. Manufacturers would be permitted to inform national, State, and local medical associations of the availability of investigational drugs and devices. Is also would establish humanitarian use of medical devices, and set statutory approval times for products covered by the title.
- **Title III – Revitalizing The Investigation Of New Products.** Establishes in law that clinical investigations of new drugs and devices may begin 30 days after the Secretary receives notification. Requires the Secretary, after consultation with industry and patient advocacy groups, and consideration of the recommendations of the International Conference on Harmonization, to publish in the *Federal Register*, the type and amount of information to be included in the notification, effective one year after enactment.
  The title requires the Secretary to publish within 120 days of enactment new regulations permitting development changes in devices, including manufacturing changes, without the additional approval of an application. In addition, if requested, FDA must meet within 30 days with the sponsor of a preclinical or clinical investigation to discuss proposed research protocols, and provide a written review of the proposal.
- **Title IV – Effective, Accountable, And Fair Product Review.** This title applies to applications for approval for new drugs, biologics, devices, food and color additives, animal drugs, and animal feeds containing new drugs. It provides statutory authority for the Secretary to contract with outside organizations and individuals for the evaluation of new product applications. The proposal establishes a mechanism for promptly determining product classification and the agency component responsible for regulating the product.
  Within one year of enactment, the Secretary must publish in the *Federal Register* criteria for the type and amount of information relating to safety and effectiveness to be included in an application for approval. Title IV establishes statutory deadlines for product reviews. If the Secretary fails to act within a specified time period for a product that meets the marketing requirements of the European Union or the United Kingdom, then the application shall be deemed approved.
  Title IV grants FDA the authority to contract out for external application reviews, and if such a review determines that an application should be approved, then it will

be deemed approved unless the agency publishes a notice denying approval and stating its reasons. If, after July 1, 1998, the agency fails to meet its statutory time periods for action on at least 95 percent of the applications in a particular product category, then FDA must contract with outside experts and organizations to review the new applications for which the agency has failed to meet its statutory time obligations. In addition, outside accredited organizations would be permitted to conduct good manufacturing practices (GMPs) inspections and the Secretary would be prohibited from requiring environmental impact assessments unless there is a reasonable probability that the manufacture, consumption, or use of a product will have adverse environmental effects.

Title IV addresses the issue of "off label" product promotion by permitted sponsors to disseminate certain types of scientific information about unapproved uses of drugs and devices. Manufacturers must disclose that the material contains information about uses not approved by FDA. The product's official label containing its approved uses would have to be attached.

The title also would establish an alternative application that would permit a medical society to petition FDA for approval of new uses of an already approved drug or device. The petition would have to document that the new use (1) has existed in clinical practice for at least five years; (2) is common among clinicians experienced in the field; and (3) represents standard medical practice. Whether the petitioners would have to substantiate the safety and efficacy of their product's new use is not specified. The agency would have 180 days to grant or deny the petition and would bear the burden of demonstrating why the new use posed a significant risk to patients. In addition, Title IV would place limits on FDA's requirements for demonstrations of product effectiveness, outcomes, and cost-effectiveness to those claimed by the manufacturer on its product label.

- **Title V – Drug, Biological Products, Devices Export Reform** The proposal would incorporate the Gregg/Kennedy substitute amendment to S. 593, the Export Reform and Enhancement Act of 1995 (see above).
- **Title VI – Drug and Biological Products Regulatory Reform.** This title would clarify FDA's authority to require only "one" adequate and well-controlled clinical study (see discussion of H.R. 1995 at footnote 50).

The proposal clarifies that product sponsors would be permitted to use pilot and small manufacturing facilities to produce drugs and biologics for clinical testing and harmonize certain regulations so that unless the Secretary determines that products are not well-characterized, most biologics would need only a product license for approval to begin marketing.

Under the provisions of Title VI, manufacturers of drugs and most biologics would be permitted to make minor changes in their manufacturing processes without prior approval from the agency. Batch and lot certification rules for insulin and antibiotics, already recommended for elimination by FDA, would also be abolished. In addition, this title would regulate most biologics as drugs and replace the requirement for a separate establishment license with the GMP requirements now applicable to drug manufacturing. New and emerging tissue technologies would be subject to new regulations issued by the Secretary.

- **Title VII – Device Regulator Reform.** Title VII would eliminate 510(K) premarket notification requirements for all Class I devices and certain Class II devices identified by FDA; provides for advisory committee review before a device can be formally classified as a Class III device; and permits minor modifications to be made in devices without the submission of a premarket notification.
  The proposed definition of what would constitute "substantial evidence" of a device's effectiveness would limit the Secretary's authority to require manufacturers to conduct more than one clinical trial. Under the terms of the proposals, device manufacturers would only be required to conduct "a [single] well-controlled clinical investigation" to demonstrate effectiveness, if FDA describes in writing the need for such a study.
  The bill would limit device tracking to Class II and Class III devices that, if they fail, would produce life-threatening or permanently debilitating consequences attributable to the device. Postmarketing surveillance of all devices would be made discretionary on the part of the Secretary, and distributor reporting would be eliminated.
- Title VII would require the Secretary, when making safety and effectiveness determinations of medical devices, to accept data based on testing of an earlier version of the device when only minor modifications of the device have been made during testing. FDA would be required to recognize national and international performance standards when evaluating the safety and effectiveness of a device.
- **Title VIII – Animal Drug Regulatory Reform.** This title would revise new animal drug approval standards by redefining the statutory definition of "substantial evidence" to mean data from at least one scientifically sound study. Field investigations to support "substantial evidence" would be required only if FDA demonstrated in writing that no other form of testing would be adequate to show the product's effectiveness.
  The agency would be given greater flexibility to approve combination animal drugs by not requiring manufacturers to demonstrate that the combination has a synergistic effect. The Secretary may dis-approve an animal drug if it is determined that the labeled use will result in unsafe residue levels. FDCA would be amended to permit the Secretary to establish separate GMP's for human and animal drugs.
- **Title IX – Food Regulatory Reform.** The proposal would establish an alternative process for the introduction into commerce of an indirect food additive (e.g., packaging, food machinery). Sponsors would notify the Secretary at least 90 days prior to the product's introduction and would demonstrate that the labeled use of the product is safe. The Secretary would be required within 90 days either to approve or to disapprove the notification and publish this decision in the *Federal Register*. If such a notice is not published then the indirect food additive would be deemed approved. An indirect food additive would be defined as a substance that is in contact with food, but is not intended for consumption as a food ingredient.

Additional drug reform legislation likely will be introduced during the second session of the 104th Congress. A House version is expected to be ready for introduction in early 1996, with new rounds of hearings likely to follow. Some members have vowed to make FDA reform a top priority, but disagreements over content of a comprehensive reform proposal, affecting so many diverse interests, may make it difficult for lawmakers to reach a legislative compromise before the end of the year.

Congress, advocacy groups, and the biotechnology and pharmaceutical industries will continue their respective efforts to influence drug marketing policy in the United States. While drug regulation was evolving from an era that offered little consumer protection to the present environment of rigorous safeguards, the American health care system came to rely on an ever-growing supply of safe and effective drug products. Regardless of the direction drug reform takes, confidence in the regulatory system can be maintained only if consumers believe that the medicines that are available are of high value and low risk.

Chapter 2

PRESCRIPTION DRUGS: PRICING DIFFERENCES BETWEEN INSURED AND UNINSURED CONSUMERS

Christopher J. Sroka

ABSTRACT

The prices paid by the uninsured for prescription drugs have become a concern for Congress, particularly because a significant portion of the uninsured are elderly. It is generally believed that the uninsured, especially the elderly, pay significantly higher prices for prescription drugs than other consumers. Under this premise, some bills have been introduced with the goal of lowering prescription drug costs for the elderly. Some plans seek to achieve this without expanding Medicare coverage to include prescription drugs. Alternatively, there are proposals to add a prescription drug benefit to Medicare.

A characteristic of the pharmaceutical market is the potential for sellers to charge different prices to different buyers. This can occur both at the manufacturing and at the dispensing level. The buyer can be an individual, a health plan, or a health-delivery institution. The price charged to a particular buyer depends on how sensitive that buyer is to the price of pharmaceuticals. Buyers who are very price sensitive will attempt to pay a lower price than those buyers who are relatively insensitive to pharmaceutical prices.

Of the buyers in the pharmaceutical market, uninsured consumers are least likely to react to the prices quoted to them. Most of the decisions concerning the use of prescription drugs are left to the physician with very little input from the consumer. Furthermore, consumers are not informed of pharmaceutical prices until the prescription is dispensed. Consequently, they cannot alter their consumption of pharmaceuticals in response to price changes. This makes it easier for sellers to charge the uninsured relatively high prices.

The situation is different for insured consumers. Unlike uninsured consumers, insured consumers pay only a portion, and in some instances none, of the drug price. The insurer is the principal buyer, and it intervenes in the pharmaceutical market in an attempt to lower the prices it pays. The insurer can persuade physicians to utilize the lowest cost treatment and can negotiate significant discounts from pharmacies. Thus, the size and resources of the insurer give it an advantage over the consumer, especially the uninsured consumer. As a result, the price paid by the insurer for prescription drugs tends to be lower than the price paid by uninsured consumers.

Both pharmacies and pharmaceutical manufacturers are able to charge different prices to different buyers. However, only pharmacies are able to charge different prices to uninsured and insured consumers. Manufacturers differentiate their prices among wholesalers, large hospitals, managed care institutions, and certain retail pharmacy chains. This differentiation is the result of the considerable ability of large buyers to bargain on the basis of prices.

Because so many of the uninsured are senior citizens, the focus of most proposals dealing with the issue of prescription drug prices has been on this segment of the population. One approach is to address the prices paid by the elderly for prescription drugs. Another approach is to give the elderly financial assistance. A third approach is to extend the coverage of Medicare to include prescription drugs. Lastly, Congress could take no action, leaving the currently situation to continue as it has for many years.

MOST RECENT DEVELOPMENTS

On February 10, 1999, the Prescription Drug Fairness for Seniors Act (H.R. 644) was introduced in the House of Representatives and was referred to the Commerce and the Way and Means Committees. The purpose of this bill is "to protect Medicare beneficiaries from discriminatory pricing by drug manufacturers and to make prescription drugs available to Medicare beneficiaries at substantially reduced prices." Under this bill, pharmaceutical manufacturers would be required to supply pharmacies with the quantity of drugs sold to Medicare beneficiaries at the same price at which the federal government purchases the same drugs.

The Making Affordable Prescriptions Available for Seniors Act (H.R. 723) was introduced on February 11, 1999, and referred to the Commerce Committee. This bill would establish a program to assist the elderly in purchasing prescription drugs. The program would be restricted to persons 65 years or older who do not have any form of insurance coverage for prescription drugs and whose income does not exceed 175 percent of the federal poverty guidelines. The bill does not specifically state how the program will be administered. However, it authorizes the Secretary of Health and Human Services (HHS) to administer the program in the most cost-effective manning, including, but not limited to, the use of vouchers, coupons, or direct reimbursement of the provider.

Another relevant bill is the Medicare Prescription Drug Coverage Act (H.R. 886), introduced on March 1,1999, and referred to the Commerce and the Ways and Means Committees. This bill instructs the Secretary of HHS to develop a proposal to expand the benefits of Medicare to include prescription drugs. The proposal must designate how the additional benefits would be funded.

BACKGROUND AND ANALYSIS

Introduction

A significant characteristic of the pharmaceutical market is the presence of price discrimination. Price discrimination occurs when the seller of a product has the ability to charge different prices to different buyers of the good. The extent to which this occurs depends on the market power of the seller relative to each buyer. Those buyers against whom the seller has a high degree of market power will be charged a higher price than those buyers against whom the seller has a low degree of market power.

A seller's market power increases as the buyer's price elasticity of demand decreases. Price elasticity refers to the sensitivity of a buyer's behavior to changes in the price of a particular good. Buyers whose demand is highly elastic will be very sensitive to price changes; small changes in the price of a good will cause the buyer to change significantly the amount of the good that it purchases. Buyers whose demand is relatively inelastic will be very insensitive to price changes; even large increases in the price of a good will not cause the buyer to significantly change the amount of the good that it purchases. Thus, a seller whose customers have primarily an elastic demand will have a high degree of market power; the seller can raise the price of the good without affecting the number of buyers purchasing the good or the quantity that each buyer purchases.

Several factors determine price elasticity. First, the more substitutes that are available for a good, the more elastic the demand will be for that particular good. When there are many substitutes for a good, the buyer can respond to price increases by purchasing substitutes. However, when there are no substitutes, buyers can only continue to purchase the good or not purchase the good altogether. Second, the more necessary the good, the less elastic the demand for that good. When a good is a necessity, it is unlikely that the buyer will forgo purchasing the good, even if there is a significant increase in price. One exception to this is the choice between two or more necessities, in which case the need perceived to be the most urgent will be satisfied to the disadvantage of the others. For example, there are anecdotal accounts of elderly foregoing medication for food.

Buyers in the pharmaceutical market have varying needs for pharmaceuticals and differing abilities to substitute one pharmaceutical for another. Consequently, price elasticity varies across different types of buyers. This gives sellers of pharmaceuticals, both at the manufacturing and at the dispensing levels, different degrees of market power and the ability to charge different prices to the different types of buyers. Analyzing the price sensitivity of each major entity in the pharmaceutical market can explain which groups are more likely to pay higher prices.

Uninsured Consumers

Among the buyers in the pharmaceutical market, the uninsured consumers have the most inelastic demand. This group consists of those consumers who do not have health insurance or whose health insurance does not provide significant pharmaceutical coverage. These consumers utilize retail pharmacies (chain, independent, mail-order, or mass retailers) to have their prescriptions dispensed and they pay for these pharmaceuticals out of their own pocket. Thus, they are both the buyer and the user of prescription drugs. When compared to other buyers in the pharmaceutical market, the uninsured are the least able to alter their consumption in response to price changes.

All consumers of prescription drugs are unable to make key decisions regarding prescription drug use. Physicians decide whether drugs will be used to treat a patient because patients usually do not know what other treatments are available. Furthermore, physicians decide which drug to prescribe to treat the patient because patients usually are unaware of the competing drugs available in each therapeutic class (commonly referred to as "me-to" drugs).

Physicians also decide how much, how often, and for how long a drug will be consumed, since most patients do not have the expertise to make these decisions. Hence, for a change in the price of a drug, consumers are unable to alter their consumption of that drug on their own. Their only recourses are to not consume the drug at all or to spread out the dosage. However, these are not practical options, since not consuming the drug or spreading out the dosage means that the patient will not receive adequate relief for the ailment.

Consumers can choose which pharmacy will dispense the prescription. However, here too, the patient is insensitive to prices. Pharmacies do not reveal the price of the prescription prior to dispensing the drug to the consumer. It is not possible to respond to the price of a drug (or any other good or service) if the price is not known. Consumers are unable to "shop around" to various pharmacies to find the lowest price for a prescription drug. Consequently, the consumer may choose a pharmacy based on factors other than price, such as the location of the pharmacy, quality of service, and pharmacy convenience (e.g., drive-thru service or 24-hour service). While the above limitations exist for all consumers, they are particular problems for uninsured consumers. For insured consumers, the insurer is the buyer of the pharmaceuticals, and it will intervene in the market to compensate for the above limitations. Uninsured consumers do not have this advantage.

If the price of a pharmaceutical were to increase at either the manufacturing level or at the dispensing level, the uninsured consumer would be unable to substitute the drug with an alternative treatment or to "shop around" to find a lower-priced pharmacy. Furthermore, the consumer would not likely forgo the drug since it is practically a necessity. Consequently, uninsured consumers have relatively inelastic demand for prescription drugs. That is, any changes in the price of a prescription drug will not cause uninsured users to alter their consumption of prescription drugs. This gives those who sell prescription drugs to the uninsured the ability to charge relatively high prices.

Insured Consumers and Insurers

Insured consumers face the same limitations as uninsured consumers. Like uninsured consumers, the decisions of whether drugs will be used, which drugs will be used, and how much of a drug will be used are left to the physician, since the consumer has less expertise than the physician. Insured consumers under a coinsurance plan or a deductible plan, like uninsured consumers, will not know the amount they will have to pay to the pharmacy until after the prescription is dispensed. (Although consumers with a co-payment plan will know beforehand exactly what price they will pay; it will be the amount of the co-pay.) Thus, the behavior of insured consumers also is insensitive to the prices of pharmaceuticals. However, this is relatively unimportant for the insured consumer because the insured consumer only consumes the drug and plays a small role in purchasing the drug.

While insured consumers are the users of prescription drugs, it is the insurer that is the principal buyer of prescription drugs. Insured consumers may pay a deductible or a relatively small co-payment, but the insurer pays a significant portion of the price. Unlike the ordinary consumer, the insurer is able to influence the decision-making process for prescription drugs. The size and informational resources of the insurer enable it to intervene in the pharmaceutical market to keep its prescription drug prices low. There are various ways by which insurers attempt to achieve this.

One way insurers influence the market is through the use of formularies. Formularies are lists of the insurer's preferred drugs; that is, the drug or drugs in each therapeutic class that the insurer wants the consumer to use. Drugs are included in the formulary based on various factors, including price. In many cases, insurers require physicians that belong to preferred provider organizations (PPOs) or managed care institutions to prescribe only those drugs included in the formulary. Insurers also may restrict coverage to those drugs listed on the formulary.

In addition to utilizing a formulary, insurers can influence which pharmacy the insured consumer uses and how much will be charged. Some insurers cover prescription drugs only if they are obtained from mail-order pharmacies because mail-order pharmacies tend to operate at lower costs than traditional retail pharmacies. Insurers attempt to negotiate a discounted price from pharmacies for dispensing prescription drugs. Many pharmacies grant these discounts because rejecting them means losing the patronage of that insurer's customer base.

The insurer is relatively price sensitive compared to the uninsured consumer. This ability to respond to prices stems from the insurer's ability to substitute. If the price of a drug listed on the formulary were to increase, the insurer can replace that drug with a "me-too" drug or a generic drug, if available. If a pharmacy were to refuse to accept the price set by the insurer, the insurer can steer its large customer base to another pharmacy that is willing to accept the price. The insurer is able to substitute drugs and pharmacies because, in contrast to the uninsured consumer, the insurer has information regarding drug prices and drug alternatives. Consequently, the insurer is in a better position than the uninsured consumer to respond to the price of pharmaceuticals.

The prices paid directly by insured consumers are lower than those paid by uninsured consumers since insured consumers are not paying the entire bill out-of-pocket; a portion or all is being paid by the insurer, who is the principal buyer. However, it also is the case that the total price paid for drugs for use by insured consumers (that is, the price paid by the insurer plus any payment by the insured user) also will tend to be lower than the total price paid by the uninsured consumer. Because the insurer's demand is sensitive to price, sellers of pharmaceuticals are limited with respect to the price that they charge insurers. As mentioned earlier, this is not true with respect to uninsured consumers because their demand is relatively insensitive to prices. Thus, uninsured consumers will tend to pay higher prices for prescription drugs than insured consumers and their insurers.

Pharmacies

Pharmacies are both purchasers and sellers of pharmaceuticals. They have a demand for purchasing drugs from manufacturers and wholesalers that is relatively inelastic. They also have the ability to price discriminate when dispensing drugs to consumers.

With respect to purchasing pharmaceuticals, pharmacies are relatively insensitive to the prices charged by manufacturers and wholesalers. Their demand is relatively inelastic because pharmacies must stock a wide selection of pharmaceuticals and, thus, have relatively little power to negotiate prices with health plans and wholesalers. Pharmacies must be prepared to fill almost any prescription that a consumer may have. Unlike insurers, they do not have the option of developing a formulary and deciding to carry only certain drugs. Thus, they are somewhat inflexible in their buying decisions and are willing to pay the price charged by the pharmaceutical wholesaler or manufacturer. On a side note, pharmacies may carry more generic drugs than brand-name drugs and encourage both doctors and patients to agree to the substitution of generic drugs when available. Using generic drugs lowers the pharmacy's costs and increases its profit as a percentage of sales.

With respect to dispensing pharmaceuticals, the market power of pharmacies varies with the type of consumer. As mentioned previously, insurers attempt to limit how much they pay for prescriptions. Consequently, pharmacies have relatively little market power vis-à-vis insured consumers. In effect, they must accept the set price set by the insurer or else forgo the customer base that belongs to that insurer's health plan.

While pharmacies have limited market power with respect to insured consumers, the same is not true about uninsured consumers. As mentioned above, uninsured consumers have relatively inelastic demand. Therefore, pharmacies have considerable market power toward uninsured consumers. Pharmacies have the ability to change the price charged to uninsured consumers without it resulting in any significant changes in the behavior of uninsured consumers. Unlike with insured customers, a pharmacy can neither gain nor lose uninsured customers by changing its price. This is due mostly to the fact that pharmacies do not disclose their prices prior to dispensing the drug. A decrease in the price one pharmacy asks for a particular drug will not induce a consumer of another pharmacy to switch to the price-lowering pharmacy because the consumer in not informed as to which pharmacy is charging the lower price. Thus, the pharmacy has no economic incentive to discount its price for the uninsured like it has with respect to insured customers. Furthermore, the pharmacy has the ability to compensate for discounts given to insured customers by raising the prices charged to uninsured consumers.

It is important to note that although pharmacies have the *ability* and an *economic incentive* to charge higher prices to the uninsured than the insured, it is uncertain whether pharmacies actually do this and the extent to which it is done. However, in a recent civil antitrust suit against the drug manufacturers, one pharmacy owner testified that cash-paying customers were charged more for brand-name prescription drugs than customers affiliated with a health or managed care plan because of discount agreements with the insurance plans (*In Re: Brand Name Prescription Drugs Antitrust Litigation*, N.D. Ill., No. 94, C 897, 1/19/99).

Pharmaceutical Manufacturers

Like pharmacies, pharmaceutical manufacturers have the ability to charge different prices to different buyers of pharmaceuticals. Competing brand-name ("me-too") drugs, generic drugs, and managed care plans are forces that shape the pricing decisions of pharmaceutical manufacturers. However, the manufacturers do not differentiate their prices between insured and uninsured users because manufacturers do not sell directly to consumers. Instead, they charge different prices to different groups of large intermediary buyers, with some buyers negotiating larger discounts than others. The ability to negotiate such discounts depends on the relative price sensitivity of the buyer and its ability to exercise its relatively significant market power. Thus, price discrimination by the manufacturer may be the result of the market power of the buyer rather than the seller.

Large hospitals and managed care institutions tend to negotiate larger discounts from drug manufacturers than large pharmacies and wholesalers. This is due mainly to the use of formularies by hospitals and managed care facilities. Formularies list the specific drugs that the institution will stock. Often, these institutions negotiate a lower price from a manufacturer in return for including the manufacturer's drug on the formulary. The drug is obtained form a wholesaler at the discounted price and the manufacturer reimburses the wholesaler for the cost of the discount (this is known as a "charge back system"). If a manufacturer were to refuse the discount, it sometimes can be replaced on the formulary with a competing "me-too" drug that will offer a discount. Thus, this power of substitution gives large hospitals and managed care facilities a relatively elastic demand; that is, their behavior is highly price sensitive to the prices of pharmaceuticals. As a result, manufacturer have a low degree of market power with respect to hospitals and managed care facilities and tend to give discounts to these institutions.

Wholesalers and large pharmacy chains that buy directly from the manufacturer are less able to respond to prices than hospitals and managed care facilities. In contrast to these institutions, pharmacies and wholesalers do not have the ability to substitute. Pharmacies, and the wholesalers that supply them, must be prepared to fill any prescription presented by the pharmacist. This means stocking a wide (if not complete) range of products, including both name brand drugs and their generic equivalents, and all drugs within the same therapeutic class. Consequently, pharmacies and wholesalers are relatively insensitive to the prices charged by pharmaceutical manufacturers. Regardless of the price charged, pharmacies and wholesalers must purchase the drug if they are to serve their customer adequately. Manufacturers have less economic incentive to grant discounts to pharmacies and wholesalers, unlike the case with hospitals, managed care facilities, and health plans.

It is important to note that the demand of all purchasers becomes more elastic with respect to generic drugs. Often, for a given generic drug, there are several firms that manufacture the drug. When dispensing a generic drug, there is not restriction as to which manufacturer's version of the generic drug must be used, so long as it is equivalent to what was prescribed. Thus, all purchasers who buy from generic manufacturers have the ability to substitute; if they do not like the price charged by one generic manufacturer, they can purchase the same drug from a different manufacturer at a lower price. Consequently, generic drug manufacturers are likely to have less market power than manufacturers of brand-name drugs.

Some would argue that the prices charged to wholesalers and large pharmacies are excessively high; however, one cannot support or dismiss such a statement with certainty. Furthermore, it is unlikely that manufacturers choose to charge different prices or that it is beneficial to do so. Rather, they are required to grant discounts because of the significant market power of large buyers and because of competition form brand-name and generic drug manufacturers. Thus, the price discrimination may reflect the influence of certain buyers and the competition among manufacturers, not necessarily any sort of illegal behavior. A similar conclusion was reached in a recent civil antitrust lawsuit against major pharmaceutical manufacturers (*In Re: Brand Name Prescription Drugs Antitrust Litigation*, N.D. Ill., No. 94, C 897, 1/19/99).

POLICY IMPLICATIONS

The issue of prices that the uninsured pay for prescription drugs has received considerable attention in Congress. One reason is that a significant number of the uninsured are elderly. Several proposals exist for assisting the elderly who do not have insurance coverage for prescription drugs, with each proposal taking a different approach to the issue. One proposal, the Prescription Drug Fairness for Seniors Act, approaches the issue by directly attempting to influence prices. A second proposal, the Making Affordable Prescriptions Available for Seniors Act, would give financial assistance for the elderly to purchase prescription drugs. A third approach is to extend the coverage of Medicaid to include a prescription drug benefit.

Prescription Drug Fairness for Seniors Act

The Prescription Drug Fairness for Seniors Act (H.R. 664) is a recent proposal to assist the elderly who have no prescription drug coverage. In essence, the bill seeks to induce pharmaceutical manufacturers to price discriminate in favor of retail pharmacies. The bill would require drug manufacturers to sell to pharmacies the quantity of drugs dispensed to Medicare patients at either the lowest price paid by any government agency, or the "best price" obtained by any other buyer, whichever is lower. Because the federal government purchases pharmaceuticals in such a large quantity, it can negotiate significant discounts with drug manufacturers. This bill would allow pharmacies to benefit from this purchasing power, effectively reducing the price that they pay for some of their drugs (the amount that they dispense to Medicare beneficiaries). In turn, it is anticipated that pharmacies will pass on these savings to Medicare patients in the form of lower prices.

Although the bill benefits pharmacies by lowering some of their acquisition costs, it does not ensure that the cost savings will be passed on to the Medicare consumers. As mentioned earlier, the relatively inelastic demand of uninsured consumers gives pharmacies significant market power. The bill does not address this issue, nor does it provide a mechanism to ensure that the pharmacies would not exercise their market power.

The Making Affordable Prescriptions Available for Seniors Act

Introduced the day after the Prescription Drug Fairness for Seniors Act, the Making Affordable Prescriptions Available for Seniors Act (H.R. 723) establishes a program to assist low-income elderly with purchasing prescription drugs. The assistance can take the form of vouchers, coupons, or direct reimbursement to the provider. The bill is very general, and it does not specifically designate how the program will work. In any case, the program would result in some sort of cash transfer that would offset the cost of purchasing prescription drugs for low-income elderly. The bill limits government assistance to $500 per person per year. The bill provides a subsidy to the consumer, but does not constrain the seller with respect to the prices charged.

Medicare Coverage of Prescription Drugs

One proposal that has receive much attention is the coverage of outpatient prescription drugs by Medicare. Currently, Medicare does not provide coverage for outpatient prescription drugs. Such coverage must be purchased by senior citizens through Medigap plans. Only very poor senior citizens have outpatient prescription drug coverage under the Medicaid program.

The specific details of an outpatient prescription drug benefit for Medicare could vary. It could be full coverage or, alternatively, it could target benefits to one segment of the population (e.g., near poor elderly who do not have Medicaid). The benefit likely would include deductibles and coinsurance. Additionally, a Medicare benefit for outpatient prescription drugs might utilize price controls to some extent. Essentially, the program could operate much like a private health plan does with respect to prescription drugs.

Unlike the Prescription Drug Fairness for Seniors Act, a Medicare drug benefit would utilize the government's market power at the dispensing level as well as the manufacturing level. Like any other insurance company, the federal government would be in a position to set the amount that it would pay pharmacies for prescriptions dispensed to Medicare beneficiaries. In effect, the plan would bring to a significant group of the uninsured (i.e., the elderly) advantages similar to those that insured consumers have.

The expansion of Medicare to include outpatient prescription drugs would not necessarily eliminate the problem of the uninsured; it would simply change the number and demographics of the uninsured. There are people who are not eligible for Medicare and who do not have any insurance coverage for prescription drugs (e.g., minimum-wage and low-wage workers, and workers employed by small businesses). This approach would not address the prices that they pay for prescription drugs. They still would have a relatively inelastic demand for pharmaceuticals, making them insensitive to potential price increases. Furthermore, because of the behavior the remaining uninsured still would be insensitive to prices, pharmacies could compensate for any price restrictions on dispensing to Medicare beneficiaries by charging higher prices to the remaining uninsured.

Promoting Price Competition

As mentioned previously, consumers are not informed of the price for a prescription until after the prescription is dispensed. This poses a significant barrier to price competition in the pharmaceutical dispensing market. Pharmacies have the ability to keep their prices charged to the uninsured significantly above cost. There is no economic incentive to compete in price because consumers know neither the price that they will pay nor the price being charged by competing pharmacies.

Again, it is important to note that although pharmacies have the ability and an economic incentive to charge significantly higher prices to the uninsured, they may not actually be doing so. Even if pharmacies are charging higher prices to the uninsured, it may be the case that the prices charged to the uninsured are not significantly higher than the cost of acquiring and dispensing the drug. In such a case, policies aiming to reduce drug prices for the uninsured need to be directed not toward pharmacies, but rather toward other aspects of the pharmaceutical market.

If it is the case that pharmacies are charging significantly higher-than-cost prices to the uninsured, disclosing the price of prescription drugs before they are dispensed could have a dramatic effect on the price of pharmaceuticals for the uninsured. Price disclosure could take various forms, such as posting pharmacy's prices at the pharmacy counter or advertising the prices that the pharmacy charges. It already is occurring with the growth of Internet-based pharmacies. Two such pharmacies, Drugstore.com [http://www.drugstore.com] and PlanetRx [http://www.planetrx.com], list the prices they charge to uninsured consumers for each prescription drug. The prices charged to insured consumers are not listed because that price varies according to each individual's health plan.

Prescription drugs are almost perfectly homogeneous goods; a prescription for Claritin dispensed from one pharmacy is exactly the same as a prescription for Claritin dispensed from another pharmacy. Economic theory states that when there is more than one seller of a homogeneous good, then prices fall to close to the cost of providing the good. Each seller would continue to undercut their competitors' prices to attempt to lure more customers. Since the goods sold are almost identical, no seller can "lock in" customers; customers can easily obtain the same good from the lowest price competitor. Prices are undercut continually until all competitors are selling the good for a price close to the cost of supplying it.

For this type of competition to occur, however, consumers must be informed about the prices of the good. Thus, disclosing pharmaceutical prices beforehand would most likely lead to the situation described above. Pharmacies would engage in price competition that does not currently exist in the pharmacy market. If pharmacies currently are pricing significantly above cost, then prescription drug prices would decrease to a level close to the cost of supplying them. If pharmacies currently are pricing close to cost, then price disclosure would have very little or no effect.

To say that pharmacies currently do not compete in prices does not imply that pharmacies do not compete at all. Pharmacies still compete with one another with respect to location, convenience, quality of service, and various other non-price factors. However, non-price competition does not result in lower prices for uninsured consumers, and in some instances may result in higher prices.

LEGISLATION

H.R. 664 (Allen)

Requires pharmaceutical manufacturers to sell pharmaceuticals to pharmacies at a price equal to or lower than the lowest price paid by any federal agency. Lowered price would apply only to those drugs dispensed for Medicare beneficiaries. Introduced February 10, 1999; referred to Committees on Commerce and on Ways and Means.

H.R. 723 (Kennedy)

Authorizes that Secretary of Health and Human Services to establish a pharmacy assistance program to aid low-income persons of 65 years and older with no existing prescription drug coverage. Requires manufacturers who develop drugs through research done at National Institutes of Health or under section 12 of the Stevenson-Wydler Technology Innovation Act of 1980 to pay the federal government 7 percent of the gross sales of that drug. Introduced February 11, 1999; referred to Committee on Commerce.

H.R. 886 (Frank)

Requires the Secretary of Health and Human Services to submit to Congress a proposal for providing and funding Medicare coverage of prescription drugs. Introduced March 1, 1999; referred to Committees on Ways and Means and on Commerce.

FOR ADDITIONAL READING

Schweitzer, Stuart O. *Pharmaceutical Economics and Policy*, New York Oxford University Press, 1997, 246 p.

U.S. Congressional Budget Office. *How Increased Competition from Generic Drugs Has Affected Prices and Returns in the Pharmaceutical Industry,* July 1998, 75 p.

Chapter 3

PRESCRIPTION DRUGS: FACTORS INFLUENCING THEIR PRICING

David J. Cantor

In general, prescription drug prices are determined by the forces of supply and demand in the market. But this process of price determination is very complex, involving the interaction of powerful and, perhaps, not-so-powerful parties on both sides of the market. The market power of large, research-based pharmaceutical manufacturers is offset by that of the generic drug producers and larger payers for prescription drugs: the insurance companies, the government, and various health care providers (such as hospitals and staffed HMOs). At the retail level, too, there are pressures on various types of retailers – independent and chain drugs stores, mass merchandisers that have pharmacies, and mail-order pharmacy services – that have different degrees of influence on prices they pay to their suppliers, while facing substantial pressure from large payer organizations to reduce retail prices.

The pricing of prescription drugs also is of concern more broadly to society as a whole. On the one hand is the ideal goal of insuring quality *and* affordable health care services to all persons. On the other hand is the need to provide adequate professional and financial incentives to all providers of health care services – including research-based pharmaceutical companies – to ensure their near- and long-term supply.

Society's concerns with respect to prescription are reflected in legislative efforts to achieve balance between the interests of research-based drug companies and the consumers' interest in having a wide range of lower-priced generic equivalents as soon as possible. In his opening statement to a hearing of the Senate Judiciary Committee on March 5, 1996 to assess the effectiveness of P.L. 98-417, The Drug Price Competition and Patent Term Restoration Act of 1984 (that is often referred to as the Hatch-Waxman Act), Senator Orin Hatch commented: "The foundation of this Act was simple. It reflected a finely tuned balance which reflected the dynamics of the health care marketplace." The Act, he said, continues to provide incentives for drug companies to undertake research on new drubs while enabling low-cost, generic equivalents that are relied upon by consumers to come quickly to market.[1]

General Characteristics Explaining Price Determination in the Prescription Drug Market

To say that prescription drug prices are determined by supply and demand forces is to simplify the process in the extreme. It would be inaccurate to simply attribute the level of drug prices solely to the market power of the large, research-based drug companies that enjoy patent protection, although this clearly is a major factor. Offsetting the influence of the research-based companies are the generic drug producers and the large payers for prescription drugs: the insurance companies, the government, and various health care providers (such as hospitals and staffed HMOs). All of these players in the market interact with one another to various degrees.

A Conceptual Approach to Understanding Price Determination in the Prescription Drug Market

Prescription drug pricing is not merely determined by the coming together in the marketplace of buyers and sellers who, in the idealized model of perfect competition, negotiate prices on an equal footing. To the contrary, the different buyers and sellers come to the market with varying degrees of negotiating power that skews the pricing advantage to one side or the other. There are two concepts in economics that are particularly helpful in exploring the functioning of the prescription drug market: price discrimination and bilateral monopoly. While neither of these economic concepts describes precisely the characteristics of the real marketplace for prescription drugs, each gives a reasonably good, although simple, picture of the players in the prescription drug market and, therefore, an explanation for price determination.[2]

Price Discrimination

Price discrimination involves the ability of the seller to segregate different groups of buyers from one another. These buyer groups are distinguished by dissimilar degrees of responsiveness to price; those who are highly price sensitive will respond to a small drop in the price with a relatively large increase in the quantity demanded. Given the ability to separate each class of buyers from all the others, the seller can charge different prices to each of the classes. This model breaks down if there are a large number of sellers, because the buyer groups would be able to shop around. The model of pure price discrimination assumes

[1] U.S. Senate. Committee on the Judiciary. *News Release: Statement of Senator Orrin G. Hatch, Senate Judiciary Chairman. "A Decade Later: The Drug Price Competition and Patent Term Restoration Act).*March 5, 1996, 4 p. Other legislative proposals that could impact on price include: S. 1191; The Consumer Access to Prescription Drug Act of 1995, introduced by Senator Pryor on August 11, 1995; and, S. 1277; The Prescription Drug Equity Act of 1995, introduced by Senator Brown on September 27, 1995.

[2] This report does not address possible legal aspects or issues that may arise in the context of the prescription drug market.

there is only one seller, a monopolist. As will be seen herein, this rigid assumption can be relaxed to allow for a small number of relatively large sellers.

Bilateral Monopoly

A market characterized as a bilateral monopoly consists of two parties: a single seller and a single buyer. Price is determined by the relative market power of the two participants. They party that is more powerful has greater influence in setting the price. Therefore, price is indeterminate in the bilateral monopoly model, unlike models of price determination in most other types of markets.

FACTORS INFLUENCING PRICING DECISIONS OF RESEARCH-BASED PHARMACEUTICAL COMPANIES

Research-based drug companies clearly have considerable latitude in setting prices for their various products. They are the firms that engage in basic or applied research leading to the discovery of potentially new and commercially viable products. If successful in their basic/applied research, they obtain patents for their products, which afford them what is called market exclusivity. In principle, they – like any seller in any market – would price their products so as to maximize profits. Given patent protection, these companies would like to behave as if they were monopolists, charging the highest possible price consistent with achieving their profit objectives.

But market exclusivity does not mean monopoly status. Within a given pharmaceutical category, patented drugs may have similar therapeutic substitutes. For example, Glaxo-Wellcome's very popular ulcer treatment drug, Zantac, competes with Merck's Pepcid; both of these drugs still are under patent. Zantac also is in competition with SmithKline Beecham's Tagamet, and with over-the-counter versions of both Pepcid and Tagamet. The market structure is more properly defined as an oligopoly, in which a relatively few firms have significant influence over the price in the market.

Owing to the relatively small number of large producers, each company is likely to take the price of the patent-protected competition into consideration in establishing its "launch price."[3] This is the price at which the drug is put on the market after obtaining Food and Drug Administration (FDA) approval to market the product. As a result, it is likely that a new drug for which there are relatively close substitutes would be prices lower than otherwise.[4] If they did not take into account what economists refer to a mutual interdependence, the would risk price instability in the market; that is, sellers of therapeutic substitutes might engage in

[3] The Boston Consulting Group. *The Changing Environment for U.S. Pharmaceuticals: The Role of Pharmaceutical Companies in a Systems Approach to Health Care*. Boston, 1993. p. 8f. (Hereafter cited as: The Boston Consulting Group. *The Changing Environment for U.S. Pharmaceuticals.)* This report was commissioned by Pfizer, Inc., one of the research-based pharmaceutical companies.

[4] Schwetizer, Stuart O. and William S. Comanor. The Cost of Pharmaceuticals, in Andersen, Ronald M., Thomas H. Rice, and Gerald F. Kaminski, editors. *Changing the U.S. Health Care System*. San Francisco, Jossey-Bass Publishers, 1996. p. 110f

ruinous price competition.[5] Taking into account the pricing of competing patented products already on the market does not imply something other than a profit-maximizing strategy. It simply recognizes that the market structure is defined as an oligopoly and not as a monopoly.

There may be cases where there are not other patented drugs in a given therapeutic category. The first research-based drug to come to market within a category – typically referred to as a "pioneer" drug – and the so-called "orphan drugs" – those for which the number of patients is very small and, therefore, which might be regarded as not commercially feasible- are examples of situations in which there is no competition. In these situations, the manufacturer would enjoy monopoly status, and, absent other pressure, could price its products accordingly. Still, when new drugs enter the therapeutic category, the "pioneer" drug producer would have to recognize that the monopoly status it enjoyed is subject to oligopolistic competition from new substitutes.

Not only are there pressures on price from other research-based companies, but, as has been alluded to above, the emergence of large payers in the market places constraints on the prices that all drug producers can charge. As a result, the research-based companies are likely to take into account other factors in the decisions to both market the drug at all and setting its "launch price." In particular, the research-based companies would probably consider the effective period of market exclusivity afforded by patent protection. Market exclusivity determines how long they can avoid the added competition and erosion of market share from generic equivalents.

While all new patents issued after June 8, 1995, will have an effective term of 20 years from the date of filing with the enactment of the Uruguay Round Agreements Act of 1994,[6] some part of this period will be lost to the patent holder owing to the applied research and development time and the FDA approval review. The former involves conducting extensive clinical trials of a new drug over a period of years to determine that the new product is both safe and effective for its intended therapeutic application. Only after developing a substantial safety and effectiveness data base from the clinical trials can the patent holder submit a new drug application (ND) to FDA. At this point, another period of time is consumed by FDA in the review of the submissions. While there can be variations in the length of time involved in both the clinical trials and the FDA review and approval process, the time consumed reduces the *effective* term of the patent.[7] The Pharmaceutical Research and Manufacturers of America (PhRMA), the trade association representing research-based drug companies, claimed that FDA required an average of 19.2 months to review and approve each of 28 new drugs in

---

[5] Although the research-based companies might avoid price competition, they likely would compete in other qualitative ways. For example, one drug may have to be taken two or three times daily, while another might have to be taken only once daily.

[6] U.S. Library of Congress. Congressional Research Service. *Patent Terms and Early Publication: Comparison of H.R. 359, H.R. 1733, and the 1994 URAA Patent Term Provisions*. Report No. 95-1136 A, by Dorothy Schrader. Washington, 1995. p. 2. Patents in force prior to June 8, 1995 would have an effective term of either 17 years from the date of award or 20 years from the date of the filing of the application for a patent.

[7] The Drug Price Competition and Patent Term Restoration Act of 1984 (P.L. 98-417) – the Hatch-Waxman Act – provides for an extension of the effective term of the patent for a period of up to five years to compensate for the time consumed in the FDA approval process. Hatch-Waxman is not superseded by the Uruguay Round Agreements Act, although the matter is being litigated.

1995.[8] Citing a Tufts University study, PhRMA asserts that the total length of time required to both conduct clinical trails and obtain NDA approval is 15 years.[9]

A longer period of market exclusivity may help to offset the competitive forces from within both segments of the supply side of the market – both the research-based and the generic drug companies – and the influence of the large payers. More importantly, the longer period of market exclusivity implies that research-based companies can accumulate greater profits over time. At a minimum, each of these companies in achieving its goal of profit maximization must recover all the manufacturing, marketing, general and administrative costs as well as those incurred in the FDA approval process, or else they will not supply the product.[10]

THE ROLE OF GENERIC DRUG PRODUCERS IN THE MARKET

The research-based drug producers typically do not respond, at least initially, to competition from generic drug producers. That is, the price of research-based product does not necessarily fall once its patent expires. The influence of generics on prices of research-based companies may be felt only after several generic equivalents come onto the market.[11]

One reason that research-based companies do not lower prices immediately in reaction to the introduction of generic drug equivalents is a variant of price discrimination. Physicians and consumers who attach great importance to brand-names or who have generous health insurance plans may conceivably be willing to demand and, therefore, pay more for a research-based drug than others. Consequently, even though the research-based company is likely to lose market share to generics, it can still charge all or nearly all of its original price while retaining those consumers who are less sensitive to price. The size of this group of consumers could decrease as generic prices fall.

When generic producers come into the market upon expiration of the patent, they represent a new source of competition to the research-based drugs. But unlike the research-based drug producers, they do not set their prices relative to their costs of production. Rather, the generic's "launch price" may be related to the price of the research-based product rather than to their own costs of production. Studies indicate that the immediate introduction of the generic is at a price roughly 30 percent less than the research-based drug.[12] Over time, as more generic equivalents come into the market, the generic price drops. What is clear, however, is that the research-based drug provides a kind of pricing umbrella for the generic.

[8] Pharmaceutical Research and Manufacturers of America. *Press Release: FDA Approves 28 New Drugs; Review Time is 19.2 Months*. Washington, January 1996. p. 1.

[9] *Ibid.* The Tufts University study cited is: DiMasi, Joseph A. Trends in Drug Development Costs, Times, and Risks. *Drug Information Journal*, v. 29, 1995. p. 375-384.

[10] These costs include the fees required to have FDA review their new drug applications. These fees were mandated in the Prescription Drug User Fee Act of 1992 (P.L. 102-571).

[11] The Boston Consulting Group. *Sustaining Innovation in U.S. Pharmaceuticals: Intellectual Property Protection and the Role of Patents*. Boston, 1996. p. 35. (Hereafter cited as: The Boston Consulting Group. *Sustaining Innovation in U.S. Pharmaceuticals.)* This reports was commissioned by PhRMA, 12 research-based pharmaceutical companies, and one biotechnology company.

[12] The Boston Consulting Group. *Sustaining Innovation in U.S. Pharmaceuticals*. p. 35; Moore, Judy. *The Pharmaceutical Industry: A Background Paper for the National Health Policy Forum*. Washington, The George Washington University, 1996. p. 8; and, Schondelmeyer, Stephen W. *Economic Impact of GATT Patent Extension on Currently Marketed Drugs*. Minneapolis, University of Minnesota College of Pharmacy PRIME Institute, 1995. Figure 2 (no page number given)/

Thus, both classes of companies appear to follow strategies that tend to avoid precipitous declines in price upon introduction of generic equivalents into the market.

Although the entry of generic products does not necessarily result in lower prices of research-based drugs, this segment of the industry leads to a lower weighted-average price of pharmaceuticals in the overall market. Heath care providers have the option of prescribing lower priced alternatives to those drugs that enjoyed patent-protected market exclusivity.

More importantly, owing to P.L. 98-417, The Drug Price Competition and Patent Term Restoration Act of 1984 – that is generally referred to as the Hatch-Waxman Act, the drop in the average price of pharmaceuticals occurs earlier than if Hatch-Waxman had not been enacted. Prior to Hatch-Waxman, generic producers could not develop generic equivalents until after the relevant patents expired. The Hatch-Waxman Act provided a statutory mechanism that enabled generic drug producers to bring their equivalent products to market immediately upon expiration of the patent (including any patent term restoration period). The basic requirements for FDA approval of generic equivalents are the submission of evidence that the primary ingredients in the generic drug are bio-equivalent to the research-based drug and that the generic is absorbed into the body at essentially the same rate as the research-based drug. The generic drug companies do not have to develop the same clinical trial database to demonstrate the effectiveness of their products. The result is that the costs incurred in gaining FDA approval to market generic drugs is substantially lower costs is the introduction of generics into the market more promptly. The Boston Consulting Group estimates that the saving in time theoretically could be in the range of five to eight years.[13]

This saving in time clearly represents a benefit to price sensitive consumers. They can purchase the generic equivalent sooner and at a lower price. Moreover, as more generic equivalents for a particular research-based drug come on the market, the generic drug price falls even more.[14]

The research-based companies argue that the ability of generics to enter the market sooner under Hatch-Waxman effectively reduces the period of their market exclusivity. This, in turn, results in a higher "launch price" for their products.

THE ROLE OF LARGE PLAYERS FOR PRESCRIPTION DRUGS

In recent years, the power of prescription drug users – and, in particular, of the institutions that *pay* for the drugs – has increased and emerged as a major countervailing force against the presumed high prices of research-based pharmaceutical manufacturers. These institutions include: insurance companies, hospitals, HMOs and other managed care organizations, and government.[15] In part, the growth of power of these groups can be attributed to the relatively speedy introduction of new generic products into the market. Ironically, while the generic producers might tie their prices to those of the research-based companies, their products make it easier for larger payers to bargain prices down. But it also

---

[13] See: Moore, Judy. *The Pharmaceutical Industry: A Background Paper for the National Health Policy Forum.* Washington, The George Washington University, 1996. p. 8; and, The Boston Consulting Group. *Sustaining Innovation in U.S. Pharmaceuticals.* p. 30.

[14] Schondelmer, Stephen W. *Economic Impact of GATT Patent Extension on Current Marketed Drugs.* Minneapolis, University of Minnesota College of Pharmacy PRIME Institute, 1995. Figure 2 (no page number given).

[15] Tully, Shawn. Why Drug Prices Will Go Lower. *Fortune*, May 3, 1993. p.56.

is a result of their size, and their ability to bargain more effectively with the large sellers than small groups of individual consumers. Their size enables them to negotiate price as bilateral monopolists.

Hospitals and HMOs and other managed care organizations exert influence on drug prices through the establishment of formularies. In essence, formularies are lists of drugs that these organizations rely upon for dispensing and to achieve financial objectives.[16] Managed care organizations and insurance companies attempt to shift patients to drugs listed on the formulary by monitoring the extent to which doctors prescribe them. Those doctors who do not meet the insurers' criteria are reportedly subject to pressure from so-called pharmacy benefit managers.[17] Insurers also provide incentives to policy holders to use mail order pharmacies that at least offer administrative cost savings to the insurance companies. Mail order pharmacies, which also have formularies, are large enough to bargain for lower wholesale prices.[18] Given the captive patient base of the large payers, the use of formularies enables these organizations to bargain intensively with the drug companies on the basis of price.

There is a great deal of anecdotal information indicating that the large payer may have sufficient power to negotiate significantly lower drug prices with the research-based companies. In 1994, a large Los Angeles Times report presented data showing that hospitals could buy various drugs at prices as much as and perhaps more than 90 percent below the wholesale price charge to retail druggists.[19] The report indicated that a Proventil Inhaler manufactured by Shcering was sold to hospitals at a price of $1.55 as contrasted with a price of $18.84 to a retail drug store. Similarly, HMOs and other managed care facilities are reported to be increasingly aggressive in dealing with pharmaceutical manufacturers with respect to price. These organizations are able to exert influence on price by establishing highly restrictive formularies; for example, the managed care organization, United Healthcare, is reported as limited its formulary listing to only one drug in each therapeutic category.[20]

Government exerts its influence on prices by requiring drug manufacturers to provide rebates to states for Medicaid and Veterans Administration drug purchases. The Boston consulting Group (BCG) indicates that Medicaid rebates are at least 15.7 percent of the manufacturers' weighted average price for all products. BCG also states that a minimum 24 percent discount is price is required to be given to the Veterans Administration.[21]

Disparate *Relative* Bargaining Power Among Retail Drug Sellers

Even within the retail prescription drug distribution network, three is considerable disparity in the *relative* bargaining power of the different participants with the drug companies. The retail outlets – primarily, the independent pharmacists, the chain drug stores,

[16] For additional information on the role of formularies, see: U.S. Library of Congress. Congressional Research Service. *Prescription Drug Prices: The Effects of Generic, Formularies and Other Market Changes.* Report No. 93-740 E, by Sylvia Morrison. Washington, 1993. p. 6.
[17] The Boston Consulting Group. *Sustaining Innovation in U.S. Pharmaceuticals.* p. 40.
[18] The Boston Consulting Group. *The Changing Environment for U.S. Pharmaceuticals.* p. 21.
[19] Fritz, Sara. Prescription Drug Pricing Hurting the Poor, Elderly. *Los Angeles Times,* January 24, 1994. p. A24.
[20] Freudenheim, Milt. The New Drug-Price Squeeze. *The New York Times, March 13, 1996.* p. D1.
[21] *Ibid.* p. 10.

the mass merchandisers and food stores with pharmacies, and the mail order facilities generally are large enough to maintain their own wholesale distributions facilities. In recent years, the independent pharmacies have formed buyer cooperatives to achieve economies of scale.[22]

A recent survey of chain and independent druggists provides some evidence that these two segments of the retail drug industry have no significant price advantage over each other.[23] The average price charged in 1994 for a prescription by the independent pharmacist was $25.54; the chain druggist charged a slightly higher average price of $25.62. More recent data indicates that chain and independent druggist have roughly the same gross margin on prescriptions; the gross margin of the chain store is about 24 percent, while the gross margin of the independent pharmacist is nearly 28 percent.[24]

Both the independent and chain drug segments of the retail pharmacy industry asset that the only significant discounts to retailers are with the mail order pharmacy facilities; they also contend that the mail order pharmacies do not pass the discounts on to the consumer.[25] Within the independent and chain drug stores, some outlets could conceivably obtain larger discounts than others. Representatives of the mail order pharmacy facilities would to comment on any discounts they may negotiate or their pricing policies owing to pending litigation.[26] Nevertheless, based on their public position that opposes legislative efforts to eliminate discounting,[27] one may reasonably assume that mail order pharmacy facilities do negotiate relatively substantial discounts.

The relative power of the mail order pharmacists vis-à-vis drug manufacturers may derive most importantly from the role of insurance companies and the incentives they offer policy holders to use mail order services. These incentives include relatively low or no co-payments to customers. Mail order services afford administrative cost saving to insurers. The mail order services also have lists of preferred drugs – formularies – that they offer at lower prices when prescriptions do not have to be filled as written.[28] There also are insurance plans that *require* policy holders to use mail order and other facilities to obtain pharmacy benefits. These exclusive contracts are cited as the main factor affecting prescription business in both chain and independent pharmacies.[29] As a result, mail order pharmacies may have substantially more power in the market than independent and chain pharmacy outlets to bargain intensively with drug manufacturers on the basis of price.[30]

---

[22] The Boston Consulting Group. *The Changing Environment for U.S. Pharmaceuticals.* p. 21 f.

[23] 1995 Prescription Trends Survey. *American Druggist*, June 1995. pp. 23 to 26.

[24] Maline, Nancy. Staying on Top of the Game. *Drug Store News For The Pharmacist*, May 1995 p. 30 f. The gross margin is the difference between the acquisition cost of the prescription drug and the retail price.

[25] Memorandum from National Association of Retail Druggists (NARD) and National Association of chain Drug Stores (NACDS) dated October 26, 1994. *Model Bill on Equal Access to Pharmaceutical Manufacturers' Discounts.* Alexandria, 1994. 1 p; and, telephone communication with NARD on March 1, 1996.

[26] Information obtained in telephone communication on March 1, 1996 with a representative of The American Managed Care Pharmacy Association (AMCPA) that represents mail order pharmacy facilities.

[27] American Managed Care Pharmacy Association. *AMCPA Policy Statement. Negotiated Pricing With Pharmaceutical Manufacturers.* Arlington, 1994. 3 p.

[28] Mail order services may contact doctors to obtain authorization to fill prescriptions with the preferred products in their formularies.

[29] 1995 Prescription Trends Survey. *American Druggist*, June 1995. p. 26.

[30] The Boston Consulting Group. *The Changing Environment for U.S. Pharmaceuticals.* p. 21.

CONCLUDING OBSERVATIONS: HOW DOES THE END-USER FARE IN THE PRESCRIPTION DRUG MARKET?

Prescription drug pricing is clearly a complex process. The research-based drug companies might ideally want to exercise "monopoly power" resulting from patent protection. But they are subject to pressures from their counterparts that hold patents on products that, in many instances, can be used to treat the same medical problem. Generic companies put some pressure on the research-based companies once patents have expired. But, given that they typically enter the market at some percentage reduction from the research-based drug prices, their influences on research-based companies may be less than what might be expected.

The increased concern over the rise in health care costs in the past decade at least and the resulting emphasis on cost containment gave rise to a growing number of large payer groups with the ability to bring significant economic pressure upon suppliers of prescription drugs to lower their prices. As a result, the rates of increase in both wholesale and retail drug prices have tended to decline since 1981.[31]

On reflection, what stands out in the discussion is the fact that drug prices are being actively negotiated between manufacturers, insurers, and distributors (including retail outlets). Passive acceptance of drug prices pertains only to certain groups of end-users: those insured persons who have to meet an out-of-pocket minimum expenditure before insurers enter the picture, and uninsured persons. For most people, the price paid for prescription drugs is both small in amount and relatively constant. Retail pharmacies are paid for the most part by insurance companies Even in the managed care market environment, pharmacists negotiate the payments they receive from insurance companies.

To say that only certain groups of end-users confront list prices for prescription drugs directly is not to suggest by any means that the individuals in those groups are insignificant. To a large extent, those groups include the elderly, and especially those on fixed retirement incomes. If for no other reason than age, they tend to spend more on medications than younger persons. Not having health insurance with prescription drug coverage independently of or in combination with Medicare, that does not cover prescription drugs, could be a significant financial burden for these people. This raises, then, a different question: is the concern with prescription drug prices a matter of large oligopolistic companies taking advantage of their market power, or is it a matter of providing affordable and portable health insurance that includes prescription drug benefits to all? The market seems to have dealt with the former concern; the latter is, arguable, a separate matter entirely.

---

[31] The Boston Consulting Group observes that the increases in the Producer and Consumer Price Indexes for drugs fell from about 12 percent in 1981 to about 3 or 4 percent in 1994. There appears to be some evidence that drug prices may be rising in the range of 3 to 5 percent over the past few years, but even this rate is much lower than the price increases in the early 1980s. See: The Boston Consulting Group. *Sustaining Innovation in U.S. Pharmaceuticals*. p. 43; and, Weber, Joseph. Drug Prices: So Much For Restraint. *Business Week*, March 4, 1996. p. 40.

Chapter 4

PRESCRIPTION DRUG PRICE COMPARISONS: THE UNITED STATES, CANADA, AND MEXICO

David J. Cantor

ABSTRACT

The question of differential prices of prescription drugs across U.S., Canadian, and Mexican national borders in invariably raised in any discussion of public policy related to the regulation of the pharmaceutical industry and, especially, the research-based pharmaceutical industry. The implication of the question is that the American consumer is being gouged by the drug manufacturer at the pharmacy.

The reality is that retail prescription drug prices in the United States are higher than in neighboring countries. While it is likely that the pharmaceutical companies price their products in these countries with a view to maximizing profits, consistent with what the market will bear, it also is demonstrably clear that the structure of the markets in the three countries are very different, making it difficult, if not impossible, for a single price to be charged in all three countries. In particular, government plays a significant role in the marketing of prescription drugs in both Canada and Mexico as compared with its role in the United States. Also, U.S. government regulation preventing the importation of retail lots of prescription drugs may give rise to the unintended consequence of creating a barrier to price equalization across national borders.

PRESCRIPTION DRUG PRICE DIFFERENTIALS: THE UNITED STATES AND CANADA

On average, and based on the most comprehensive data available – for 1991 in a report compiled by the General Accounting Office (GAO)[1] – prescription drugs in the United States were prices about 34 percent higher than the same products in Canada.[2] Average price for the

---

[1] U.S. General Accounting Office. *Prescription Drugs; Companies Typically Charge More in the United States Than in Canada. GAO/HRD-92-110.* Washington, 1992. 37 p. (Hereafter cited as: GAO. *Prescription Drugs.*)

[2] The concept of the same product includes the same quantity dispensed, the same form the product (e.g., tablets, capsules), and the same dosage. See, GAO. *Prescription Drugs.* p. 10.

products sold in the United States was $45.17, ranging from $2.35 (for Deltasone, 5mg. Tablets) to $304.32 (for PCE, 333 mg. Tablets). The average price for the same products sold in Canada was $33.78, ranging from $1.29 (for Deltasone, 5 mg. Tablets) to $211.98 (for PCE, 333 mg. Tablets). The comparisons were based on data collected in both countries for 121 prescription drugs in the same quantities for each product.

It should not be assumed that U.S. prices were higher on every product. Of the 121 products, 22 were priced lower in the United States than in Canada. Of the 99 products with higher U.S. prices, the differential was less than 1o percent in 11 cases. Thus, in about one-fourth of the products, the U.S. price was either moderately higher or lower than the same product in Canada. At the same time, it should be noted that the price differential exceeded 100 percent in 21 cases; of these, the differential was greater than 200 percent in eight instances.

The products selected by GAO for its analysis were the most frequently dispensed drugs in their most commonly used dosages and packages sizes by U.S. drugstores.[3] The U.S. prices were obtained from private U.S. databases, and are the wholesale acquisition costs paid by the drugstores. Given the list of drugs, the Canadian prices were the Canadian factory prices listed by the Ontario Drug Benefit Formulary (ODB).[4] The ODB is a provincial government plan; its formulary – the list of drugs covered under the plan – indicates the maximum amount of reimbursement to the druggist for each prescription drug.[5]

GAO offers two principal reasons for the differential in the drug prices in the two countries. First, Canadian law controls prices of both new drugs entering its market and any increases in the prices of pharmaceuticals already on the market. Second, provincial government drug benefit plans, in which the provinces are third-party payers, confer on government market power in determining prices.[6] For example, the Ontario Drug Benefit plan serves 40 percent of the prescription drug market, according to GAO, enabling it to exert significant pressure on prices that it will pay.[7]

Prescription Drug Price Differentials: The United States and Mexico

PhRMA, the trade association representing the research-based pharmaceutical companies in the United States, acknowledges that prescription drug prices in Mexico are significantly lower in the United States.[8] It offers two main reasons for these price differentials: international income inequality and the lower value of the peso vis-à-vis the dollar.[9] The change in the value of the peso is to all intents and purposes self-explanatory: a decline in the value of the peso increases the prices of U.S. goods imported into Mexico. The lower income

---

[3] *Ibid.*
[4] *Ibid.*, p. 11.
[5] *Ibid.*, p. 16.
[6] *Ibid.*, p. 15 f.
[7] *Ibid..*, p. 17.
[8] Price data for prescription drugs in Mexico are not available in the same detail as the GAO study of Canadian drug prices.
[9] Pharmaceutical Research and Manufacturers of America. *Industry Issue Brief: International Price Comparisons.* Washington, 1994. p. 1-3.

levels in Mexico prevent or inhibit U.S. manufacturers from charging the same price on both markets.[10]

The PhRMA position on price differentials in the two markets may help to explain why the level of demand in Mexico could be lower than in the United States at any price. But it ignores business decision criteria on the supply side of the market. In an idealized free market, the proposition that people with low incomes may not demand large quantities of a product at any given price as compared with persons with high incomes does not mean that suppliers would simply make the same product available to the former group at lower prices. The suppliers in such a market are thought to be motivated by considerations of profit, if not maximum profit. As a result, unless the supplier can cover all costs of production – including embedded costs of research, development, and testing, they are not likely to enter the given marketplace.

Perhaps of greater importance in explaining price differentials in drug prices in Mexico and the United States is the fact that price controls and government procurement policies on pharmaceuticals are in place in Mexico, and have been for some time.[11] Since implementation of NAFTA and the introduction of new drugs in the Mexican market, the price differentials between the two national markets have narrowed somewhat. Still, price controls remain in place. The Mexican government is the largest purchaser of manufactured pharmaceuticals in Mexico, and, according to PhRMA, tends to favor domestic manufacturers in its purchasing decisions. The Mexican government sells its purchased drugs through the social security system in the country, a system that includes delivery of health and other services. The latter distribution system accounts for more than 40 percent of the retail market for pharmaceuticals, according to PhRMA. These policies constitute a subsidy to the consumer of pharmaceuticals, which also helps to explain price differentials in the two national markets.

The subsidy to consumers does not necessarily mean that producers are selling their product in the Mexican market at lower prices than they might otherwise charge in the idealized free market. First, because it is a consumer subsidy, it is entirely possible that the Mexican government retails its supply at prices below its cost. Second, and possibly as a result of the consumer subsidy, the actual manufacture of pharmaceuticals is to a large extent concentrated in Mexico. Mexican firms along with transnational firms operate in Mexico. The transnational companies may have located in Mexico to take advantage of lower in put costs to be able to manufacture product and sell that output in Mexico even at controlled prices that cover costs of production. A relatively recent report on the Mexican pharmaceutical industry suggests that the country is largely self-sufficient in drug production.[12] This report tends to confirm the hypothesis that even foreign-based companies would establish manufacturing operations in Mexico to avail themselves of the market.

---

[10] Information obtained in a telephone conversation with PhRMA staff on June 2, 1995. The same assertion was made in congressional hearing in 1992 by an officer of the Upjohn Corporation. See: U.s. Library of Congress. Congressional Research Service. *Pharmaceutical Pricing: Does Federal R&D Support Justify Federal Review of Prices?* CRS Report 93-471 E., by Sylvia Morrison. Washington, 1993. p. 17.

[11] For a more extensive discussion of these policies, see: Grant, Jeanne. Headaches for Pharmaceuticals. *Business Mexico*, August 1991. p. 8 f.

[12] Toledano, Salvado Herrera. Drug Production and Free Trade. *Business Mexico,* August 1991. p.14.

Additional Comments on the Explanations or Price Differentials

The question can be raised: if the manufacturers can realize profits in countries with price controls and/or government purchasing plans, why do they charge higher prices elsewhere? In a pure market economy, the objective of any firm is to *maximize* profits. When markets can be segregated so that consumers in one area cannot buy in another, the seller may be able to increase its profits by engaging in what economists call *price discrimination*. The prescription drug market in the United States can be segregated from the Canadian, Mexican, or any other foreign market. Under regulations promulgated by the Food and Drug Administration (FDA), it is *illegal* for any retail purchaser to import drugs approved for sale in the United States from other countries.[13] The rationale for this is that, while the specifications for the product is identical in both or several countries, FDA cannot certify that the product sold at retail to the buyer was manufactured in an FDA-certified facility. The FDA approval process for new and generic drugs *includes* the approval of the facilities where the drug would be manufactured for commercial distribution in the United States. While some manufacturing facilities in Canada and elsewhere have been certified by FDA, they ship products in bulk and wholesale lots, and do not sell to individual consumers. Thus, U.S. government policy relating to maintaining the safety and effectiveness of our drug supply may create conditions under which prescription drug manufacturers can charge different prices in different markets in order to maximize their profitability.

The significant role of provincial and national governments as a third-party payer of drugs in Canada and Mexico stands in relatively sharp contrast to the relatively smaller role of government and other large buyers and/or payers of prescription drugs in the United States. As noted above, 40 percent of the prescription drug market in Ontario is served by the Ontario Drug Benefit Plan; its power to influence price is significant, because it can exclude specific products from its formulary.

The role of the government as a payer for prescription drugs is not so great in the United States as it is in Canada and Mexico. Institutional facilities – hospitals (including federal facilities), staffed HMOs, and clinics – accounted for about one-fifth of the market for drugs in 1995. Typically, these organizations buy and dispense drugs based on written orders of doctors. Chain drug stores, independent pharmacies, mass merchandise outlets (such as Wal-Mart), and food stores accounted for about 70 percent of the market in 1995.[14] The institutional facilities have greater control over the products they use and, therefore, the prices they pay. While drug stores and other retail outlets are associated with managed care program to a large extent, they do not establish formularies and, therefore, have to stock virtually all pharmaceutical products. The retail outlets have considerably less power to influence price than their institutional counterparts, because they cannot exclude products from their inventory.

---

[13] U.S. Department of Health and Human Services. Food and Drug Administration. *Book on Importing Drugs Is Misleading and Could Cause Harm.* TALK PAPER. T91-1, January 9, 1991. Rockville, MD, 1991. 3 p.; and, U.S. Department of Health and Human Services. Food and Drug Administration. *Policy on Importing Unapproved Aids Drugs For Personal Use.* TALK PAPER. T88-51, July 27, 1988. Rockville, MD, 1988. 3. p.

[14] Dillon Read Equity Research. *Industry Report: Specialty Pharmaceuticals: Generic Drug and Drug Delivery Industry Overview.* New York, Dillon, Read & Co., Inc., 1996. p. 43.

With few exceptions, no such public sector constrains on the pricing of prescription drugs exist in the United States.[15] This is not to say, however, that there are no constrains on the pricing of prescription drugs by pharmaceutical companies.[16] First, with the exception of the first patented product approved for marketing in the United States for a particular medical problem, the availability of other therapeutic remedies for the same medical problem introduces an element of competition among different manufacturers of research-based drugs.[17] Second, staff health maintenance organizations (HMOs) and health insurance plans are able to exert pressure on drug manufacturers to control prices. Third, while bringing generic equivalents to market may be easier in Canada than in the United States,[18] generic drugs are increasingly more commonplace in the United States. Owing to their lower prices vis-à-vis research-based drugs, insurance companies and managed care organizations offer significant price inducements to their policyholders/members to use generic drugs whenever possible. Staffed HMOs and hospitals also maintain formularies listing those drugs that their medical staff may or are encouraged strongly to prescribe; price is a factor in the listing of drugs in the formulary.

In summary, there is no question but that prescription drugs in Canada and Mexico are less expensive than in the United States. But it would appear that the characteristics of the market significantly influence prices in both countries. U.S. government regulations related to the safety and effectiveness of drugs impose a barrier to the free-flow of prescription drugs between all three countries in principle.[19] Potentially as a result of this factor, sellers are able to charge different prices; the forces of competition that would tend theoretically to equalize prices in both markets are unable to function. That government is one of the largest payers for drugs in Canada and Mexico also gives it significant power to establish prices there; apart from its being a major payer for drugs, it also determines what drugs it will pay for. In both cases, it appears that government policy is a major factor giving rise in part to drug price differentials in these countries.

---

[15] The primary *public sector* constraints are those in the Medicaid and the Veterans Administration health benefit programs.

[16] For a fuller discussion of prescription drug pricing, see: U.S. Library of Congress. Congressional Research Service. *Prescription Drugs: Factors Influencing Their Pricing*. CRS Report 96-296 E, by David J. Cantor. Washington, 1996. 11 p.

[17] For example, Tagamet, Zantac, and Pepcid are prescribed to deal with the same medical issue. They differ in qualitative ways, such dosage and frequency of use.

[18] GAO. *Prescription Drugs*. p. 19 f.

[19] The effectiveness of this barrier to trade depends upon the degree to which Customs officials enforce the regulations propounded by FDA at the border.

Chapter 5

PRESCRIPTION DRUGS: IMPORTATION FOR PERSONAL USE

Donna U. Vogt and Blanchard Randall IV

ABSTRACT

The 107th Congress, concerned about the high costs of pharmaceuticals in the United States, is considering legislation that would give U.S. citizens the legal right to import less costly prescription drugs from foreign countries. The House, in the FY2002 appropriations for the Department of Agriculture (H.R. 2330), adopted an amendment, sponsored by Representative Gutknecht that would let persons, who are not commercial drug importers, import prescription drugs for personal use. Under the amendment, drugs must be Food and Drug Administration (FDA) approved, non-narcotic, and manufactured in an FDA-registered facility. In the Senate, a different proposal to allow drug imports (S.1229) was introduced by Senator Wellstone. I would allow patients to import prescription drugs if they are FDA-approved, non-narcotic, made in FDA-registered facilities, originate from specified countries, and are accompanied by a special import form. FDA would have to keep records of the drugs imported. These proposals would change FDA's current "personal use policy," which lets patients with life-threatening conditions (i.e., AIDS, cancer, etc.) bring small quantities of unapproved drugs into this country for personal use, tone that lets patients import approved prescription drugs for personal use. The proposals were introduced when the past and present Secretaries of Health and Human Services (HHS) declined to implement last year's Medicine Equity and Drug Safety Act (MEDS), legislation that would have let pharmacists and drug wholesalers import drugs originally made in the United States. According to the Secretaries, the MEDS Act would have raised health risks and not lowered the cost of prescription drugs. Also, they were worried that the program might make it easier for counterfeit drugs to enter the country.

INTRODUCTION

In recent years, the cost of prescription drugs has become a major issue for Congress. At present, U.s. consumers, particularly the elderly and uninsured, oftentimes pay more for prescription drugs than citizens in other countries. This price disparity has prompted some Americans to purchase prescription drugs through the Internet, by mail-order, or by traveling outside the United States, often to nearby Canada or Mexico.

To address these concerns, the 106th Congress passed the Medicine Equity and Drug Safety Act (MEDS). The MEDS Act would have let pharmacists and drug wholesalers re-import FDA-approved prescription drugs previously manufactured in the United States. However, Congress aid that the new law could not be implemented unless the Secretary of Health and Human Services (HHS) could show that the Act would result in a cost savings for imported prescription drugs and not pose additional risks to public health. (See Text Box.) Saying they were unable to meet these conditions, both the past and present Secretaries of HHS declined to implement the law stating that prescription drug safety could not be adequately guaranteed if re-importation were allowed under the MEDS Act.[1] Secretary Tommy G. Thompson further explained that the costs associated with documenting, sampling, and testing of imported drugs, as the Act requires, would make if difficult for consumers to get any significant price savings.

Summary of Drug Import Provisions in Agriculture Appropriations Act for FY2001

Medicine Equity and Drug Safety Act (MEDS). The 106th Congress passed the MEDS Act in October 2001, as part of the FY2001 agriculture appropriations law (P.L. 106-387). An amendment to the Federal Food, Drug, and Cosmetic Act (FFDCA), the established a five-year import program to allow pharmacists and drug wholesalers to import less costly prescription drugs into the United States. The following summarizes two of the legislation's major clauses as enacted:

Regulations and Limitations. Under the MEDS Act, the Secretary of HHS was to have promulgated regulations that would have guaranteed that all drugs imported under the program would be FDA-approved, tested for authenticity, and be properly labeled before distribution.

Conditions. Before the Act could be implemented, the Secretary had to demonstrate to Congress that its implementation would pose no additional risk to public health and safety, and would result in a significant reduction in the cost of drugs for U.S. consumers.

Prescription Drug Import Fairness Act of 2000. This Act, also passed as part of the FY2001 agriculture appropriations law, prevents FDA from sending warning letters to persons who import the drugs for personal treatment unless the agency specifies how the import violates the law.

The MEDS Act was never implemented by either Secretary of HHS. The Prescription Drug Import Fairness Act, however, currently is in effect.

Subsequently, some Members of the 107th Congress have looked for other legislative ways to deal with the drug pricing issue. On July 12, 2001, the House agreed to an amendment by Representative Gutknecht to the FY2002 appropriations bill for the

[1] "Secretary Thompson Determines That Safety Problems Make Drug Reimportation Unfeasible," *HHS News*, Press Release, July 10, 2001. [http//:www.hhs.gov/news].

Department of Agriculture (H.R. 2330), that would let U.S. citizens who are not in the drug importation business import FDA-approved, non-narcotic prescription drugs, if they meet the requirements in the bill. While these measures are similar (i.e., both would allow patients to import FDA-approved, non-narcotic prescription drugs), they also have their differences. The House-passed amendment would let persons import prescription drugs for personal use for any country. The Wellstone bill, however, would only let persons import drugs from specified countries,[2] and only if accompanied by an import form. The Senate bill also would require RDA to keep records of all drugs imported.

BACKGROUND

Under the Federal Food, Drug, and Cosmetic Act (FFDCA), all drugs have to be proven safe and effective before they can be marketed in the United States. To gain FDA approval, foreign or domestic drug manufacturers must first submit New Drug Applications (NDAs) that include reports of clinical studies documenting safety and efficacy. As the NDA is being evaluated, the agency inspects the plant and the production line where the new drug will be manufactured to ensure that it will be made to specification and in accordance with good manufacturing practices (GMPs). Also, it approves the companies that supply the raw ingredients that go into making the final product. As these inspections are carried out, other FDA officials check the drug's labeling to make sure that it is both accurate and comprehensive. Pharmaceuticals imported into the United States, whether they were originally made here or abroad, must be FDA-approved and properly labeled. Imported drugs have to be accompanied by information telling where they were made, the name and address of the importer, and evidence that the drugs were made in an FDA-inspected facility following proper GMPs. Imported pharmaceuticals that do not meet the U.S. standards are considered "unapproved" drugs and cannot be imported legally. To reduce the chance that adulterated or subpotent drugs could enter a U.S. retail pharmacy, Congress passed the 1987 Prescription Drug Marketing Act (P.L. 100-293). The law made it illegal for anyone other than the original manufacturer to import a drug back into the United States.

Today, both U.S. Customs and FDA officials have broad authority to deny entry to imported drug products that "appear" to violate U.S. regulatory requirements. For enforcement purposes, the FDA separates imported prescription drugs into three categories: (1) drugs for commercial distribution; (2) prescription drugs that arrive by mail or common carrier; or (3) prescription drugs that are brought into the country by persons passing through customs.

FDA's Current Mail and Personal Use Import Policy

Although it is illegal to import unapproved drugs into the United States, the FDA, for years, has maintained a policy that lets patients bring a small amount (i.e., a 90-day supply) or non-FDA approved drugs into this country for compassionate sue. The so-called "personal use import policy" makes it easier for patients with life-threatening diseases (such as AIDS)

[2] Australia, Canada, European Economic Area (including the European Union, Norway, Iceland, and Liechenstein), Israel, Japan, New Zealand, South Africa, or Switzerland.

to bring therapies back into this country to be treated by their personal physician.[3] Under the policy, drugs cannot be imported commercially, and patients must affirm in writing that the drug is for personal use and provide the name and address of their physician. Enforcing the personal use policy often requires a lot of discretion on the part of FDA and Customs inspectors. When drugs are brought into this country for personal use today, they either are carried in by persons, or arrive via the mail, after being purchased from pharmacies operating over the Internet.

When the personal use import policy was established, it was never intended to be a way for patients to bring lower priced drugs into this country; nor was it a means for patients to buy drugs that already are available in the United States. While the policy has not changed, where it once let patients import drugs for compassionate use, today it is being used to import drugs to treat all kinds of medical conditions, by patients seeking lower prices prescription drugs from other countries.[4] Over time, FDA's import policy, and its discretionary enforcement, have led to a dramatic increase in drug imports. Today, this increase has become a major concern of both FDA and the Customs Service.

Earlier this year, in order to determine the amount and types of drugs being imported through the mail, the FDA and Customs conducted a five-week survey of drugs entering the United States by mail in Carson City, California. According to the agencies, many of the drugs detained during the survey were for treating health conditions that normally require a doctor's diagnosis.[5] This funding raised the concern that patients who would obtain prescription drugs without a doctor's prescription may be exposing themselves to serious risks. During a Jun 7, 2001 congressional hearing on drug import policy, the FDA said that it was on the verge of recommending that the Secretary of HHS end the practice of allowing drugs imported via the mail, as long as there was an exception for drugs intended for compassionate use.[6] The large number of drugs entering the country by mail has become an enforcement problem, and FDA's concern is that government inspectors cannot, with any assurance, determine whether the products being shipped are safe.

THE GUTKNECHT AMENDMENT

When the House considered the FY2002 appropriations bill for the Department of Agriculture, it agreed to an amendment sponsored by Representative Gutknecht, that would allow individuals to bring FDA-approved drugs into the United States for personal use. The text of the amendment says:

> None of the amounts made available in this Act for the Food and Drug Administration may be used under section 801 of the Federal Food, Drug and Cosmetic Act to prevent an individual who is not in the business of importing prescriptions drugs within the meaning of section 801(g) of such Act from importing a prescription drug that (1) appears to be FDA-approved,

[3] U.S. Food and Drug Administration. [http:www.fda.gov/ora/import/pipinfo.htm].

[4] U.S. citizens who want to have their prescriptions filled by Canadian pharmacies must have the prescription confirmed by a Canadian physician before the pharmacy will fill it.

[5] Hubbard, William K., Senior Associate Commissioner for Policy Planning and Legislation, Food and Drug Administration. Statement before the Subcommittee on Oversight and Investigations, Committee on Energy and Commerce, Jun 7, 2001.

[6] Ibid.

(2) does not appear to be a narcotic drug; and (3) appears to be manufactured, prepared, propagated, compounded, or processed in an establishment registered pursuant to section 510 of such Act.[7]

The amendment likely would make it easier for U.S. citizens to bring less costly prescription drugs into this country for personal use. It prohibits the commercial importation of prescription drugs, as well as the importation of narcotic products. The amendment would allow all drugs that appear to be FDA-approved to be imported. FDA believes that it would still have the authority to stop drug imports from entering this country, but only if it proved that the imported drug violated the law.

THE PERSONAL PRESCRIPTION DRUG IMPORT FAIRNESS ACT (S. 1229)

Only July 24, 2001, Senator Wellstone introduced a bill entitled the Personal Prescription Drug Import Fairness Act. In essence, the bill would create a legal framework for FDA's current policy that allows patients to import small amounts of drugs for compassionate use and extend it for treatments of other health conditions. It would amend the FFDCA to require the Secretary of HHS, in consultation with the U.S. Trade Representative and the Commissioner of Customs, to promulgate regulations to let individuals, either in person or by mail, bring a 90-day supply of prescription drugs into the country for personal use. All drugs imported under the measure, would have to be FDA-approved, be made in FDA-registered facilities, come from designated countries, be in a finished form, and could be resold in this country.

Prescription drugs, either brought in by individuals or mailed into this country, would have to be accompanied by a new "import form." The form must include the name, address and telephone number of the patient, the pharmacy that dispensed the drug, and the place where it was manufactured. It also must include the name of the patient's doctor in the United States responsible for treatment with the prescription drug, or evidence that the drug is for the continuation treatment that began outside of the United States.

Under the bill, the Secretary would be required to maintain records of each prescription drug imported. Additionally, the Secretary would have to make publicly available a list of FDA-approved drugs that could be imported for personal use that: 1) are manufactured outside of the United States; and 2) are U.S. made but intended for export.

[7] Section 801(g) was enacted by the Prescription Drug Import Fairness Act of 2000 to keep the FDA from sending individuals who import drugs for personal use warning letters about the illegality and potential health risks of imported drugs, unless the agency specifies how the import violates the law. Section 510 requires the registration of drug manufacturing facilities, whether or not they are in the United States or abroad.

Legislative Issues

Prescription Drug Costs

Supporters of the proposals contend that, as long as drug price disparities continue between countries, consumers will benefit from being able to purchase lower cost pharmaceuticals from other countries. Given that many foreign governments impose strict controls on drug prices, it would be difficult to determine a set of circumstances that might eliminate the price differences that currently are driving demand for foreign prescription drugs.

Product Integrity and Inspections Issues

Some believe that FDA's current compassionate use policy favors the import of unapproved drugs over approved drugs. To address this, the House amendment would change the policy so that a greater number of prescription drugs could be imported. In addition, it would not impose any special requirements on prescriptions obtained from foreign pharmacies. In these changes become law, FDA claims that it would be unable to guarantee the integrity of these drugs since its inspectors would have a hard time examining every parcel and determining the quality of its contents. Under such circumstances, FDA has stated that it would be "buyer beware" for consumers who decide to import prescription drugs. The Senate bill provides for a more formal system for checking the safety of imported drugs, but also does not guarantee the integrity of the drugs by FDA standards. All imported drugs would need an import form disclosing the name of the patient, the address of the dispensing pharmacy, the name of the health care provider or evidence that the drug was for treating a health condition that began overseas, and where the drug was made. However, the success of such a system would, in all likelihood, depend on consumers being able to make purchases and obtain approved drugs without undue administrative hardships.

Lack of Physician Involvement

FDA is concerned that under the House-passed bill many patients who order prescriptions drugs via Internet pharmacies do not necessarily do so with a doctor's prescription. In some instances, there may be no doctor-patient relationship whatsoever. At times, prescription drugs can produce side effect known only to professional health care providers. Without professional oversight, some drugs can pose serious health risks. The Senate bill would require the name of the patient's doctor, or evidence showing that the drug is for treatment that began outside of the United States.

FDA Enforcement Issues

The United States has the most rigorous system for ensuring drug safety in the world. Before drugs can be marketed, they have to be FDA-approved, labeled properly, manufactured in FDA inspected facilities, and sold through licensed distributors and pharmacists. Currently, the FDA has broad authority to stop the importation of a drug if the agency suspects it is unapproved or does not appear to meet U.S. standards. The House-passed amendment states that a drug can be imported if it "appears to be FDA-approved." If the amendment becomes law, FDA is concerned that it would first have to allow drugs to enter the country that appear to be approved, and then prove that the imported drug was not FDA-approved before denying entry. This could make it more difficult for the agency to keep adulterated or counterfeit drugs from entering the country if they appear to be FDA-approved and comply with U.S. regulations.[8] The Senate bill, on the other hand, would require FDA to keep records of all prescription drugs imported for personal use. In addition, the agency would have to compile and make public a list of FDA-approved drugs, manufactured both inside and outside the United States that can be imported into the country. FDA contends that these requirements would add extensive monitoring responsibilities for the agency and might not necessarily increase the safety of imported prescription drugs.

[8] Hubbard, William, K., Senior Associate Commissioner for Policy, Planning, and Legislation, Food and Drug Administration. Letter to the Honorables W.J. "Billy" Tauzin, Chairman, and John Dingell, Ranking Minority Member, Committee on Energy and Commerce, House of Representatives, July 17, 2001.

Chapter 6

PRESCRIPTION DRUG PRICES: THE EFFECTS OF GENERICS, FORMULARIES, AND OTHER MARKET CHANGES

Sylvia Morrison

ABSTRACT

The Waxman-Hatch Act of 1984 shortened and simplified the Food and Drug Administration's approval process for generic drugs. The resulting surge in the availability of low-cost generics, combined with growth in the use of formularies[1] by health care providers, is likely to reduce pharmaceutical prices, except prices for new breakthrough drugs.

BACKGROUND: SUPPLY IN THE PRE-1984 PHARMACEUTICAL MARKET

New prescription drugs normally are originated by brand-name pharmaceutical manufacturers. The manufacturers test the drugs over a multi-year period, first on animals and the on humans, for effectiveness and safety. They present their test result to the Food and Drug Administration (FDA), which must approve all drugs before they may be sold.

Generic drugs are inexpensive, pharmaceutical equivalents of brand-name products. In 1982, generics held a market share (in units) of just 2 percent.[2] One reason was that the FDA then required generic manufacturers to carry out the same lengthy and expensive tests as

---

[1] A formulary is a list of medications that are designated by a health care provider as most cost-beneficial. Health care providers instruct their doctors to prescribe formulary medications in preference to others as much as possible.

[2] By 1989, the market share (in units as opposed to dollars) of generics had grown to 33 percent. (Why Generic Drugs are O.K. *U.S. News and World Report*, September 18, 1989, p. 71.) In a CRS seminar in April 1993, pharmaceutical industry analyst Hemant Shah estimated that generics accounted for 37.5 percent of all new prescriptions in 1991, and he predicted that use of generics will rise to 40 percent of all new prescriptions in 1993, and by 2000 will probably exceed 60 percent.

originating manufacturers, even though the medication the generic was copying had already been shown to be safe and effective.[3]

A second reason for the small market share held by generics in 1982 was that as late as 1975, most States had laws that forbid pharmacists to substitute a generic drug product for the brand-name drug prescribes, unless the prescribing physician had given explicit permission for the substitution.[4] All such anti-substitution laws now have been repealed.[5]

Thus, prior to 1982, original medications experienced little or no competition even after their patents had expired except for competition from "me-too" drugs[6] offered by rival brand-name manufacturers. The kind of competition "me-too" drugs did offer typically was not price competition. On the contrary, the rival companies producing "me-toos" often priced them higher than the original drugs because the reason given for producing "me-toos" was that, in some respect, they improved upon the original medication.[7]

How Waxman-Hatch Changed the Pharmaceutical Market

In 1984, Congress swung wide the market door for generic drugs by passing the Drug Price Competition and Patent Term Restoration Act (P.L.98-417), usually called the Waxman-Hatch Act. The Act required generic drugs only to demonstrate that (1) the generic is *bioequivalent* to the brand-name drug – that is, it contains an approximately equal dose of the main ingredient; and (2) the generic is as bioavailable as the original drug – that is, it is absorbed by the body at approximately the same rate.[8] In short, the Act authorized generic drug manufacturers to avoid much of the lengthy and expensive testing the law requires for original drugs. Now generic manufacturers can place their versions of drugs on the market at considerably lower prices than those of the original medications immediately after the brand-name patents expire. Currently, pharmaceutical industry spokesmen report, a generic version of a drug absorbs half of the market for a drug within two years of its entry into the market.[9]

---

[3] In 1972, the FDA adopted a "paper NDA" policy for generics. The policy allowed generic manufacturers to submit reports published in scientific journals as the main supporting documentation for new drug applications, but only for generics made after 1962.

[4] Evaluation of Impact of Drug Substitution Legislation. *Journal of the American Pharmaceutical Association*. Vol. NS 16, No. 2, February 1976.

[5] Source: Telephone interview with staff at Pharmaceutical Manufacturers Association.

[6] New chemical entities designed to treat illnesses for which there are already drugs on the market sometimes are described as "me-toos" or "me-toos" may be chemical imitators of pioneer drugs that are altered or improved enough that they are eligible for separate patents. Some critics charge that "me-toos" rarely add any important attribute to the therapeutic market, but rather represent an attempt by rival companies to grab a portion of the market developed by the originating company. Others note that such attributes such as reduced side effects or a more convenient dosage schedule, which "me-toos" often provide, offer real advantages to the pharmaceutical consumer, and that competition tends to reduce prices.

[7] William S. Comanor. The Political Economy of the Pharmaceutical Industry. *Journal of Economic Literature*. Vol. XXIV, September 1986, p. 1187.

[8] At the same time, Waxman-Hatch provided patent extensions of up to five years to medications that had been or would be long-delayed by FDA evaluation.

[9] Still, the price advantage generics offer the consumer does not appear to draw the entire market for a drug away form the higher priced originator, even after a considerable time on the market. In a recently published three-year study, the Office of Technology Assessment (OTA) found that six years after patent expiration, the average brand-name drug still commanded more than 50 percent of the market in physical units. U.S. Congress, Office of Technology Assessment. *Pharmaceutical R&D: Costs, Risks and Rewards*. Washington, D.C. February 1993. p. 30.

A brand-name company may produce, as many are doing, generic versions of its own patented medications by simply licensing manufacture of a generic to a subsidiary of its own company.[10] The brand-name manufacturer's generic version of its own drug has both the advantage offered by the generics (lower price than the original drug), and the advantages held by the brand-name product (proven efficacy, safety, and brand-name recognition).

DEMAND IN THE PRE-FORMULARY PHARMACEUTICAL MARKET

With respect to demand – a consumer's decision to buy a medication, or to buy one medication rather than another – there have been forces at work that make price less influential in a consumer's decision to buy medications than it would be in his decision to buy almost anything else.

The first of these forces is the buyer's inclination to regard his health or that of a family member as top priority – that is, worthy of being put first before other considerations, including price. Second, in the purchase of prescription drugs, the person who pays is usually not the person who decides what to buy. The consumer believes, or at least hopes, that the doctor knows better than he which medication will benefit him most and he considers the doctor not only an expert on drugs on the market, but an objective evaluator of them. The doctor may or may not know the cost of the prescription he has written; the literature indicates that frequently he does not.[11] He may not know whether there is a generic substitute on the market, or what that may cost. Hence, unless the patient raises the issue of cost-effectiveness with his doctor or inquires from his pharmacist, he may pay for whatever drug the doctor customarily prescribes, whether it is the most cost-effective drug or not.[12]

The third factor that acts to distort demand is pharmaceutical coverage as part of a health insurance package. As Dr. Judith Wagner of OTA has written:

> While it protects consumers from uncontrollable and catastrophic expenses, health insurance also reduces the effective price of health care services and products. By reducing patients' out-of-pocket costs, health insurance makes them less sensitive to price than they otherwise would be.[13]

MANAGED COMPETITION AND FORMULARIES

A formulary is a list of drugs that an advisory committee of a health care institution (such as a hospital, health maintenance organization [HMO], or mail-order drug provider) has agreed contains those medications for each illness that provide the greatest benefit for the lowest cost. The advisory committees are made up mainly of doctors but sometimes include pharmacists.

---

[10] Almost 80 percent of U.S. generic drugs are manufactured by brand-name firms. Source: Jeffrey Yorke. FDA Ensures Equivalence of Generic Drugs. *FDA Consumer,* September 1992. p. 11.

[11] Shawn Tully. Why Drug Prices Will Go Lower. *Fortune*, May 13, 1993, p. 60.

[12] William s. Comanor. The Political Economy of the Pharmaceutical Industry. *Journal of Economic Literature*. Vol. XXIV, September 1986, p. 1210.

[13] U.S. Congress, Office of Technology Assessment. *Pharmaceutical R&D: Costs, Risks and Rewards*. Washington, D.C. February 1993. p. 26.

The Omnibus Budget Reconciliation Act of 1993 (OBRA 93) reversed OBRA 90 by authorizing States to devise formularies for their Medicaid programs. State advisory committees are to be appointed by the Governors.

If, as some predict, a system of managed competition[14] emerges as the dominant form of health care from the current political discussions about the reform of the American health care system,[15] the practice of selecting drugs by formulary is likely to become more common. With formularies in use by a growing number of HMOs,[16] hospitals, and mail-order drug companies, the patient's habit of taking a prescription given to him by his private doctor tot he local pharmacy likely will change to the practice now familiar to a number of HMO subscribers. A doctor who is a member of the patient's medical group will prescribe a medication that is included in the group's formulary. The HMO then will sell the drug to the patient at a price typically lower than that offered by a local pharmacy, or perhaps for a small co-payment.

A spokesman for Kaiser Permanente, America's largest HMO, said Kaiser provides its physicians with a formulary and, since the HMO sells the drugs it prescribes to its patients, it carries out "oversight of clinical variations;" that is, it tracks doctor's records to discover to what extent Kaiser doctors are adhering to the formulary in prescribing.[17] Kaiser restricts access to doctors by detail men,[18] and, in fact, carries out "counter-detailing" to ensure that doctors understand the reasons for prescribing the drugs included in the company's formulary. Kaiser's purpose in doing this is to concentrate its drug purchases and sales among the medications it has chosen for its formulary so that in bargaining with manufacturers for price, Kaiser can be regarded as a high-volume customer – one that will be given the best possible price.[19] As of May 1993, 96 percent of Kaiser's prescriptions were coming from the formulary list, and 75 percent were generics.[20]

The practice of prescribing almost exclusively from the formulary list, if it becomes the norm – and we cannot know now to what extent it will – will heighten competition in the pharmaceutical market to an extent that has not been experienced before now. Health care providers doubtless will follow various policies in administering their formularies, but pharmaceutical manufacturers will have to compete with each other for quality and price to get their products listed in formularies.

---

[14] Managed competition is a system for providing health care in which consumers would choose form among a variety of competing health care plans and would be given financial incentives for selecting the most cost-effective. For more information, see *Health Care Reform: Managed Competition*, CRS Issue Brief IB93008 by Mark Merlis. Updated regularly.

[15] President Clinton is widely reported to favor the managed competition option over two other types of national health care that also are reported to be considered as options. These are the "single-payer" option (Federal or State-provided insurance) and "play or pay" in which employers who fail to offer a private plan that would meet Federal Standards would pay a payroll tax that would fund Federal coverage for the uninsured. Neither of these latter two options likely would be likely to spawn as many formularies as would the managed competition option. For discussion of these latter two options, see *Health Care Reform: Mandated Employer Provided Coverage,* CRS Brief IB87168 by Beth Fuchs. Updated regularly.

[16] 36.8 million persons now are reported to be enrolled in HMOs. *Prudential Securities Health care Regulatory Update*. January 12, 1993, p. 3.

[17] Medications not included in a formulary list may be permitted as exceptions if considered necessary by prescribing physicians.

[18] It has long been a practice of pharmaceutical companies to send "detail" men or women to visit doctors, introduce new products, and provide free samples.

[19] Drugs are one of the fastest growing outlays HMOs have. Drug costs per member grew on average 17 percent from the 1990 level. *Prudential Securities Health Care Regulatory Update*. January 12, 1993, p. 6.

[20] Tully, Shawn. Why Drug Prices Will Go Lower. *Fortune*, May 3, 1993, p. 62.

RESERVATIONS ABOUT FORMULARIES

Certain reservations have been expressed about the use of formularies. The first is the inducements almost certainly will be offered to the members of the committees that select the drugs for the formularies of various organizations. The status of the law that might prohibit committee members from accepting inducements is not clear, and it is unknown whether any sanctions against accepting inducements might be applied by the medical community.

Second, many analysts cite the "paucity of well-designed comparative studies on drug safety and efficacy, and insufficient resources at the local level to support the evaluation process."[21] The literature notes that lately liability-conscious doctors tend to prescribe the drugs they have had satisfactory experience with.[22] A questions arises as to whether such preferences might override objective evaluations of competing drugs.

Third, in a managed competition environment where health care providers will have to compete for patients, the pressure to keep prices low by buying the cheapest but not necessarily the best drug will be high.

Finally, the pressure of competition to secure a place on the formularies will not apply to new, breakthrough drugs, which, owing to patent protection, will be unique, at least until a "me-too" imitator enters the market. The competitive pressure of the formularies should mean, however, that "me-toos" no longer will be offered at a higher price than the original drug, but rather a price that will make them competitive in the contest for a place on the formulary list.

---

[21] Donald T. Rucker. Ph.D. and Gordon Schiff, M.D. Drug Formularies: Myths-in-Formation. *Medical Care*, October 1990, Vol. 28, No. 10, p. 928.

[22] William S. Comanor. Op. Cit., p. 1210.

Chapter 7

OUTPATIENT PRESCRIPTION DRUGS: ACQUISITION AND REIMBURSEMENT POLICIES UNDER SELECTED FEDERAL PROGRAMS

Heidi G. Yacker

ABSTRACT

Varying reimbursement methods determine the payments for outpatient drugs supplied under different federal programs. The Veterans Health Care Act of 1992 limits the prices that drug manufacturers can charge the Development of Veterans Affairs (VA); several other government agencies, including the Department of Defense (DOD), are able to purchase pharmacy supplies through the VA supply system. The Medicaid program reimburses providers directly for covered pharmaceuticals, establishing upper payment limits on approved drugs and receiving rebates from manufacturers. The Medicare program provides limited coverage for outpatient drugs. For those drugs it covers, Medicare reimburses providers at the rate of 95 percent of the average wholesale price. This report discuses the reimbursement methods used to pay for outpatient prescription drugs by the VA, DOD, Medicaid and Medicare. It will be updated as necessary.

INTRODUCTION

The federal government provides coverage for outpatient prescription drugs under several program. The largest programs are administered by the Department of Veterans Affairs; the Department of Defense; Medicaid, the joint federal-state entitlement program that pays for medical services on behalf of certain groups of low-income persons; and Medicare, the nation's health insurance program for the elderly and certain disabled individuals. The Medicare program provides only limited outpatient drug coverage.

DEPARTMENT OF VETERANS AFFAIRS (VA)

The VA maintains a system of medical facilities from which all pharmaceutical supplies, including prescription drugs, are dispensed to beneficiaries. It also supports a mail service prescription program as part of the outpatient drug benefit. The system serves approximately 3.65 million veterans. According to VA analysts, spending for pharmaceuticals will be approximately $1.8 billion in FY1999.

The Veterans Health Care Act of 1992 (VHCA, P.L. 102-585) established the Federal Ceiling Price Program, limiting the price manufacturers could charge for drugs purchased for the VA, the Department of Defense, the Public Health Service (including the Indian Health Service) and the Coast Guard. In order to receive reimbursement under the Medicaid program (as well as from the agencies listed above), manufacturers are required to provide covered drugs to the four protected agencies at a discount of at least 24 percent below the non-Federal Average Manufacturers Price (non-FAMP), minus any cash discounts, rebates, or similar reductions. The non-FAMP is calculated using the weighted average price paid by non-federal wholesalers over the previous 12 months. Thus, the Federal Ceiling Price (FCP) is calculated using the following formula:

$$(0.76 \times \text{non-FAMP}) - \text{additional discount} = \text{FCP}$$

The FCP is the highest price that can be charged to the protected agencies for covered drugs, which are defined as all products that a drug company holds or markets under an original New Drug Application (NDA) as approved by the Food and Drug Administration, including certain single source and innovator multiple source drugs,[1] biological products, and insulin. This provision does not apply to generic drugs.

VHCA also required that, in order to be reimbursed under Medicaid, manufacturers of brand-name drugs must make all their covered pharmaceutical products available for sale mainly to the federal government. All federal agencies (and a few other entities) may purchase pharmaceuticals from the FSS. In FY1996, the VA purchased $922 million in pharmaceuticals from the FSS.[2] The VA's National Acquisition Center (NAC) is the sole negotiator for the government with drug manufacturers in establishing the prices for the approximately 23,000 drugs listed on the FSS. The prices must be equal to or better than the best price charged to the manufacturer's most favorable comparable customer. Because the VA's NAC is not bound in its negotiations with manufacturers to the FCP limits, the Federal Ceiling Price and Federal Supply Schedule prices are not necessarily the same. In fact, many prices are more than 50 percent below the non-FAMP.[3] However, the FSS price is higher than the FCP, the four protected agencies are not required to pay more than the FCP.[4]

Although most purchases are done through the FSS, the VA also negotiates contracts independent of the FFS. Through Blanket Purchase Agreements (established under FSS

---

[1] A multiple source drug is defined as one marketed or sold by two or more manufacturers or labelers; it can also be a drug marketed or sold by the same manufacturer or labeler under two or more different proprietary names, or both under a proprietary name and without such a name.

[2] U.S. General Accounting Office. *Effects of Opening the Pharmaceutical Schedule Are Uncertain.* GAO/T-HEHS-95-171, July 10, 1997. p. 1.

[3] Ibid, p. 4.

[4] Ibid.

contracts) and other national contracts with manufacturers, the VA guarantees a volume purchase (either for their beneficiaries exclusively or for beneficiaries in additional federal programs) in exchange for discounts below the FSS prices.

In addition to these contracts for goods, the VA also awards a contract for distribution under the Pharmaceutical Prime Vendor Distribution Program. Under the current award, with very few exceptions, all drugs are distributed by one company. This contract included a *negative* 2.25 percent service fee for drugs distributed through facilities, and a negative 2.9 percent for VA's Consolidated Mail Outpatient Pharmacies.

DEPARTMENT OF DEFENSE (DOD)

DOD provides drugs to approximately eight million active duty personnel, retirees, and their families through three points of service: military treatment facility (MTF) outpatient pharmacies, TRICARE managed care contractor retail pharmacies, and not the National Mail Order Pharmacy Program (NMOP). The pharmacy benefit is generally not available to Medicare-eligible retirees. As described above, DOD is covered by the Federal Ceiling Price Program established by VHCA.

Although some purchases of pharmaceuticals are made though the FSS, DOD negotiates independent contracts for the majority of their purchases. The pharmaceutical group of the Defense Supply Center in Philadelphia (DSCP) is the single entity that negotiates DOD's distribution and pricing agreements (DAPAs) with more than 200 drug manufacturers. Their starting point for negotiations is the 24 percent discount on the non-FAMP that are required under VHCA. DOD estimates that DAPA negotiated prices for drugs are approximately 24 percent to 70 percent below the average wholesale price (AWP).[5] DSCP contracts directly with a wholesale prime vendor to store drugs and deliver requested pharmaceuticals directly to MTFs. In FY1997, MTF pharmacies dispensed approximately 55 million prescriptions at a cost of approximately $1 billion.[6]

The National Mail Order Pharmacy Program (NMOP) deliver up to 90-day supplies of drugs directly to beneficiaries at their homes for patients with long-term or chronic conditions. The DAPA prices, once only available to MTFs, are now used when purchasing drugs for the mail-order program.

Under TRICARE programs, insurers under contract with DOD provide prescription drug coverage to enrolled beneficiaries. In FY1997, the NMOP and TRICARE contractor retail pharmacy programs spent approximately $245 million for prescription drugs.[7]

MEDICAID

Under Medicaid federal requirements, outpatient prescription drug coverage is an optional service. However, all 50 states and the District of Columbia provide some level of coverage. Unlike the VA and DOD, the federal Medicaid program does not directly negotiate

---

[5] The average wholesale price (AWP) is the price reported by the *Red Book* or other national compendia.

[6] U.S. General Accounting Office. *Fully Integrated Pharmacy System Would Improve Service and Cost-Effectiveness.* GAO/HEHS-98-176, June 1998. p. 3.

[7] Ibid.

contracts to purchase drugs from manufacturers. Instead, in most cases, the federal government establishes price limits that are used by states for drug reimbursement. Manufacturers provide rebates to states based on their Medicaid sales in that state during specified time periods. According to the Health Care Financing Administration (HCFA), in FY1996, Medicaid served approximately 36.1 million beneficiaries and paid $10.y billion in prescription drug benefits.

Payment for multiple source outpatients drugs is made subject to upper limits established by HCFA, plus a reasonable dispensing fee established by the state. Upper payment limits will be established only if (1) all formulations of the drug approved by the Food and Drug Administration (FDA) are evaluated as therapeutically equivalent, and (2) the drug is listed by at least three suppliers in current cost compendia of those drugs available for sale nationally. The upper payment level for thee drugs is 150 percent of the published price (as listed in any of the published drug pricing compendia) for the least costly therapeutic equivalent, plus a reasonable dispensing fee.

Guidelines also exist for "other drugs." There are brand-name drugs certified by a physician as medically necessary for a particular recipient, or a drug other than a multiple source drug for which a limit has been established. In these cases, Medicaid applies a payment level that is the *lower* of:

(1) the estimated acquisition cost plus a reasonable dispensing fee, or
(2) the provider's usual and customary charges to the general public.

Within federal limits, states can design their own prescription drug programs and attempt to limit their expenditures.

In addition to these price limits, states receive rebates from drug manufacturers under the Medicaid Rebate Program established by the Omnibus Budget Reconciliation Act of 1990 (P.L. 101-508). Under this program, in order to be eligible for federal Medicaid matching funds, pharmaceuticals manufacturers must enter into *national rebate agreements* (as opposed to the *pricing* agreements established by the VA and DOD) with the Secretary of Health and Human Services on behalf of the states (although the Secretary can authorize states to enter into contracts directly with manufacturers). The formula for calculating the multiple source rebate is:

a. the total number of units of each dosage form and strength paid for under the state plan in the rebate period, *multiplied by*
b. the greater of:

    (1) the difference between the average manufacturer price (AMP)[8] and the best price[9] ***or***
    (2) 15.1 percent of the AMP.

[8] The average manufacturer price is average priced paid to a manufacturer by retail pharmacies, or by wholesalers, for drugs distributed to the retail pharmacy class of trade.

[9] The best price is defined as the lowest price available from a manufacturer during the rebate period to any wholesaler, retailer, provider, HMO, nonprofit entity, or government entity (excluding prices charged under VHCA, prices charged under the Federal Supply Schedules, prices used under state pharmaceutical assistance programs, and depot prices or single award prices of federal government agencies).

An additional rebate is given by the manufacturer for any price increase that is higher than the increase in the consumer price index (CPI).

Rebates for "other drugs" are determined by multiplying the total number of units of each dosage form and strength paid for under the state plan in the rebate period by 11 percent of the AMP.

Rebates are not required for Medicaid managed care plans.

Drugs are reimbursed in the following manner. Beneficiaries submit prescriptions to their pharmacy. The pharmacy submits a claim for reimbursement to the state Medicaid program. The claim indicates the manufacturer of the drug and the dosage dispensed. The state Medicaid office reimburses the pharmacist using the payment levels described above. Data accumulated by the state Medicaid office is submitted quarterly to each participating manufacturer holding a rebate agreement with Medicaid. The data include the total number of dosage units of each of the manufacturer's drugs that has been dispensed to Medicaid beneficiaries in that state during the quarter. This information is used to calculate the rebate (using the formula described above) that the manufacturer remits to the state.

MEDICARE

The Medicare program generally does not provide coverage for outpatient prescription drugs. For those that it does cover (see below), payments are made under Part B of the program. Like Medicaid, Medicare does not contract with manufacturers to acquire prescription drugs for its beneficiaries. Rather, it reimburses the providers of these drugs. According to HCFA, in FY1997, Medicare, which covered approximately 38 million beneficiaries, paid $2.75 billion for outpatient prescription drugs.

Medicare makes payments directly to physicians for drugs that cannot be *self-administered* and are "incident to" a physician's professional service. Coverage is generally limited to those drugs that are administered by injection.

Despite the general limitation on coverage for outpatient drugs, the law specifically authorizes coverage for certain classes of drugs: those used in conjunction with home infusion or inhalation equipment, those used for the treatment of anemia in dialysis patients, immunosuppressive drugs for patients who have received organ transplants under Medicare, certain oral cancer and associated anti-nausea drugs, and certain immunizations. For these drugs, Medicare pays the physician or supplier (e.g., pharmacist) directly.

Drugs are identified using codes from HCFA's Common Procedure Coding System (HCPCS) that define the *type* of drug and a standard dosage amount where applicable. However, unlike the NDCs used under the federal ceiling price program, HCPCS do not identify specific drugs.

Medicare enters into contracts with local carriers and the four regional durable medical equipment carriers (DMERCs) to establish Medicare allowed amounts for covered drugs. There are not national limits set. The Balanced Budget Act of 1997 provided that the maximum allowable payment for outpatient prescription drugs is 95 percent of the average wholesale price (AWP). Carriers determine the AWP using such sources as *Red Book* or other publications or databases used by the pharmaceutical industry. Prior to 1999, if a drug had both brand and generic sources available, reimbursement was based on 95 percent of the median AWP for generic sources. In some cases, however, a brand-name product's AWP is lower than the median generic price. Therefore, in 1999, Medicare began calculating the AWP for multiple source drugs at the *lower* of the median generic AWP, or the lowest brand-name AWP.[10]

[10] U.s. Department of Health and Human Services. Office of the Inspector General. *Comparing Drug Reimbursement: Medicare and the Department of Veterans Affairs*. November 1998. p. 1.

Chapter 8

THE U.S. DRUG APPROVAL PROCESS: A PRIMER

Blanchard Randall IV

HISTORICAL BACKGROUND

The United States has perhaps the world's most stringent standards for approving new drugs. These standards, and the statutes that support them, evolved slowly during the past century as lawmakers strove to keep pace with advances in pharmacology, and growing consumer demand for safer drugs. Until early in the 20th century, there were no federal laws requiring drug manufacturers to verify the quality of the medicinals they sold in America. Untested remedies and popular cure-alls were widely sold, most with no assurance of their quality, safety, or medical benefit. Growing increasingly skeptical of the burgeoning patent medicine trade, health advocates in the early 1900s began pressing for reforms that would give consumers some protection from the growing number of unproven health claims appearing in product advertising and labeling.[1] In response to these concerns, Congress passed the Food and Drugs Act of 1906.[2] While the new law prohibited manufacturers from introducing misbranded and adulterated foods and drugs into interstate commerce, it did not require pharmaceutical companies to prove their drugs were safe.

Following the infamous "elixir of sulfanilamide" incident,[3] where more than 100 patients died from taking a drug containing a poisonous solvent, Congress passed the Federal Food, Drug, and Cosmetic Act (FD&C Act) of 1938.[4] Besides adding new quality standards for both food and drugs, the law, for the first time, required drug manufacturers to provide evidence that their products were safe before they could be approved by the U.s. Food and Drug Administration (FDA) for marketing.

A call for revamping the nation's drug laws came again in early 1960s when the world learned that thalidomide, anew drug being taken by pregnant women to treat morning

---

[1] Jassen, Wallace F. Pharmacy . . . and the Food and Drug Law. A significant Relationship. *American Pharmacy*, v. NS21, no. 4, April 1981, p. 30.

[2] Food and Drugs Act, Pub. L. no. 384, ch. 3915, 34 stat. 768 (1906).

[3] FDA Backgrounder. *Milestones in U.S. Food and Drug Law History*. May 3, 1999. [http://www.fda.gov/opacom/backgrounders/miles/html].

[4] Federal Food, Drug, and Cosmetic Act, Pub. L. no. 717, 52 stat. 1040 (1938).

sickness, was responsible for birth defects in thousands of babies born in western Europe.[5] Thalidomide's approval was pending in the United States at that time, but an FDA drug reviewer had serious reservations about the drug's safety. While these concerns prevented the drug's marketing in the United States,[6] the incident's publicity led to lengthy congressional hearings on the pharmaceutical industry, and eventual passage of the 1962 Kefauver-Harris Amendments.[7] These amendments not only tightened up existing safety testing requirements for drugs, they also required manufacturers to prove their product's effectiveness. Since then, federal law has required drug companies to prove that their products are both safe and effective before the FA can approve them for marketing.

During the 1980s, Congress enacted several landmark drug laws that have had a lasting impact on the regulation of pharmaceuticals. While none of these legislative measures were aimed at changing the Act's basic safety and efficacy provisions, per se, in one way or another, they all left their mark on the drug approval process. In 1983, Congress passed the Orphan Drug Act (P.L. 97-414), which offers drug makers financial and marketing incentives to develop drugs for treating rare diseases. The following year it enacted the Drug Price Competition and Patent Term Restoration Act of 1984 (P.L. 98-417).[8] Better known as the "Hatch-Waxman" law, it established a statutory mechanism to facilitate more rapid approval of generic drugs. At the same time, it gave drug companies added years of patent protection as compensation for marketing time lost during FDA review.[9] In 1988, these same patent benefits were given to producers of animal drugs under the Generic Animal Drug Patent Term Restoration Act (P.L. 100-670).

During the early 1990s, both consumer groups and the pharmaceutical industry became increasingly concerned about the length of time it was taking FDA to approve new drug products. In response, Congress looked for legislative ways it could speed up the drug review process without lowering approval standards, especially those that might compromise patient safety. With this goal in mind, it passed the 1992 Prescription Drug User Fee Act (PDUFA).[10] Under the user fee law, drug companies are assessed several different types of fees. The law stipulated that the extra revenues had to be used to hire additional reviewers and support staff, and upgrade FDA's information technology in order to reduce the time it took to review and approve drug marketing applications.

According to annual performance reports for PDUFA, approval times for new drug applications declined steadily after the law was enacted. Nonetheless, by the mid-1990s, the drug industry and other FDA reform advocates were contending that the rate of approval could be increased even further if more sweeping statutory changes were adopted. After much debate and political compromise, Congress passed the 1997 Food and Drug Administration Modernization Act (FDAMA), the most comprehensive overhaul of the nation's food, drug,

---

[5] Grigg, William. The Thalidomide Tragedy – 25 Years Ago. *FDA Consumer*, v. 21, no. 1, February 1987. p. 17.

[6] In 1998, FDA approved thalidomide for treating leprosy.

[7] P.L. 87-781.

[8] For a comprehensive description of the Hatch-Waxman patent law see: CRS Report RL30765, *Patent Law and Its Application to the Pharmaceutical Industry: An Examination of the Drug Price Competition and Patent Term Restoration Act of 1984*, by Wendy H. Schacht and John R. Thomas.

[9] Drug companies usually file for patent protection as soon as a new compound is discovered. As such, the testing period and FDA review, often several years, counts as part of the total period of patent protection.

[10] P.L. 102-571.

and medical device laws in more than 30 years.[11] The reform measure not only reauthorized the 1992 user fee law, it also included numerous other provisions, many of them specifically tailored to limit or modify FDA's regulatory authority over foods, drugs, and medical devices.[12]

With the FDA Modernization Act, Congress adopted several measures it decided were needed to streamline clinical research and make it easier for drug companies to test and market new products. For example, in lieu of the full reports drug manufacturers traditionally required to submit with marketing applications, Congress directed the FDA to issue guidance describing when companies would be allowed to submit abbreviated study reports instead. The agency also was instructed to set up a program to encourage further development of surrogate endpoints as predictors of a drug's therapeutic benefit.[13] In addition, Congress gave drug companies an additional six months of marketing exclusivity for testing the use of their drugs in pediatric patients. It also amended the FD&C Act so that the efficacy of a drug could, at FDA's discretion, be verified by only one, adequate and well-controlled study, along with confirmatory evidence.[14]

FDAMA also included provisions for the 'fast-track' approval of high priority drugs for treating life-threatening diseases, and expanded patients' rights to access investigational therapies.[15] However, while all of these measures, including the requirement for pediatric testing,[16] were touted as needed legislative reforms, they were, for all practical purposes, little more than a codification of policies that FDA already had proposed or adopted through rulemaking.

---

[11] P.L. 105-115. For more detailed information in the FDA Modernization Act see: CRS Report 98-263, *Food and Drug Administration Modernization Act of 1997 – The Provisions,* by Richard Rowberg, B. Randall, Donna Porter, Bernice Reyes-Akinbileje and Donna Vogt, Science, Technology, and Medicine Division and Diane Duffy, American Law Division.

[12] Congress placed the regulation of medical devices under the Federal Food, Drug, and Cosmetic Act in 1976.

[13] The acceptance of 'surrogate endpoints' was established FDA in its 1992 accelerated drug approval regulations. (See: *Federal Register*, v. 57, no. 239, December 11, 1992. p. 58942.) Generally, surrogate endpoints are laboratory findings or physical signs that may not, in themselves, be a direct measurement of how a patient feels, functions, or survives, but nevertheless is considered likely to predict therapeutic benefit.

[14] P.L. 105-115, Section 115. The provision says that "if the Secretary determines, based on relevant science, that data from one adequate and well-controlled clinical investigation and confirmatory evidence (obtained prior to or after such investigation) are sufficient to establish effectiveness, the Secretary may consider such data and evidence to constitute "substantial evidence" . . . for the purposes of meeting the efficacy requirement. Prior to the FDA Modernization Act, FDA traditionally required at least two confirmatory studies to prove a drug's effectiveness.

[15] Even before FDAMA, FDA's review priorities always favored drugs for treating serious and life-threatening diseases. Moreover, the agency adopted rules in 1987 that make it easier for patients with serious medical complications to assess experimental therapies (See: *Federal Register*, v. 52, no. 99, May 22, 1987.) In 1992, FDA ushered in its "parallel-track" policy that allows patients access to investigational drugs at the same time they are being used in clinical trials (See: *Federal Register*, v. 57, no. 73, April 15, 1992.) Later that year, the agency issued "accelerated approval" regulations for drugs to treat serious and life-threatening diseases (See: *Federal Register*, v.57, no. 239, December 11, 1992.).

[16] U.S. Dept. of Health and Human Services. Food and Drug Administration. Regulations Requiring Manufacturers to Assess the Safety and Effectiveness of New Drugs and Biological Products in Pediatric Patients; Final Rule. *Federal Register,* v. 63, no. 231, December 2, 1998. p 66632.

The Drug Approval Process

How 'Drug' is Defined Under Federal Law

The term "drug" has been officially defined in federal law for the better part of a century. The definition has been amended several times, however, mainly to extend its statutory reach. When Congress first outlawed the sale or transportation of adulterated or misbranded medicines under the Food and Drugs Act of 1906, it defined "drug" to mean:

> all medicines and preparations recognized in the United States Pharmacopoeia or National Formulary for internal or external use, and any substance or mixture of substances intended to be used for the cure, mitigation, or prevention of disease of either man or other animals.[17]

Decades later, when Congress passed the Federal Food, Drug, and Cosmetic Act of 1938, it made a significant change in the way drugs would be characterized under the law.[18] With the 1938 amendments, the definition of drug was broadened so that the term would include not only substances that were intended to cure, mitigate, or prevent disease, but also any "articles" intended to affect the structure or function of the human body in some way, could be deemed to be a drug by FDA for regulatory purposes.[19] The definition has remained the same every since, and under current law, the term drug means:

> articles recognized in the official United States Pharmacopoeia, official Homeopathic Pharmacopoeia of the United States, or official National Formulary; . . . and articles intended for use in the diagnosis, cure, mitigation, treatment, or prevention of disease in man or other animals; and articles (other than food) intended to affect the structure or any function of the body of man or other animals; and articles intended for use as a component of any articles specified in [these] clauses.[20]

As a result of the 1938 law, all new drugs in the future would have to be tested for safety before they could be approved by the FDA for marketing. Along with the new pre-market testing requirements, Congress added new language to the act defining how "new drugs" would be characterized from that point on. The statute also included the requirement that new drugs would have to become "generally recognized" as safe before they could be approved for marketing. The only exception was drugs previously marketed under the provisions of the 1906 Food and Drugs Act. These so-called "old" drugs were "grand fathered," and considered exempt from the new safety testing requirements.[21] Under the 1938 act, a new drugs was defined as:

---

[17] Pub. L. No. 384, Ch. 3915, Section 6.

[18] Pub. L. No. 717.

[19] Sometimes an item that usually is not considered a drug can become one if it is used in a way that affects the structure of the body of man. For example, common toothpaste, which would ordinarily be defined as a cosmetic since it can "cleanse, beautify, or promote attractiveness," also can be regulated as a drug when the product contains fluoride and is labeled and promoted for reducing tooth decay.

[20] FD&C Act, Section 201(g)(1).

[21] Under the 1938 FD&C Act, Congress drew a legal distinction between "new drugs," and so-called "old drugs." Old drugs, those that entered medial use before 1938, were "grand fathered," and considered exempt from retroactive safety testing.

> Any drugs the composition of which is such that such drug is not generally recognized, among expert qualified by scientific training and experience toe valuate the safety of drugs, as safe for use under the conditions prescribed, recommended, or suggested in the labeling thereof . . . or any drug the composition of which is such that such drugs, as a result of investigations to determine its safety for use under such conditions, has become so recognized, but which has not, otherwise than in such investigations, been used to a material extent or for a material time under such conditions.[22]

When Congress expanded the definition of drug under the 1938 FD&C Act, it chose the word "articles" to describe the kinds of substances that if offered for the diagnosis, cure, or treatment of human disease, potentially could be covered by the statute. In other words, the term drug can be applied to virtually any item (i.e., articles) that is marketed in interstate commerce, and is labeled or promoted for medicinal purposes. In the United States, the sale or marketing of pharmaceuticals without FDA approval is a violation of the FD&C Act.

The circumstances under which a substance might be regulated as a drug, has been debated ever since Congress defined the term. Generally speaking, products taken for their pharmacological effects, such as prescription or over-the-counter (OTC) medications, clearly meet the statutory definition of drug. For certain other products, however, even though they also are marketed as being therapeutic, the legal definition of drug may not apply. A good example would be certain food products, particularly dietary supplements. While dietary supplements are labeled and promoted for a number of suggested health benefits, they are not regulated as drugs, and, as such, need not undergo any safety and efficacy testing. Instead, Congress has deemed the products to be foods and has directed that they be regulated as such.[23]

Drug Safety and Effectiveness

All drugs – be they available by a doctor's prescription or sold more widely as OTC products – must be proven safe and effective before they can be approved in the United States. While prescription and nonprescription drugs are quite different, particularly in terms of their ingredients, labeling and availability, many of the statutory requirements for marketing approval apply to both classes.[24] While the law requires drugs to be proven safe and effective before they can be approved by FDA, it does not specify just how safe and effective the drug must be. Moreover, even though safety and efficacy have to be confirmed through clinical testing, there is no guarantee that the drug will be equally safe and effective for all patients once it enters the mainstream of general medicine.

Even though the FD&C does not specify the same level of safety and efficacy for all pharmaceuticals, it does stipulate that FDA can approve anew drug for marketing only when its safety has been demonstrated by, "adequate tests by all methods reasonably applicable to show whether or not such drugs is safe for use under the conditions prescribed, recommended

[22] The FD&C Act (1938), Section 201(p).

[23] For more information on the regulation of dietary supplements see: CRS Report RL30887, *Dietary Supplements: Legislative and Regulatory Status*, by Donna V. Porter, March 14, 2001.

[24] Hutt, Peter Barton and Richard A. Merrill. *Food and Drug Law, Cases and Materials.* 2nd Ed. Westbury, New York, The Foundation Press, Inc. 588 p.

or suggested in the proposed labeling thereof.[25] The agency also is prohibited from approving a new drug if, based on the clinical evidence submitted, there is, "a lack of substantial evidence that the drug will have the effect it purports or is represented to have under the conditions of use prescribed, recommended, or suggested in the proposed labeling thereof.[26] The key phrase, "substantial evidence" is defined in the act to mean evidence:

> . . . consisting of adequate and well-controlled investigations, including clinical investigations, by experts qualified by scientific training and experience to evaluate the effectiveness of the drug involved, on the basis of which it could fairly and reasonably be concluded by such experts that the drug will have the effect it purports or is represented to have under the conditions of use prescribed, recommended, or suggested in the labeling or proposed labeling . . .[27]

When Congress passed the FDA Modernization Act of 1997, it avoided making wholesale changes that would undermine the basic statutory requirements for drug approval in the United States. Instead, it looked for other ways the testing and approval process could be sped up, while leaving the prerequisites for safety and efficacy alone. To this end, Congress reduced some of the paperwork involved in filing marketing applications, and clarified the number of clinical studies drug makers would need to do in order to gain FDA approval. The legislation also directed the agency to issue guidance describing when drug companies would be allowed to file "abbreviated study reports" in lieu of the "full" reports, they were previously required to submit.[28] Moreover, as noted, unlike in the past where data from a least two, corroborative, well-controlled clinical studies were needed to confirm a drug's effectiveness, under FDAMA, data from only one adequate and well-controlled clinical investigation, along with confirmatory evidence, can be sufficient to meet the law's "substantial evidence" requirement.[29]

Preclinical Research and Testing

When a new chemical compound is discovered, the drug manufacturer or sponsor[30] carries out a series of preliminary experiments to find out how the substance works, and whether it may be, one day, safe enough for use in patients. The testing process typically begins in the company's laboratory where scientists perform preliminary tests to see whether the drug has any affect on a disease or its symptoms in an appropriate animal mode. At this early stage in testing, a drug is said to be undergoing preclinical evaluation. By federal law, all experimental drugs must be tested in animals before they can be given to patients in clinical trials.

---

[25] Section 505(d).
[26] Ibid.
[27] Ibid.
[28] P.L. 105-115, Section 118.
[29] P.L. 105-115, Section 115. When FDA issued its guidance in August 1999, it said that "full study reports should [still] be submitted for all clinical and human pharmacology investigations that contribute to the evaluation of effectiveness for the proposed indication, or that otherwise support information included in labeling."
[30] The term "sponsor" usually means the person or agency who assumes responsibility for an investigation of a new drug.

During preclinical testing, the drug manufacturer's main goal is to determine if the chemical compound is reasonably safe for initial use in humans, and whether it has enough pharmacological activity to justify further commercial development. To answer these questions, compounds with promising therapeutic potential are evaluated using a variety of testing methods that include not only live animals, but also *in vitro* (i.e., test tube) tests, tissue cell cultures, and computer driven data analysis systems. These studies can provide basic information about a drug's toxicity, and in some instances, preliminary data about which dosage levels might prove to be unsafe in humans. The drug's effects in animals are examined in detail, including the amount absorbed into the bloodstream, and the rate at which it is metabolized and eliminated by an intact, living organ system. In addition, these tests can provide valuable information about the new drugs' possible carcinogenic, mutagenic (causing genetic mutation), and teratogenic (abnormal fetal development) effects.

The Investigational New Drug (IND) Application)

During preclinical research and testing, the majority of compounds being evaluated are, for a variety of reasons, found to be unworthy of further consideration. For those that merit further development, the results of the animal tests and lab work will be used to design a detailed protocol for eventual clinical trials in human subjects. When the decision is made to go forward with human clinical trials, the manufacturer must file an Investigational New Drug (IND) application with the FDA. The IND application is not a request for permission to market anew drug; instead, it is an exemption from the statutory prohibition against shipping experimental drugs in interstate commerce without FDA approval. Drugs with approved INDs, however, can legally be shipped and administered to patients enrolled in clinical investigations.

When a drug manufacturer or other sponsor files an IND, they must submit all information and data from preclinical studies, an explanation of the investigational drug's intended medical use, and a full description of the clinical trial protocols designed to document the drug's safety and effectiveness. The IND must specify how many patients will be involved in the clinical trials, how the drug will be administered (i.e., oral versus injectable), and the dosage level that will be given. Information about the drugs' chemical composition and manufacturing process also is required. An IND also must include the names and qualifications of the clinical investigators involved, and where the studies will be conducted. The FDA has 30 days to review an IND, and if it has no objection to the protocol's design, the sponsor can begin clinical testing. In situations were FDA has concerns about an application, it can place the IND on "clinical hold."[31] Once an IND has been placed on clinical hold, the investigation can proceed only with the agency's approval.

FDA regulation acknowledge several types of INDs, depending on the needs of the drug sponsor, or the kind of clinical investigation involved. Commercial INDs are those typically filed by a drug manufacturer so they can begin clinical testing. In 1987, however, the agency issued regulations establishing to so-called "treatment IND." Also known as "compassionate INDs," these exemptions are granted so that patients with serious or life-threatening diseases or conditions can gain access to promising experimental drugs for treatment purposes without

[31] 21C.F.R. 312.42. Imposing and lifting clinical holds.

being part of the formal clinical trial. To be granted treatment IND status, the experimental drug must be under active clinical investigation, cannot be promoted or sold during the clinical trials, and the manufacturer must be actively pursuing marketing approval. Moreover, in situations where treatment INDs are involved, the drug company must agree to make the drug available, and the patient's doctor must be willing to administer the drug and then monitor and record its effects.

During manufacturers or sponsors usually arrange with physicians, hospitals, or clinical centers to carry out and/or direct the clinical investigations. By FDA regulation, every investigation involving human test subjects must be overseen by an Institutional Review Board (IRB).[32] IRBs are required to have at least five members, with varying backgrounds (e.g., medical, ethicist, clergy, and physicians), who have the experience and expertise to evaluate the ethical aspects of the proposed study and protect the rights and welfare of the human subjects involved. Review boards have the authority to approve, modify, or disapprove research protocols. Before a clinical trial can begin, IRB members also must ensure that the informed consent obtained from the study subjects complies with the requirements in the Protection of Human Subjects regulations.[33]

Clinical Trials

When the FDA has reviewed an IND's animal test data and concluded that the investigational drug is safe enough to be tested in humans, clinical (human) studies can begin. These studies, or clinical trials, are usually carried out in three phases. Phase I studies focus on assessing the drug's safety in a group of healthy volunteers, usually at a very doses in fewer than 100 patients. These preliminary tests are intended to help pharmaceutical companies find out whether small doses of the drug cause any immediate safety problems that could make continuation of the trial impossible. The information gathered from these small trials will make it easier for investigators to determine whether the drug's dosage needs to be adjusted before it is given to a large number of study participants in the testing phases that lie ahead. At this juncture, if no serious or unexpected complications have emerged, the clinical testing moves on to Phase II.

In general, Phase II trials are randomized, well-controlled, double-blind clinical investigations. While controlled studies are important to verify further a drug's safety, their main purpose is to find out whether the drug is effective or not. Typically, the studies are designed, or set up, so that a group of patients who are given the active drug – the "treatment" group – is compared to a "control" group of patients who share similarities in age, sex, and disease characteristics, but are given a placebo, or dummy pill instead. Investigators have several different kinds of controls they can use, depending on the study's objective, knowledge of the disease being treated, and whether there are viable, alternative therapies available. Further, these trials also are "blinded," meaning that neither the investigators nor the patients know which group of patients is receiving the active drug or the placebo. Phase II studies typically involve several hundred patients.

---

[32] 21 C.F.R. Part 56, Institutional Review Boards. Also, under C.F.R. 312.66, clinical investigators must assure that an IRB that complies with the requirements of Part 56 will be responsible for the initial and continuing review and approval of the proposed clinical study.

[33] 45 C.F.R. 46.

Phase III clinical trials can involve both controlled and uncontrolled studies and may include as many as several thousand patients. These trials produce additional information about safety and effectiveness, help define the drug's overall benefit-to-risk ratio, and determine how its official labeling will be worded. The larger studies are intended to provide more information on the drug's side effects, whether it interacts with foods and/or other medications, and whether certain patient populations should avoid its use altogether.

Quite often, investigational drugs seem to be relatively safe and effective in the early stages of testing. However, when the drug is administered to a much larger patient population, particularly during later, more tightly controlled trials, only then will the unanticipated, potentially serious side effect begin to show up. In a similar context, compounds that looked as though they might be very effective based on preliminary data, are sometimes shown to offer patients little or no therapeutic benefit in later controlled studies. Also, drug makers know that once a drug's clinical trials have been completed, and a marketing application has been filed, the FDA will examine their test results very carefully. Whether the drug will be approved ultimately rests with the agency's interpretation of the safety and efficacy data generated during the clinical trials.

The New Drug Application (NDA): FDA Review

If clinical studies confirm that a new drug is relatively safe and effective, and will not pose unreasonable risks to patients, the manufacturer files a New Drug Application (NDA), the actual request to manufacture and sell the drug in the United States. The NDA must include all data from animal and laboratory testing, comprehensive information about the drugs' chemistry and pharmacology, and the complete results of all clinical investigations.[34] Samples of the finished product and copies of the drug's proposed labeling must also be included. In addition, the application must include information about the facilities where the drug will be produced, and provide assurances that the finished product will be made in accordance with current good manufacturing practices (GMPs).[35] When an NDA is reviewed, agency statisticians and epidemiologists closely examine the drug's safety and efficacy data. At the same time, samples of the drug undergo laboratory analysis, while other officials check to make sure that the product's official labeling is comprehensive, scientifically accurate, and not misleading. The entire review process can take months to several years to complete, depending on the size and complexity of the application.

By law, FDA does not require drug companies to prove that a new drug will be 100 percent safe and effective for all patients before it can be approved for medical use. For pharmaceutical products, such absolute certainty is unfeasible, if not impossible to obtain. There is no such thing as a completely risk-free drug; and all produce unwanted side effects in a small percentage of patients. Instead, when the FDA examines a drug's safety and efficacy profile, it focuses on the quality and totality of the clinical trial data. Once the agency analyzes the data, it decides from a statistical standpoint, whether the product's "benefit-to-

[34] The information contained in an NDA used to fill numerous, mostly paper, volumes. In today's computer environment, the same filing can be done in electronic format.

[35] Section 5081(a)(2)(B) of the FD&C Act declares that a drug must be deemed adulterated if the methods, facilities, and controls used for its manufacture, processing, packaging, are not in conformity with current good manufacturing practices (GMPs). GMP regulations for drugs are codified at 1 C.F.R. 210 and 211.

risk" ratio is sufficient to support its approval. In general, FDA tries to apply this "benefit-to-risk" policy the same way for all marketing applications. From time to time, however, the agency will approve a drug with a higher risk profile, particularly if the drug may benefit patients with a serious life-threatening disease, and there is no other alternative therapy available.

When an NDA is reviewed, FDA officials often will meet simultaneously with the sponsor to discuss possible deficiencies the application may have. For example, if the agency has serious concerns about the sufficiency of the drug's safety and efficacy data, it may insist the company do additional studies or data analysis. Only when these studies are done, and the agency is satisfied with the additional data, will the application be considered for approval. Questions that involve minor discrepancies must be resolved to FDA's satisfaction before final approval is given. Under the FD&C Act, FDA has 180 days to either approve or disapprove an NDA.

The FDA can refuse to approve a drug's marketing application for any number of reasons, most of which relate to serious deficiencies in the sponsor's NDA. By law, approval can be denied if the application does not include adequate tests, done by conventional methods, to prove that the product can be used safely for the medical conditions described or suggested in its labeling. In addition, the application could be denied if the clinical data were insufficient, in FDA's judgment, to show that the drug was effective. Where safety and effectiveness are not an issue, final approval could be delayed if the agency has concerns that the facilities and controls used for production and packaging are inadequate to preserve the finished product's pharmacological integrity (i.e., its identity, strength, quality, and purity).

When the review reaches its final stage, FDA will notify the manufacturer that the drug either is approved for marketing, would be approved if some last-minute changes are made, or cannot be approved because the test data do not support the drug's safety and efficacy. At this point in the review process, refusing to approve an application is fairly unusual. Should this happen, however, the drug's sponsor can choose to withdraw the application or request a hearing.[36] If a hearing is granted, the sponsor bears the burden of convincing the agency to reconsider its decision to deny approval.

Generic Drug Approval

The review and approval of generic drugs is quite similar to that of brand-name products.[37] According to the FDA, generic drugs are identical to brand-name pharmaceuticals in dosage form, safety, strength, route of administration, quality, performance characteristics and independent use.[38] Most brand-name drugs are developed and marketed with the benefit of patent protection. Drug patents give innovator pharmaceutical companies a period for marketing exclusivity, which allows them to recoup their research and development costs. When a drug's patent(s) or marketing exclusivity expires, however, other manufacturers are free to produce the drug in its generic form. Under the Drug Price Competition and Patent

---

[36] 21 C.F.R. 314.200. Hearing Procedures for New Drugs.

[37] *From Test Tube to Patient: Improving Health Through Human Drugs.* An FDA Center for Drug Evaluation and Research, Special Report. September 1999. p. 62.

[38] See: FDA, Office of Generic Drugs, [http://www.fda.gov/cder/ogd.index.htm].

Term Restoration Act of 1984, manufacturers of generic drugs are allowed to submit abbreviated new drug applications (ANDAs) to market their products.[39]

An ANDA is considered "abbreviated" because the sponsor is not required to reproduce the clinical studies that were done for the original, brand name product. Instead, generic drug manufacturers must demonstrate that their product is the same as, and bioequivalent to, a previously approved brand name products.[40] Generally, bioequivalence is established by producing scientific data verifying that the generic drug will deliver into the bloodstream of health test volunteers, the same amount of active ingredient, in the same amount of time, as the innovator's product. In addition to bioequivalence, generic drug makers must also provide assurance that their products meet all U.S. Pharmacopoeial standards, and are properly labeled. Finally, the facilities where the finished product will be made must undergo FDA inspection, and the manufacturer must certify that the finished product will be made in accordance with good manufacturing practices and procedures.

All approved drug products, both brand name and generic, are listed in FDA's *Approved Drug Products with Therapeutic Equivalence Evaluations,* the so-called "Orange Book."[41] Named for the color of its cover, the *Orange Book* is a cumulative agency publication that lists drug products that are bioequivalent, including new drugs, generic drugs, and some antibiotics. It also includes information about approved nonprescription drugs, drug patent listings, and time periods for market exclusivity.[42] Using a coded lettering system, the *Orange Book* identifies the approved drugs the agency considers to be therapeutically equivalent – those designated by the "A: codes, and those it believes have documented bioequivalence problems – indicated by the "B" codes. By making this sort of information available, including on-line, the *Orange Book* gives physicians, dispensing pharmacists, and patients an unbiased source to help them decide when therapeutically equivalent generic drugs can be substituted for brand name products.

POST-MARKETING SURVAILLANCE

As a health protection agency, the FDA is responsible for monitoring the safety of pharmaceutical products once they are approved for marketing in the United States. To do this, the agency relies on several post-marketing surveillance systems, designed to watch for safety problems that sometimes arise, especially in newly approved products that are being prescribed for the first time. Under FDA's adverse drug reporting system, the legal obligation to report side effects or adverse experiences is different for pharmaceutical companies than it

---

[39] See footnote 8.

[40] 21 C.R.R. 320.1(e). FDA regulations state that drug bioequivalence means the absence of a significant difference in the rate and extent to which the active ingredient or active moiety in pharmaceutical equivalents or pharmaceutical alternatives becomes available at the site of drug action when administered at the same molar dose under similar conditions in an appropriately designed study.

[41] See FDA's: *approved Drug Products with Therapeutic Equivalence Evaluations.* [http://www.fda.gov/cder/ob/default.htm].

[42] Market "exclusivity" refers to a period of time, often several months or years, that pharmaceutical companies are given to market a drug, during which the FDA is not allowed to approve the same product made by another manufacturer. In the 1980s, Congress granted drug makers periods of market exclusivity under the Orphan Drug Act and the Drug Price Competition and Patent Term Restoration Act. More recently, under the 1997 FDA Modernization Act, Congress gave drug companies 6 additional months of exclusivity for determining the safe use of drugs in pediatric populations.

is for health professionals and consumers. By regulation, pharmaceutical companies must report all serious and unexpected adverse drug experiences they become aware of, no matter the source, to the FDA within 15 days.[43] However, even though doctors, health care professionals, and consumers are encouraged to report adverse drug experiences as well, their participation in the post-marketing surveillance process is strictly voluntary.

Post-approval monitoring of drug safety is essential for several reasons, not the least of which is watching for adverse effects that often do not show up until the drug is on the market. In early clinical investigations, experimental drugs are usually tested on a relatively small number of study participants, usually a few hundred, to several thousand patients. Under these limited, tightly controlled conditions, a side effect that occurs in only 1 out of 10,000, or possible 1 out of 100,000 patients, may not have materialized at that point in testing. However, once the new drug reaches the market, and is prescribed for a much larger population of patients, perhaps numbering hundreds of thousands, if not millions, the probability of adverse effects increases substantially. A post-market reporting system helps FDA officials determine whether adverse effects in such large user populations are serious enough to warrant some kind of regulatory action.

In 1993, the FDA updated its post-marketing surveillance capabilities, and established a more global monitoring system under the name MedWatch.[44] According to the agency, the MedWatch program was designed to make it easier for health professionals (i.e., doctors, nurses, pharmacists, etc.), and the general public, to voluntarily report side effects and other health problems related to the use of prescription drugs, biologics,[45] and medical devices. Adverse effects associated with the use of over-the-counter drugs, dietary supplements, infant formulas, and medical foods can also be reported using the system. Adverse reactions attributable to vaccines, however, are reported to their own surveillance program, the Vaccine Adverse Event Reporting System (VAERS), rather than to MedWatch. When adverse reactions are reported to the FDA, they are entered into MedWatch's post-marketing surveillance database for further evaluation. At this stage, the collected data are analyzed to find out if there is a causal relationship between the use of a drug and the reported adverse reactions. When this determination is made, the information is forwarded to the appropriate center where FDA officials decide whether some kind of public notification is needed.

Recently, the MedWatch surveillance system has helped FDA decide whether a number of pharmaceutical products, suspected of causing serious side effects in some patients, should be allowed to remain on the market. In 1998, after post-marketing reports linked the anti-inflammatory drug Duract (bromfenac) with severe liver problems in some patients, the product was voluntarily withdrawn from the market by its manufacturer Wyeth-Ayerst Laboratories.[46] That same year, the drug Posicor (mibefradil), an anti-hypertensive, was voluntarily withdrawn by its maker Roche Laboratories, after new reports linked it with potentially harmful interactions with other drugs.[47]

---

[43] 21 C.F.R. 314.80

[44] MedWatch: The FDA Medical Products Reporting & Safety Information Program. [http://www.fda.gov/medwatch/.

[45] Biologics are products derived from living sources such as humans, animals, and microorganisms.

[46] Wyeth-Ayerst Laboratories Announces the Withdrawal of Duract from the Market. *FDA Talk Paper,* Food and Drug Administration. June 22, 1998. [http://www.fda.gov/bbs/topics/ANSWERS/ANS00879.html].

[47] Roche Laboratories Announces Withdrawal of Posicor from the Market. FDA Talk Pater, Food and Drug Administration. [http://www.fda.gov/bbs/topics/ANSWERS/ANS00876.html].

In February 2000, the drug Lotronex (alosetron HCL), a prescription drug manufactured by Glaxo Wellcome, received FDA approval for treating Irritable Bowel Syndrome (BIS) in women. Shortly thereafter, FDA became concerned when early post-marketing reports linked Lotronex to cases of intestinal damage resulting from ischemic colitis (reduced blood flow to the intestine) and severely obstructed or ruptured bowels.[48] To address these concerns, FDA convened its Gastrointestinal Drugs Advisory Committee in June to discuss various risk management options. Among the factors discussed was the fact that many IBS patients taking Lotronex did not experience adverse effects, and wanted to continue their treatment. The advisory committee recommended that immediate steps be taken to inform both physicians and patients of the adverse effects associated with the drug's use.

In August, Glaxo Wellcome responded, updating Lotronex's professional labeling, and distributing medication guides warning patients about the drug's potential health risks. In addition, the company mailed letters informing doctors and pharmacists of the new safety information. In November, after receiving more reports of serious adverse reactions, including reports of several deaths in patients taking Lotronex, the FDA offered Glaxo Wellcome the option of withdrawing the drug, or agreeing to restricted distribution under the agency's new risk management program. According to the agency, the risk management program for Lotronex had to include: safer use of the drug in appropriately informed patients; continued access to Lotronex by severely affected patients under closely monitored conditions; and continued clinical studies of the benefits and risks, and safe use of the drug.[49] After further discussions, Glaxo Wellcome decided that FDA's risk management offer wasn't in their best interest, and, on November 28, 2000 opted to withdraw Lotronex from the market.

At this point, the availability of Lotronex in the immediate future is uncertain. Despite the withdrawal, patient demand for the drug still remains high. In January 2001, the manufacturer (now GlaxoSmithKline (GSK) after a merger) and FDA officials were reportedly having discussions about the possibility of bringing Lotronex back, albeit with specific restrictions.[50] These discussions are apparently continuing as GSK and the agency try to figure how to identify risk factors for Lotronex adverse events, and the best way to incorporate those factors into a risk management plan for irritable bowel syndrome therapy. However, some have expressed strong concerns about Lotronex being reintroduced, even under a limited access plan,. In an April 18 letter to FDA, the consumer advocacy group *Public Citizen* said that the drug should only be available to patients who have used it and have not experienced adverse effects.[51]

As these examples illustrate, when reports indicate that a drug product may be causing serious side effects in patients, FDA has several objectives: analyze the magnitude of the health risks involved; find out if the drug in question is actually responsible, and decide whether these factors, taken together, justify some sort of remedial action. Depending on the severity of the reactions, and how great a health threat they pose, the agency has several

---

[48] Glaxo Wellcome Decides to Withdraw Lotronex From the Market. *FDA Talk Paper*, Food and Drug Administration. November 28, 2000. [http://www.fda.gov/bbs/topics/ANSWERS/ANS01058.htm]

[49] Glaxo Lotronex Withdrawal Follows Failed Risk Management Negotiations. *The Pink Sheet*, v.62, no 49, December 4, 2000. p.3.

[50] Grady, Denise. FDA Pulls a Drug, and Patients Despair. *The New York Times*, Health & Fitness, Section F, January 30, 2001, p.1.

[51] Lotronex Risk Factor Identification Is Prerequisite to Return, FDA Says. *The Pink Sheet*, v.63, no.17, April 23, 2001. p.10.

regulatory options to choose from. For that rare occasion where the side effects associated with a drug are so serious that they pose an "imminent hazard" to public health, Congress authorized the Secretary of Health and Human Services to suspend the marketing of a drug immediately.[52] To do this, however, the Secretary must be able to show that the drug is so dangerous that without its immediate suspension, these will likely be further injury and harm to public health.[53]. Since these criteria are very hard to meet, the Secretary has invoked imminent hazard clause in only a handful of cases.

When a drug's adverse effects aren't serious enough to justify complete market withdrawal, the FDA relies on other means to help patients understand the risks involved. A fast and common method is to issue a public announcement or general warning through the media and its own Website. If necessary, the agency sends out "Dear Health Professional" letters, which passes the latest information about adverse effects along to doctors and pharmacists. This same kind of information is also disseminated by the manufacturer through similar channels. As this is being done, the FDA will contact the manufacturer to discuss changes in the drug's professional labeling that will reflect the new safety concerns. Moreover, when the product's labeling is updated, the manufacturer may be required to use a so-called "boxed-warning," especially if the FDA decides that the new warning information has to be displayed more conspicuously.

After a time, if these efforts don't seem to be to protecting the health and safety of patients, and reports of serious side effects continue to grow, FDA can offer the manufacturer one of two things. As in the Lotronex situation above, it can request that the drug be available only though a limited distribution program, or it can urge the manufacturer to consider withdrawing the drug from the market.

CONCLUSION

Ever since Congress first outlawed the sale of adulterated or misbranded products in the early 1900s, the statutes and rules that govern the drug approval process today have grown numerous and complex. Nevertheless, by the close of the twentieth century, these very drug laws had raised testing standards, assured veracity in labeling, and provided U.S. consumers with an unparalleled supply of safe and effective medicines.

Today, the United States has perhaps the toughest drug approval standards in the world. Before new drugs can be sold, pharmaceutical manufacturers are required by law to produce large amounts of clinical data demonstrating that products are both safe and effective. In addition, safety and efficacy have to be proven through rigorous, well-controlled clinical trials, investigations that are scientifically demanding and expensive to conduct. Although the FD&C Act requires that all drugs be proven safe and effective, it doesn't specify just how safe and effective they have to be. For this reason, the FDA has a lot of discretion in deciding whether a drug's clinical data are sufficient to meet the statutory requirements for marketing approval.

The speed with which FDA reviews and approves new pharmaceuticals is measured more closely than any of its regulatory functions. As such, the agency faces ongoing pressure from

---

[52] Section 505(e), FD&C Act.
[53] See: 21 C.F.R. 2.5, Imminent Hazard to the Public Health.

Congress, the U.S. pharmaceutical industry, and patient advocacy groups to approve new drugs as quickly as possible. In the 1990s, Congress passed several bills aimed specifically at speeding up the approval process. In 1992, which many feel has contributed greatly to faster application reviews. Subsequently, again with strong industry support, it enacted the FDA Modernization Act of 1997. With this latter FDA reform measure, Congress extended the original user fee law for another 5 years, revised and streamlined certain drug testing requirements, and demanded more timely approval of pharmaceutical products.

Many of the major advances in the quality of U.S. health care over the past 50 years were brought about with the help of pharmaceutical technology. Diseases, which lacked reliable treatment just decades ago, can today be cured or at least managed through the use of safe and effective drugs and vaccines. In recent decades, as public demand for safer, more effective "high-tech" medicines has increased, so too have the costs of research and development and the price of drugs as well. As the nation's health care system comes to rely more on the use of pharmaceuticals each year, the laws and policies that affect the drug approval process become more important.

Chapter 9

PHARMACEUTICAL RESEARCH AND DEVELOPMENT: A DESCRIPTION AND ANALYSIS OF THE POCESS

Richard E. Rowberg

INTRODUCTION

Perhaps the central issue in the debate about inclusion of prescription drug benefits in Medicare has been whether such action would lead to some type of price controls for these drugs.[1] A key element of that debate is the relationship between prescription drug prices and the research and development (R&D) activities of the pharmaceutical industry.

In 2000, the worldwide, research-based pharmaceutical industry spent an estimated $26.4 billion on R&D including &22.4 billion in the United States.[2] The U.S. and worldwide totals were up by about $2.4 billion, or 10%, from 1999. For 2000, these R&D expenditures constituted an estimated 20% of the sales of these companies. In is the contention of the industry that current prices are required if that R&D is to continue at a level sufficient to develop drugs to attack many of the diseases now afflicting humankind. Critics, however, argue that those prices are higher than can be justified by R&D costs.

The purpose of this report is to help the reader understand the pharmaceutical R&D process as part of the knowledge needed to evaluate the debate about drug pricing. In addition, however, the Pharmaceutical R&D process and future prospects raise a number of issues on their own. This report provides a description of that process and analyzes a number of those key issues. The steps of the research process – drug discovery, preclinical testing, clinical trials, and post approval monitoring – are described. In addition, various factors affecting the duration and costs of the process are discussed, including the possible consequences of recent advances in biomedical research. Finally, an analysis is presented of topics pertinent to the R&D process that may be of interest to Congress.

---

[1] For a discussion of these issues see Congressional Research Service, *Medicare: Selected Prescription Drug Proposals*, by Jennifer O'Sullivan, RL30584, Updated September 14, 2000.

[2] Pharmaceutical Research and Manufacturers of America, *Pharmaceutical Industry Profile - 2000* (PhRMA, Washington, DC, 2000), 20. http://www.phrma.org/publications/publications/profile00/

Although the report discusses pharmaceutical R&D costs, it does not present an analysis of the validity of various cost estimates. Those and other areas related to pharmaceuticals R&D and prescription drugs, including patent protection ,regulation, and advertising, are now or will be covered in other CRS studies.[3]

BACKGROUND

A description of the pharmaceutical R&D process requires a brief review of the relevant biology, both to help the reader understand the origins of most human disease and how most drugs work in combating diseases. The section begins with a brief discussion of the basic biological mechanisms of living systems and how disease attacks those systems. It next presents a short discussion of the biological processes by which pharmaceuticals work in combating disease.

Biological Basis of Disease

Of the different chemical compounds that are essential for human organisms, proteins play crucial roles in most human biological functions and provide much structural support. Proteins provide structural support for the body as critical components of ligaments, tendons, and skin. Enzymes are proteins that accelerate the essential chemical reactions in the cell. Antibodies are proteins that protect cells from attack by foreign substances called antigens. Hormones that regulate cell metabolism are proteins.[4] Within the membrane (wall) of the cell, proteins act as receptors, attaching to and transporting essential chemicals into the interior of the cell. Proteins perform many other functions as well.

The instructions contained in the genetic code are translated to control of cellular behavior through the synthesis of proteins. The genes contained in the DNA molecule code instructions for the chains of amino acids which are the building blocks of proteins. Furthermore, this gene expression is itself regulated by other proteins. Proteins are large molecules, containing hundreds to thousands of atoms, and are arranged in very complex shapes. For those proteins responsible for controlling functions – enzymes, receptors, hormones, etc. both the chemical structure and the shape determine how they react with other chemicals.

Because proteins are so important to the functioning of living systems, they are naturally almost always involved when something goes wrong. In most cases the problems occur with proteins that are either enzymes, receptors, or hormones.[5] Many cancers result when proteins that control the rate at which cells divide no longer function properly, and cells begin to

[3] See for example, Congressional Research Service, *Patent Law and Its Application to the Pharmaceutical Industry: An Examination of the Drug Price Competition and Patent Term Extension Act of 1984,* by Wendy Schacht and John R. Thomas, RL30756, December 5, 1999; Congressional Research Service, *Food and Drug Administration Modernization Act of 1997,* by Richard Rowberg, et.al., 98-263, March 13, 1998, and Congressional Research Service, *Food and Drug Administration: Selected Funding and Policy Issues,* by Donna Vogt, 95-422, updated February 27, 2001.

[4] Not all hormones are proteins. Another common class of hormones are steroids such as testosterone, vitamin D, and cholesterol.

[5] For a general discussion of the role of proteins in disease, see Susan Aldridge, *Magic Molecules: How Drugs Work* (Cambridge: Cambridge University Press, 1998).

multiply in an uncontrolled manner. Infections can damage a living organism when bacteria or viruses produce toxins that inhibit protein synthesis, resulting in the death of cells. These microbes can also cause damage by invading and multiplying within cells and tissues. Fever and inflammation result through the action of the body's immune system attacking the intruders. In the case of AIDS, proteins on the human immunodeficiency virus (HIV) bind to receptor proteins on cells of the immune system. The virus is then able to invade those cells, reproduce, and eventually destroy the cells. As a result, the immune system weakens and is unable to stop other microbial invasions called opportunistic infections.

Other diseases result from problems with hormone production or utilization. Diabetes I occurs when the body does not produce the hormone insulin while diabetes II occurs when insulin production is normal but the body cannot use it. In the cardiovascular system, proteins called low density lipoprotein (LDL) deposit cholesterol stored in fat cells on body tissue including the insides of blood vessels. High density lipoprotein (HDL) deposit cholesterol stored in fat cells on body tissue including the insides of blood vessels. High density lipoprotein (HDL), on the other hand, carries the cholesterol to the liver for recycling. Therefore, if the ratio of LDL to HDL is too high, the individual is at risk for heart disease.

Identifying and understanding protein behavior, therefor, are primary objectives of research into disease and its causes. Because of the connection between genes and proteins, it is also clear that genes play an important role in disease mechanism. Indeed protein behavior that leads to disease can often be attributed to genetic mutations that result in creation of proteins that do not behave normally or of failure to create needed proteins. For example, cystic fibrosis results from a genetic mutation that prevents the formation of proteins allowing chloride to pass though cell walls. Over 4000 diseases have been identified as having a genetic origin,[6] although many of those are rare. Some are the result of single gene mutations while others result from a combination of multiple gene mutations and other factors. Because of this gene-protein linkage, genetics has been and continues to be the target of research in understanding disease and its origins.

Basics of Pharmaceuticals

Given the role of proteins in disease it is natural that the focus of most drug therapy is to inhibit protein activity that causes physiological harm to humans or to stimulate protein activity that is needed by the body but is lacking.[7] For example, aspirin works for pain mitigation by inhibiting the action of a protein that, when stimulated, is responsible for producing a chemical that results in pain. Aspirin contains chemicals that bind with that protein, preventing it from acting. As a stimulant for protein activity, drugs can bind with receptors, causing the cells on which they are located to carry out desired biochemical activity. For example, when insulin binds with its target receptor, the cells act to maintain steady levels of glucose in the blood stream. Many cancer drugs work by actions that inhibit proteins responsible for maintaining multiplication of cancerous cells, resulting in the death of those cells (as well as other rapidly dividing cells). Antibiotics kill bacteria by inactivating

---

[6] Eric S. Grace, *Biotechnology Unzipped: Promises and Realities* (Washington: Joseph Henry Press, 1997), 62.

[7] See Aldridge, *Magic Molecules,* 6-11, 73 and Jurgen Drews, *In Quest of Tomorrow's Medicines* (New York: Springer, 1998), 118-121.

enzymes on bacterial cell membranes, causing them to stop forming, or by halting the synthesis of proteins needed to sustain the microbe's life.

While the basis of most pharmaceutical action sounds straightforward, implementing such action is usually very difficult. Determining targets for drugs can be a daunting, costly task as has been repeatedly demonstrated from the history of biomedical research. For example, the research effort to discover the proteins responsible for cancerous cell growth and how they work has consumed many billions of dollars and several decades, and complete understanding still appears a long way off. Furthermore, once a target is determined, discovering a chemical that will bind with that target protein and either inhibit or aid its actions as need be is not assured.[8] As stated above, proteins have very complex shapes that determine how other molecules bind with them, and even if one can discover such molecules, the drug still may not work in humans. Human biological processes on the molecular level are extremely complicated and research efforts to understand those processes and bring about chemical therapies for disease are substantial.

Just how is that research carried out? How are the fundamentals outlined above applied to bring about the development of prescription drugs? The next section provides a description of the pharmaceutical R&D process as it is typically performed. Reference is made wherever appropriate to the biological basis of disease and pharmaceuticals just presented.

The Research Process

This section discusses the pharmaceutical research process. The section begins with a brief overview of the entire process. It then describes in more detail the basic research phase of pharmaceutical research, drug discovery, followed by a discussion of preclinical research. A description of the clinical trial phase is given next followed by a review of the post-approval process. A brief survey of the history of pharmaceutical R&D is given in Appendix A.

Overview

Drug research and development begins with the drug discovery phase. Typically, at this stage, chemical compounds – either naturally occurring (called biologics) or synthetic – are investigated in laboratory settings for their potential to bind to and modify target molecules. Once promising candidates are identified, preclinical testing begins. In this stage, actual drug development begins and pharmacological studies are carried out. Basically that research focuses on how the drug candidates react when delivered to the body.

If promising candidates emerge from these first two stages, they enter the most arduous and time-consuming portion of the R&D process, clinical trials. There are three stages to clinical trials – called phase I, phase II, and phase III – that a candidate drug must pass through before it can be considered for market approval. In phase I, the safety of the candidate drug is tested on healthy volunteers. Once safety screening is complete, testing begins on a population of patients who have the disease. Then, phase II trials and held to

[8] In the case of aspirin and penicillin, the biological basis of the drugs' actions were not discovered until many years after the drugs themselves were discovered. `

establish the parameters (end points) for the quantitative measurement of the effectiveness of the drug. Phase III trials are basically a large-scale version of phase II trials. In phase III, however, the focus is on obtaining quantitative measurements of the effectiveness of the drug, based on the end points determined in the phase II trials, and on monitoring for any important side effects.

If the results of the phase III trials provide a clear indication of the candidate drug's effectiveness and that any side effects can be reasonably managed, it is submitted to the Food and Drug Administration for approval to market. During that process, it is possible that FDA may require additional phase III trials. If approval is granted, post-marketing surveillance is carried out to monitor the drug for additional safety concerns that may not have appeared during the preapproval clinical trials. Additional trials – phase IV – may also be required at this point.

Each of these steps is complex and uncertain, and each requires a substantial commitment of time and resources. To gain some insight into those characteristics, each step will now be described in more detail.

Drug Discovery

Drug discovery usually begins with research to identify potential drug targets. Targets are biochemical compounds in the body – usually proteins, as noted above – whose action or absence of actions results in a diseased condition.[9] In some cases, drugs have been discovered without researchers knowing an underlying cause of the disease. Aspirin was discovered long before the mechanism by which it works was determined. Much more often, however, particularly in recent years, identification of drug targets has launched the search for therapies. Usually the search is aided by new knowledge of biological processes and disease mechanisms resulting from basic biomedical research, much of which is funded by the National Institutes of Health (NIH).

Diseases often have multiple biochemical causes or factors. Discovery of a single factor in such a case may not lead to a useful drug target. As noted above, the complexity of most diseases means that identification of targets is generally quite difficult. It is estimated that thousands of potential targets exist in the body.[10] By 1996, however, a survey of drug targets on which current drug therapy was based bound that only about 500 targets were being used, 45% of which were receptors and 28% of which were enzymes.[11] The remaining 27% consist of a variety of targets including hormones, DNA molecules, and cell nuclei receptors, or are unknown.

The actual process of drug discovery is characterized by a search for molecules that can bind to targets and result in an action that produces a therapeutic result. Until the last few

---

[9] Most illness and death from illness is a result of viral or bacterial infection. Proteins are still the target of antibiotic and antiviral drugs, although they belong to the invading microbes and not the host. Blocking bacterial enzymes or inhibiting protein synthesis are the principal objectives of antibiotics. Drugs that work with viruses usually bind on viral enzymes, inhibiting their action. Vaccines against infectious diseases work by presenting an antigen to the host's immune system. Antigen proteins, carried on the surface of a virus, stimulate the immune system when a virus enters (Aldridge, *Magic Molecules, 72-82*).

[10] Aldridge, *Magic Molecules*, 257.

[11] Jurgen Drews, "Drug Discovery: A Historical Perspective," *Science* 287 (2000), 1961.

decades, this search was largely a trial and error process.[12] Pharmaceutical companies would develop libraries of thousands of molecules over the years from a variety of sources.[13] When a promising target was identified, researchers would test molecules from these libraries, largely by trial and error or random screening, to look for potential therapeutic activity. Many different natural and synthetic compounds – thousands to tens of thousands – were tried in laboratory experiments, often using animals, to see whether they showed therapeutic promise. Often, the biochemical basis for any therapeutic effect was not understood, and at times a substance being screened would be found to treat an ailment different from the one for which the screening was intended.[14] In addition to being time-consuming and resource intensive, discoveries obtained in this fashion usually did not yield findings that could be generalized to aid in the search for therapies to other diseases. Consequently, while this method of drug discovery has resulted in many new drugs over the years, the industry has put major efforts into development of more rational approaches.

In recent years search methods have become more systematic.[15] Using a technique known as combinational chemistry, literally thousands of candidate drug compounds can be produced in a systemic and automatic fashion. In this situation, a candidate molecule is modified, atom-by-atom, producing a large number of similar molecules to be tested for therapeutic action. Testing itself is done using automated methods including monitoring the interactions using a high-throughput screening process.

Results that modify the targets are explored further giving rise to more information about those compounds. The use of combination chemistry expanded rapidly in the 1990s, and a huge library of potential drugs exists in those companies employing this technique.[16]

Advances in molecular biology (see box) are also having a profound effect on drug discovery. First, they are leading to a substantial increase in understanding the origin and causes of diseases. Application of molecular biology developments is changing the way researchers identify drug targets. More about this application will be discussed below. Second, biotechnology (see box) has been used to bring about dramatic increases in the production of certain drugs (e.g., insulin) whose efficacy was already established. Third, new results from molecular biology research are being used to enhance the search for other drugs.[17] As a research tool, genetic engineering (see box) is used to produce "pure" screens on which to test new drug candidates.[18] Therefore, rather than relying on a screen that may contain the target in question among others, the receptor can be synthesized and made to exist alone, allowing a more rational and effective test of the drug.[19] Recent developments in biotechnology are only just beginning to make major contributions to drug discovery, however, and they promise to revolutionize the entire pharmaceutical R&D process.

---

[12] Drews, *In quest of Tomorrow's Medicine,* 121.

[13] While most of these molecules are produced synthetically, a large fraction of prescription drugs on the market comes from natural sources. Of the 520 drugs approved between 1983 and 1994, 39% were either natural products or derivatives of natural products (Alan Harvey, "Strategies for discovering drugs from previously unexplored natural products,", *Drug Discovery Today,* 5 (July 2000), 294.

[14] National Research Council, "U.S. Industry in 2000: Studies in Competitive Performance," *Pharmaceuticals and Biotechnology,* (National Academy Press, Washington, DC, 1999), 368.

[15] Drews, "Drug Discovery: A Historical Perspective," 1962.

[16] Robert Service, "Winning combination," *Technology Review,* 101 (1998), 34-42.

[17] National Research Council, "U.S. Industry in 2000: Studies in Competitive Performance," 378.

[18] Screens are small samples of chemical or biological substances that contain drug target molecules. They are used for initial testing of drug candidates to look for those candidates that will bind with the target.

[19] National Research Council, "U.S. Industry in 2000," 381.

Molecular Biology – The study of the properties and functions of living organisms at the molecular level. The objective is to understand the behavior of the molecules that make up an organism's cells and the interactions between those molecules. The principal foci of molecular biology research are the molecular structure of genes – in particular the DNA molecule – and the structure and behavior of protein molecules.
Biotechnology – The technique of using living cells to make useful products and provide services. Modern biotechnology involves the manipulation of the molecules making up cells, such as DNA and RNA.
Genetic Engineering – A type of biotechnology that involves manipulation of genetic material to produce desired types of living organisms or to correct genetic defects.

Preclinical Testing

Once promising drug candidates have been identified, they enter the prelinical research stage. The candidates undergo laboratory and animal testing focusing on the pharmacological aspects of drug development. Of the about 5,000 to 10,000 drug candidates screened during the drug discovery stage, about 250 will typically make it to the preclinical research stage.[20] During this phase, the pharmacological concerns of toxicity, bioavailability,[21] and efficacy are investigated. In addition, at this point, an investigational new drug (IND) application is filed with the Food and Drug Administration (FDA), patents are applied for, and efforts are started to develop economic and quality manufacturing processes.[22] Safety testing takes place in animals that are administered ever increasing doses to look for onset of toxicity. Also, a key feature of this stage is to determine the best method of delivery (e.g., oral, intravenous, etc.). A drug with a low bioavailability – at or near zero – either must have its dosage increased when administered orally or it must be administered in some other way. Other tests include determining a drug candidate's shelf lifetime and shipping durability.

The first step in preclinical pharmacological testing is to determine toxicity, including the relationship between dosage and toxicity, how those effects vary over time, the organs affected, and the reversibility of any effects.[23] To determine how the effects change over time or whether there are long-term toxic effects, extended tests are performed. They usually last more than a year and attempt to determine a number of factors in addition to a cataloging of any risks of long-term use. Included are tests to determine dosage range, maximum dosage for no side effects, and largest tolerable dosage. In parallel, carcinogenicity studies, involving various dosage levels and lasting up to two years, are carried out. Other conditions studied include local side effects, allergenic reactions, and effects on reproduction.

---

[20] *Pharmaceutical Industry Profile – 2000,* 32.

[21] Bioavailability is a measure of drug's ability to move through and remain in the human body and reach the bloodstream and the drug target with a sufficient dose for therapeutic action. For a drug taken by mouth, a high bioavailability – at or near one – means that it was not metabolized by the liver and that it penetrated the walls of the small intestine to the blood stream before being excreted (Aldridge, *Magic Molecules,* 11-12).

[22] An investigational new drug (IND is a drug candidate undergoing clinical investigation or an approved drug being investigated for a new indication (use). FDA may permit an IND to be used for seriously ill patients who are not part of ongoing clinical trials.

[23] Drews, *In Quest of Tomorrow's Medicine,* 129-130.

During the safety testing, animals are used for studies of toxicity including chronic toxicity.[24] The drug's cancer-causing potential is also investigated by examining how it may damage the animal's DNA. Pregnant animals are used to look at the drug's effects on pregnancy. Animal testing is opposed by some, however, and other methods are being sought, including the use of tissue cultures, bacteria cells, and computer models. Many of these methods are now used for preliminary screening to reduce the number of animals used in safety testing.

Drug delivery is also an important objective of preclinical research. This stage involves the study of how the drug is absorbed, distributed, metabolized, and excreted by the body. Such studies are carried out on animals. In order to maximize the amount of the drug that reaches the drug target, it is necessary to develop delivery systems that minimize the absorption of the drug be healthy tissue before it can reach the target.[25] For example, many drugs that are proteins would be digested rapidly by the stomach and small intestine. Enzymes in the liver can deactivate many drugs if they circulate in the blood stream. If, as a result of such actions, a drug candidate will not work if taken orally, the major alternative at present is needle injection. Because injections cause discomfort and can be difficult to administer, much pharmaceutical R&D is directed at ways to deliver drugs to avoid needle injections. The dosage level of drugs must also be controlled so that they are effective but not toxic. In addition, timing of drug delivery may be important because of disease rhythms and natural body cycles, and to minimize toxic effects.

The final objective of preclinical research is the development of manufacturing methods.[26] Most often production is done by synthetic chemistry, but the use of genetic engineering (recombinant DNA) is growing. Other methods include fermentation[27] and extraction from natural sources (primarily plants). Once a method is chosen, production is scaled up to levels needed for clinical trials.

Clinical Trials

Of the approximately 250 drug candidates that enter the preclinical research stage for a typical drug development project, about five will emerge as INDs to be tested in the clinical trial stage. Clinical trials, which constitute the most time-consuming and costly portion of drug development, consist of three phases, each more complex than the preceding. Before clinical trials can begin, the sponsoring pharmaceutical company must have approval from FDA about trial protocols (see below).

Description

Phase I clinical trials are designed to test drug safety; in particular to determine maximum safe dose. Small, single doses are used at first, with the dosage level increasing until side

---

[24] Aldridge, *Magic Molecules,* 43-44.

[25] National Institute of General Medical Sciences, National Institutes of Health, *Medicines by Design: The Biological Revolution in Pharmacology,* NIH Report No.93-474, September 1993, 29-30 [http://www.nigms.nih.gov/news/science_ed/medbydes.html]

[26] Aldridge, *Magic Molecules,* 41-42.

[27] Fermentation – a biotechnology process – is used to produce vast quantities of certain bacteria that, in turn, are used to produce many antibiotics and other drugs such as insulin.

effects are observed. Concentrations of the drug in the blood are them measured. These tests are followed with multiple dose tests, and a range of concentrations that do not produce unacceptable side effects is determined. Typically, a phase I trial will include 10 to 100 participants, last about 1.5 years and cost about $10 million.[28] Participants are usually healthy, although if very serious side effects are a possibility, the tests may be made on the targeted patient group.

The purpose of phase II trials is to determine the parameters for the final test (phase III trials). These parameters, among others, are the class (e.g., age, gender) and condition of the patients to include in the trial, what end points to measure, and what constitutes an effective dose and duration of treatment. End points are those conditions that yield an unambiguous indication of the drug's success or failure. To test a drug's effectiveness often it is necessary to look for surrogate markers rather than, survival, absence of the disease, or some other measure of long-term success.[29] For example, in AIDS, testing for a period long enough to determine whether there is a high long-term survival rate would not be appropriate because of the large number of years it would take. Such a trial be impractical. In this case, a surrogate, such as a decline in viral particles in the blood, may be considered an acceptable market. Similarly, markers are used for chronic diseases such as diabetes because of the length of time needed to prove that the drug actually inhibits the onset of complications.

There is a risk of using surrogate markers, however, because they may not adequately predict the therapeutic effectiveness (clinical benefit) of the drug candidate. In such a case, a trial could show significant positive results based on the surrogate chosen, and the drug would be approved. When used by the general patient population, however, it is possible that drug may not improve the patients' wellbeing to any significant degree. For this reason, for any drug that uses surrogate endpoints to gain market approval, the FDA will require a clinical trial after that approval to "resolve remaining uncertainty" about the ability of the surrogate endpoint to accurately predict clear clinical benefit.[30]

Phase II involves the first use of a control group – a test group of patients to whom a placebo or another drug is given – which allows the clearest means of proving whether the drug is successful and of determining its side effects. The use of placebos is becoming less common in favor of existing treatments where possible. Control groups also provide the means of eliminating confounding factors (factors that may have the same effect as the drug being tested but are unrelated to the drug's actions). A drug effect – desired or otherwise – must show up in a statistically significant manner among the participants of the test group in order to be considered definitive.[31] Use of a control group should be a double-blind procedure: neither the patients nor the physicians administering the treatment should know which group is getting the therapy being investigated. Typically, phase II trials include 50 to 500 participants, last about two years, and cost about $20 million.[32]

Phase III trials determine the effectiveness of the drug and any important side effects. The testing in this phase is designed to match as closely as possible how the drug would be used if marketed. Often, several controlled studies (studies using control groups)take place at different locations (called multi-center studies), and each study must follow the same

[28] Justin A. Zivan, "Understanding Clinical Trials," *Scientific American*, 282 (April 2000), 71.
[29] Drews, *In Quest of Tomorrow's Medicine*, 132.
[30] 21 CFR 314.510.
[31] Zivan, "Understanding Clinical Trials,"73.
[32] Ibid., 73.

protocols. The group of patients included in the test are selected based on characteristics defined in the phase II trials. An important factor for this phase is to get patients with just the right level of illness to test efficacy – patients too ill may not live through the trial and those not ill enough may not show significant improvement.[33] While such a group is not strictly representative of the entire population of patients with that disease, it is a necessary compromise in order to ensure a feasible trial.

The goal of the phase III trial is authoritative demonstration of a drug's effectiveness as defined by the end points determined in the phase II trials. A control group is used and a statistically significant number of test group patients must attain those end points for the study to be considered pivotal. Usually two or more pivotal trials are required to secure FDA approval unless the first trial is particularly positive. A large fraction (about 80%) of the data used for FDA approval application arises from phase III trials.[34]If the results of the first phase III trial are ambiguous, a redesigned trial is usually held with a more restricted group of patients or with other changed factors. The data from the first trial usually determined the changes, if any, that need to be made in the follow-up trial.

The ideal Phase III trial is a double-blind, crossover trial. Crossover means that the test and control groups switch half-way through the trial. If the tested drug produces dramatic improvements, trials may be stopped before scheduled completion, with the approval of FDA, to make the drug available to everyone suffering from the disease. Phase III trials typically involve anywhere from 300 to 30,000 participants, run for three to five years, and cost about $45 million.[35]

General Features

During the clinical trials, companies are required to follow certain standards and procedures to ensure good clinical practice.[36] As part of the IND filed with the FDA, the company must provide a complete description of the procedures it will follow in the clinical trials, including how it will meet the standards of good clinical practice. The FDA must approve those procedures before trials begin. The FDA issues guidelines about trial procedures, but they do not have the force of law. The FDA also has oversight responsibility over the trials and has the right to stop them at any time if it believes the participants may be at excessive risk.

The FDA also requires two other conditions to be met before trials can begin: informed consent by the participants and the establishment of an Institutional Review Board (IRB).[37] Patients participating in trials must sign a written, informed consent form explaining – to the extent possible – all of the potential risks about the study. The IRB, made up of patients' advocates, health-care professionals, and nonprofessionals, must oversee the trial, permit it to begin, and stop the trial if necessary. A Date Safety Monitoring Board is also established to monitor safety and other aspects. It, too, can recommend stopping the trial before it is completed.

---

[33] Aldridge, *Magic Molecules,* 48.
[34] Drews, *In Quest of Tomorrow's Medicine,* 134.
[35] Zivan, "Understanding Clinical Trials," 75.
[36] Ibid., 70-72.
[37] U.S. Food and Drug Administration, Center for Drug Evaluation and Research, *From Test Tube to Patient: Improving Health through Human Drugs,* DHHS (FDA) 99-3168, September 1999, 25.

Costs of clinical trials, as noted above for each of the phases, are substantial and are usually borne by the drug companies. The costs include organizing and running the trials (done by physicians), data verification, analysis, and support personnel, as well as payments to physicians and nurses caring for participants. They do not include the cost of capital that, as noted below, is usually included when calculating total pharmaceutical R&D costs and is substantial. Because of the cost of these trials, pharmaceutical companies will almost always limit the drugs tested to those that have the potential for large markets.[38]

Upon completion of phase III trials, if the results prove positive, a New Drug Approval application (NDA) is filed with the Food and Drug Administration requesting approval to market the drug.[39] This application must contain a description of the drug chemistry, manufacturing processes, labeling (instructions for use of the drug), preclinical pharmacology and toxicology, pharmacokinetics (Drug action in the body) and bioavailability in humans, and data and analysis from the clinical trials. Supporting information includes a description of clinical safety, patient information, and other relevant information. These applications are quite extensive, ranging up to several tens-of-thousands of pages in length.[40]

If approval is granted, the drug can be marketed. Assessment of the drug, however, does not stop at that point. Even though phase III trials consist of a large number of participants, it is impractical to make them so large that all conceivable adverse reactions can be determined. Therefore, postmarket surveillance must be carried out to determine if there are any safety concerns that did not show up during the clinical trials. This activity usually does not use controlled studies as is the case for phase II and phase III trials, but rather relies on observations of physicians prescribing the drug. Pharmaceutical companies are required to file adverse drug reaction (ADR) reports with the FDA on a regular basis. The marketing pharmaceutical company usually recruits physicians to monitor the actions of the drug on patients to whom it has been prescribed. On occasion, serious reactions show up that result in the drug being removed from the market, such as was the case with the diabetes drug Rezulin, which caused the deaths of several people taking the drug.[41] It is also possible that FDA, as a condition of marketing approval, may require a firm to carry out a study to obtain more safety information after the drug is on the market. As noted above, such is the case for pre-approval trials that are based on surrogate endpoints. If such a study involves a clinical trial, it is labeled as a phase IV trial. It is also possible that new uses (indications) for the drug will be found during the phase IV trials.

Discussion

This section presents a discussion of three topics that are of particular importance in any consideration of the pharmaceutical R&D process: the time required to complete the process (drug development time), the cost of R&D to bring a drug to market, and the allocation of costs among the various components of the drug development cycle.

---

[38] Drews, *In Quest of Tomorrow's Medicine,* 135.
[39] For a description of the FDA, see Congressional Research Service, *Food and Drug Administration; Selected Funding and Policy Issues for FY2000,* by Donna Vogt, 95-422 SPR, February 27, 2000.
[40] Drews, *In Quest of Tomorrow's Medicine,* 137.
[41] David Willman, "The Rise and Fall of the Killer Drug Rezulin," *Los Angeles Times,* June 4, 2000, Section A1.

Development Time

As indicated above, the time it takes to go from the start of the drug discovery phase to the successful marketing of a drug is typically several years. In addition, there is substantial attrition of drug candidates along the way.

Figure 1. Drug Development Time and Attrition Rate

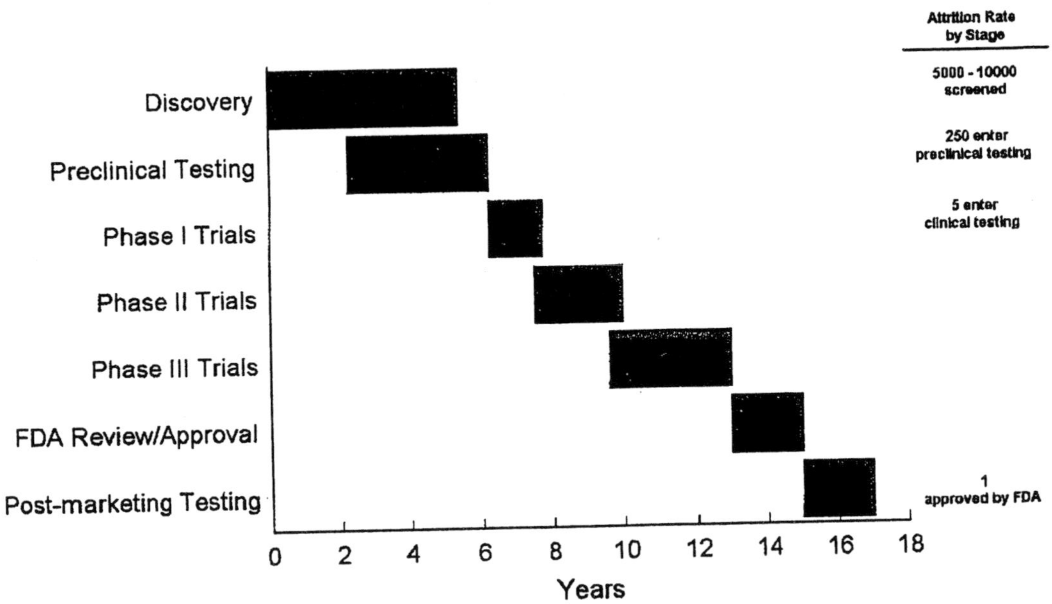

Figure 1, adapted from the Pharmaceutical Research and Manufacturers of America (PhRMA) 2000 Industry Profile, shows both of these characteristics.[42] The figure shows that the entire process takes on average about 15 years to marketing approval, with the clinical trials phase taking up about 7 years or 47% of the time. Furthermore, total drug development time has lengthened over the past 40 years.[43] In the 1960s, the average development time to approval from the onset of drug discovery (first synthesis of a drug candidate for initial laboratory screening) was about 8.1 years. In the 1970s, the average time was 11 years, in the 1980s it was 14.2 years, and in the early 1990s, it had grown to about 14.9 years. The attrition rate of drug candidates is also evident in the figure, which shows that for every drug approved by FDA, about 5,000 to 10,000 candidates were initially considered. Of course, nearly all of those candidates were eliminated by the time clinical trials commenced.

The length of the process has resulted in substantial effort over the years of trying to reduce the time taken for the various stages. For example, the chart shows that the average time for FDA approval is about two years. The average period for approval has dropped significantly in recent years, going from about 30 months in 1990 to about 12.6 months in

[42] PhRMA, *Industry Profile – 2000*, 32.
[43] PhRMA, *Industry Profile – 2000*, 34.

1999.[44] A sharp drop occurred from 1993 to 1994 and again from 1997 to 1998. The former was a result of the Prescription Drug User Fee Act of 1993, which provided FDA with the year the Food and Drug Administration Modernization Act of 1997 took effect. Nevertheless, the approval period remains relatively short – about 15% of the entire process – and the declines in recent years have not stopped the trend toward a longer drug development cycle.

The lengthy period for clinical trials has made them a major target for acceleration as well. There has been some progress on that front as the average length of trials has dropped from 7.2 years for those underway during the 1993 to 1995 period to 5.9 years for those underway during the 1996 to 1998 period.[45] Nevertheless, the need to obtain detailed information about potential side effects and the requirements for unambiguous results on an investigational drug's effectiveness mean that trials are likely to continue to require substantial periods of time – several years – for the foreseeable future.

The other major contributor to development time is the preclinical phase consisting of drug discovery and preclinical testing. How long drug discovery takes, of course, depends on how many compounds must be screened to come up with attractive drug candidates. If a candidate is discovered early in the process, the period can be considerably shortened. That is the basic reason for the wide range estimated for drug discovery – 2 to 10 years – given in the above chart. Drug discovery now is largely a rational systematic process compared to the trial and error approach that was dominant a few decades ago (see above), although the number of candidates that must be screened has not greatly changed. Indeed with the growing application of combinational chemistry, the number of candidates screened has probably grown. The "bottleneck" in drug discovery is not finding promising candidates – i.e., those that bind with the targets - but selecting those candidates that are also likely to become successful drugs.[46]

Drug researchers, however, hope that recent advances in biotechnology will result in a substantial decrease in time required for drug discovery. Biotechnology appears to be providing a way to accelerate and systematize the research process at its beginning stages during the search for candidate drugs.[47] Important goals are the development of more precise drugs with fewer side effects (so-called smart drugs), development of susceptibility markers to treat diseases before onset, production on a large scale of replacement human proteins (e.g., insulin for diabetes treatment and erythropoietin for cancer treatment), and elimination of contamination resulting from the use of human or animal raw material sources for drug chemicals.

The science of genomics – the study of the human genome - facilitates the investigation of the underlying, genetic cause of diseases and how drugs work. This approach opens up the possibility of developing theoretical frameworks to identify therapies. Technologies emerging from genomics might be able to provide ways to systematically produce and test new molecules that are candidate drugs. One such process already in use is the comparison of DNA sequenced from diseased tissue with those in DNA databases.[48] If a match is found and the protein expression characteristics of the DNA in the database are known, it may be possible to determine the proteins encoded by the diseased sample. If so, drug target

[44] PhRMA, *Industry Profile – 2000,* 33.
[45] Zivan, "Understanding Clinical Trials," 73.
[46] David Searls, "Using bioinformatics in gene and drug discovery", *Drug Discovery Today,* 5 (April 2000), 136.
[47] PhRMA, *Industry Profile – 2000, 9-13.*
[48] Ken Howard, "The Bioinformatics Gold Rush," *Scientific American,* 283 (July 2000), 59.

identification can be significantly facilitated with a consequent reduction in drug discovery time. Such comparisons are made possible by the field of bioinformatics, which applies advanced computer systems and technology to biology.

Eventually, it is likely to be possible to extend bioinformatics to play a major role in identification of drug candidates. Such computer-aided design processes have already been put to use and played a critical role in developing AIDS drugs. The HIV protease (the enzyme used by the virus to make proteins needed to infect cells) was modeled in this way and led to the protease inhibitor.[49] Full realization of this step toward computer-aided design of drugs is likely to be facilitated by identifying and determining the properties of all the proteins expressed by the human genome. This operation, called proteomics, involves both the identification of the protein and a determination of its physical structure.[50] Finally, gene therapy - the replacement of errors in the genetic code to prevent the expression faulty proteins or to ensure the expression of needed proteins – is being examined as a potential way to prevent the onset of a genetically caused disease in the first place. Because thousands of diseases are completely or primarily the result of genetic defects, such methods could prove to be very important for future drug development.

Advances in molecular biology also give promise to reducing the cost and duration of clinical trials. There is hope that the emerging field of pharmacogenomics or pharmacogenetics – understanding the genetic basis for differing drug response – will result in the development of drugs that will be more effective and have fewer adverse side effects than current drugs. Basically, this process uses the genetic profile of an individual affected by a disease to predict the response of that person to a given medicine. Researchers hope that such predictions can remove much of the uncertainty that now exists about whether a drug will work. As a result, faster and more effective clinical trials for new drug therapies should be possible, leading to more rapid drug approval.[51] Finally, drugs could be designed that are tailored to an individual.[52] In that last case, of course, the clinical trials would be meaningless. If drug development does reach this level of sophistication, different drug approval processes will be required.

While there is much promise in these advances, there are numerous and difficult challenges to surmount if they are to be widely applied to drug development. The mapping of the human genome, while a substantial achievement, is only one step. The targets of drugs, proteins, remain to be understood and surveyed in a way that will facilitate the search for new drug candidates.[53] The enterprise of proteomics will be long and costly and is just now getting underway.[54] Because protein structures are very complicated and are an essential feature in determining a protein's function, such surveys require a three-dimensional image of the protein (structural genomics). Obtaining these images requires the use of complex X-ray crystallography.

As noted above, only about 500 drug targets have currently been identified, a very small fraction of all of proteins in the body. While not all proteins will end up as drug targets, some

---

[49] Aldrige, *Magic Molecules*, 39.

[50] Carol Ezzell, "Beyond the Human Genome," *Scientific American*, 283 (July 2000), 64.

[51] Allen D. Roses, "Pharmacogenetics and future drug development and delivery," *Lancet*, 355 (April 15, 2000), 1358.

[52] Eric S. Grace, *Biotechnology Unzipped: Promises and Realities*, 88.

[53] Robert Service, "Structural Genomics Offers High-Speed Look at Proteins," *Science*, *287* (March 17, 2000), 1954-56.

[54] Ibid., 1956.

estimates are that the human genome map will eventually yield up to 10,000 new targets.[55] Another challenge is that the proteins most important for drug design, e.g., membrane proteins that control input to a cell, appear to be those most difficult to survey because of difficulties in determining their structure.[56]

Identification of drug targets, of course, is only part of the battle. Drug candidates must be discovered that bind to the target. Identifying such candidates require experimental procedures that are still very complex and subject to many failures. Furthermore, while a particular molecule might bind with a given drug target and result in apparent therapeutic action, that is no guarantee that it will be successful as a drug. Doses at toxic levels may be required to achieve the desired results. In other cases, the investigatory drug molecule may bind to other proteins, resulting in unwanted side effects.

In addition, it is too soon to tell just how effective the genetic advances will be in shortening the time required for clinical trials. The response of an individual to a drug is very complex and it is likely to take some time before researchers, regulators, and consumers will accept more specific, shorter trials to prove drug safety and efficacy. Nevertheless, recent advances are substantial and hold out much hope for a dramatically improved pharmaceutical R&D process.

R&D Costs

The cost of developing a typical drug (pharmaceutical R&D) is not well established. One source cites costs for R&D for a successful drug of about $116 million in 1976, about $287 million in 1987, about $359 million in 1990, and about $500 million in 1996.[57] All are in 1990 dollars. The 1990 figure was obtained from a study carried out by the Office of Technology Assessment and is the cost estimated before taxes.[58] The most recent figure is an estimate provided by PhRMA and is based on drugs introduces in 1990.[59] These estimates are before taxes, and cover both successful and unsuccessful drug development attempts.

Also important is how R&D costs are allocated among the various components of the R&D process. The cart shown in Figure 2, based on data from PhRMA, provides a graphical display of how those costs are allocated.[60] It is clear from the chart that clinical trials consume the major share of the costs, about 28.3% for Phases I through III, and an additional 5.8% for Phase IV. In addition, the actual drug discovery phase – synthesis and extraction and biological screening – requires about 27.1%.

General Cost Issues A major importance of the cost of pharmaceutical R&D lies in the claim made by the industry that prescription drug prices in the United States are justified by the high cost of developing new drugs. As a consequence, any debate about those prices usually includes a debate about the costs of doing pharmaceutical R&D. While it is beyond the scope of this report to present a detailed analysis of those costs, a few points can be made about them that may be important for any debate over costs.

---

[55] Aldridge, *Magic Molecules,* 257.
[56] Service, "Structural Genomics," 1956.
[57] Drews, *In Quest of Tomorrow's Medicine,* 149.
[58] U.S. Congress, Office of Technology Assessment, *Pharmaceutical R&D: Costs, Risks, and Rewards,* OTA-H-522, February 1993, 16.
[59] PhRMA, *Industry Profile – 2000, 25.*

Figure 2. R&D Cost Allocations by Stage - 1998

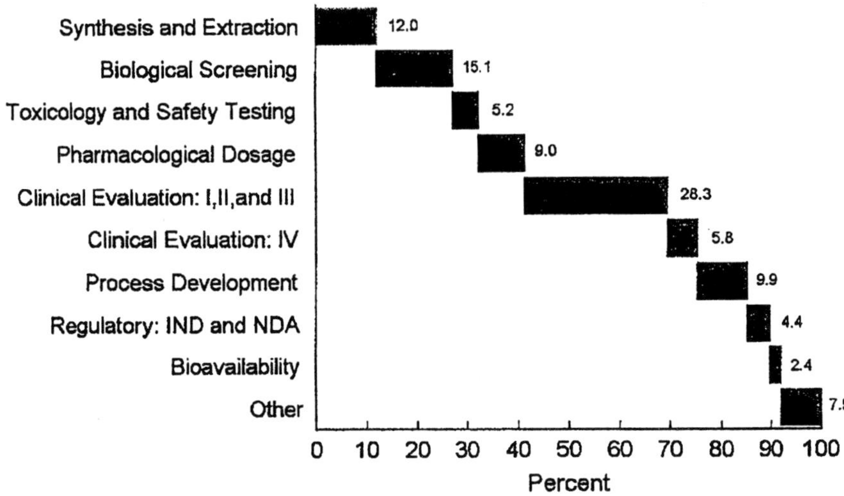

First, there have not been many detailed studies of the costs done by disinterested groups. The last such study was the OTA effort which was completed in 1993. Data used for that study were obtained on drugs developed during the 1980s.[61] No results have been reported on drugs developed in the last 10 years that might have benefited significantly from the recent advances in molecular biology.

Second, the calculation of those pharmaceutical R&D costs that have been reported all contain a factor accounting for the cost of capital.[62] This cost element accounts for the opportunity cost of money invested in the R&D process. In other words, the funds used for R&D could have been used for other investments (opportunities) that will yield a return. Those 'lost' opportunities are accounted for by including the forgone returns as part of the cost of performing R&D. Including such costs is a standard accounting practice used by all of industry in computing R&D costs. In the OTA estimate, opportunity costs constitute about 65% of the total R&D cost for a typical drug. The key element in calculating the foregone returns is the cost of capital, which is determined by the discount rate assumed. A change of a few percentage points in that rate can make a substantial difference in the total R&D cost.[63] While most analysts agree with the inclusion of opportunity costs, there is dispute over the size of the discount rate assumed. Industry officials generally agreed with the rates used by OTA but some critics argued they were too high.[64]

Third, there is a disagreement about whether pretax or after-tax costs are the more appropriate figure for pharmaceutical R&D costs.[65] For the OTA study, the after-tax estimate is $194 million compared to the pretax estimate of $359 million. This difference is substantial. It should be noted, however, that the marginal tax rate used in the OTA study,

---

[60] Ibid., 26.

[61] OTA, *Pharmaceutical R&D,* 48-54.

[62] It should be remembered that costs presented in this section include the cost of capital while those in the section on clinical trials above do not.

[63] Joseph A. DiMasi, "Trends in Drug Development Costs, Times, and Risks," *Drug Information Journal,* 29 (May 1995), 375.

[64] George Anders, "Vital Statistic: Disputed Cost of Creating a Drug," *The Wall Street Journal,* November 9,1993, B1.

[65] Ibid., B5.

46%, has since been reduced to 34%. As a result, the pretax/after-tax differences calculated on current pharmaceutical R&D costs would be considerably smaller than in the OTA case, but still large. On the other hand, the OTA calculation did not account for the research and experimentation tax credit[66] or any tax credits available for orphan drug development.[67]

A fourth consideration is whether the sales of successful drugs cover pharmaceutical R&D costs. According to the industry, a 1994 study found that only three out of ten pharmaceuticals introduced from 1980 to 1984 had enough sales to cover average R&D costs per drug.[68] Those sales, however, were sufficient to cover the industry's total R&D costs. In fact, the OTA study found that the internal rate of return (IRR) for the entire pharmaceutical industry from 1976 to 1987 exceeded the returns to other firms by about two to three percentage points.[69] This IRR differs from the standard accounting return on assets that are usually reported in publically available statements from individual firms.[70] Comparison of the return on assets for the same companies for which the OTA IRR comparison was made showed that pharmaceutical companies outperformed other firms by four to six percentage points over the 1976 to 1988 period. While there has been no more recent study of IRR comparison, data on return on assets from 1995 through 1999 continues to show that pharmaceuticals as a group outpaces all other industry groups and in nearly all cases the margin is greater than two percentage points.[71] It should be noted that the pharmaceutical industry generally contends that return on assets overstates the industry's profitability because drug patents are not counted as assets in standard accounting practices used to determine this measure.

Contribution of Federal R&D Funding

Another point of discussion is the contribution of federally-funded biomedical research to pharmaceutical development.[72] Nearly all of that research is supported by the National Institutes of Health (NIH).[73] In FY2001, NIH's total budget was $20.31 billion, about 60% of which goes for basic biomedical research and most of the remainder for clinical research. NIH basic research focuses on the biological, chemical, and molecular understanding of disease. Drug development is not its mission, although drugs do result from discoveries made by NIH-funded research.[74] While in some instances testing of actual drug candidates may be

---

[66] Congressional Research Service, *The Research and experimentation Tax Credit: Current Law and Selected Policy Issues for 106th Congress,* by Gary Guenther, RL30479, Jan. 23, 2001.

[67] Orphan drugs are those for which the potential market is small – 200,000 or fewer patients. A 50% tax credit on qualifying R&D is provided for those drugs as well as seven years of market exclusivity (P.L. No.97-414, 96 Stat.2049 (1983) (codified at 21 U.S.C.§ 360aa et seq.)).

[68] PhRMA, *Industry Profile – 2000,* 25.

[69] OTA, *Pharmaceutical R&D,* 24.

[70] For an discussion of the difference between IRR and the return on assets see OTA, *Pharmaceutical R&D,* 201-235.

[71] See, for example, "Most profitable industries," *Fortune,* April 17, 2000, F-27.

[72] For an extended discussion of federal support of pharmaceutical R&D, see OTA, *Pharmaceutical R&D,* 201-235.

[73] The National Science Foundation, the Department of Energy, the Department of Defense, the Veterans Administration, and the National Aeronautics and Space Administration, and the Environmental Protection Agency also fund biomedical research.

[74] Iain M. Cockburn and Rebecca Henderson, "Publicly Funded Science and the Productivity of the Pharmaceutical Industry," *NBER Conference of Science and Public Policy,* National Bureau of Economic Research, Washington, DC, April 2000, 12.

funded by NIH,[75] in most cases it is the knowledge of the disease mechanisms gained from the NIH-funded research that allows pharmaceutical companies to proceed with drug discovery.[76] It is common for the pharmaceutical industry to develop drugs from scientific discoveries made by researchers supported by the NIH.[77] In addition, over the last 20 years, Congress has enacted a number of laws to enable cooperative research arrangements between industry and government in order to facilitate the commercial application of knowledge discovered through federally-funded research.[78] These laws have been particularly successful in the areas of biomedical research.[79]

It seems clear that the pharmaceutical R&D cost estimates reported above understate the true cost by not including federally funded R&D that contributed to the ultimate development of the drug. That is, if the pharmaceutical industry had to pay for all of the basic research now funded by NIH, it is likely that the average cost of R&D to bring a drug to market would increase, perhaps substantially.[80] While the industry does fund a significant amount of basic research, most of its R&D funding is directed at drug discovery and development, and clinical trials. Estimates of the contribution of NIH-funded research to pharmaceutical R&D costs are usually not attempted because of the great difficulty of assigning basic research costs to specific innovations. There is generally not a direct linear relationship between basic research and specific innovations, but rather the connections are quite complex.

For the NIH-funded research that is focused on specific drug development, the allocation of costs is less difficult but still uncertain. The OTA study estimated that about 14% of preclinical pharmaceutical R&D in 1988 was funded by NIH. NIH also funds clinical research, as noted above, although most of that support is usually reserved for high-risk therapies not likely to yield high profits, and that would be of limited benefit to the industry.[81] A certain fraction of NIH clinical trial funds does directly support pharmaceuticals, however, and OTA estimated that about 11% of all pharmaceutical R&D funds allocated to clinical trials in 1988 came from NIH.

These figures suggest that the cost of pharmaceutical R&D to the industry for a typical drug would increase significantly if it had to absorb all of the costs that now directly support drug development but which are funded by NIH. It would likely be an even greater increase if the costs of all of the contributing basic research now funded by NIH could somehow be allocated to drug development. The outcome of such a situation could be a noticeable increase in the price of an average drug to the extent those prices cover R&D costs. Furthermore, to the extent the total industry expenditures on R&D did not grow, the number of new drugs developed would likely decrease. Therefore, one could argue that federal funding of biomedical research is helping to keep drug prices down. This possibility is indirectly raised

[75] OTA, *Pharmaceutical R&D*, 202.
[76] Cockburn, "Publicly funded Science," 12.
[77] Jeff Gerth and Sheryl Gay Stolberg, "Drug Companies Profit From Research Supported by Taxpayers, "*New York Times*, April 23, 2000.
[78] Congressional Research Service, *Federal R&D, Drug Discovery, and Pricing: Insights from the NIH-University-Industry Relationship*, by Wendy Schacht, RL30585, June 19, 2000.
[79] Jeff Gerth, *New York Times*, April 23, 2000.
[80] If total R&D expenditures did not change, the increased cost of R&D for a typical drug under these circumstances would likely mean that fewer new drugs would be developed.
[81] Zivan, "Understanding Clinical Trials," 75.

by analysis that puts the rate of return to the industry of public biomedical research funding at 30%.[82]

This benefit appears substantial, but that is no guarantee that another allocation of public and private R&D resources – e.g., the pharmaceutical industry supporting all biomedical research – could not produce a higher return. While it is not the purpose of this report to present an analysis of this issue, it is worthwhile to present some considerations important to that analysis. If industry had to fund the basic research that contributes to drug development that is now funded by NIH, it probably would not support all of the research now funded by NIH. Industry would very likely restrict funding to that it believed most relevant to pharmaceutical development, and total national spending on biomedical R&D – public and private sectors – would be less than is now the case. In this hypothetical situation where industry would absorb all basic biomedical research costs needed for drug development, the cost of R&D to develop a typical drug would increase from current estimates. Because total spending on basic biomedical research would be lower than is currently the case, however, the return on that investment, in terms of pharmaceuticals produced, would be higher than current estimates, provided no change in output – discovery and marketing of new pharmaceuticals – occurred.

Whether productivity could remain the same under this scenario would depend primarily on the pharmaceutical industry being able to select just the basic research now funded by NIH needed to maintain industry productivity. As discussed above, such research includes both basic research that is directly related to drug development and basic research that advances general biomedical knowledge important for drug discovery. It is very unlikely that the industry would be able to make such a selection given the uncertain nature of basic research. In addition, it is possible, in this hypothetical situation, that important knowledge that would be essential to the advances of biomedicine in the more distant future – 10 to 20 years – would not be forthcoming because the research had not been done. Another concern about this scenario is what happens to the basic research results. It is unlikely that a firm would be willing to make these results widely available if it believed they were important for its economic future. As a result, researchers outside that firm would not have access to new biomedical knowledge that may be critical to other advances in medicine, with a consequent loss to the public.

Also, even though the economic benefit from NIH research quoted above appears substantial, that is no guarantee that the public is adequately compensated for the subsidy that federally funded biomedical R&D provides to the industry. There are other factors that must be accounted for to assess that issue thoroughly.[83]

Implications of Biomedical Advances

The high and apparently growing cost of pharmaceutical R&D puts a premium on any advances that will slow that growth or even reduce costs. Shorter drug development time would mean smaller direct outlays for R&D. Furthermore, because the opportunity costs (described above) accumulate on an annual basis, a shorter development time would mean that this contribution to pharmaceutical R&D costs would decline as well. The biomedical

---

[82] Cockburn, "Publicly Funded Science," 18.

[83] CRS, *Federal R&D, Drug Discovery and Pricing, 18-19.*

advances discussed above in the section on drug development time, if successful, offer that opportunity. Cost mitigation would be especially true if those advances allowed a significant decrease in the time required for the clinical trials, which are the biggest single component of the cost of drug development.

Reduced pharmaceutical R&D costs for a typical drug could, in turn, have at least two advantages. First, it is possible that lower pharmaceutical prices will result. Second, drug companies may be more willing to undertake research on drugs that have a more limited market – that is, on drugs that attack diseases that afflict only a relatively small number of people. Now, such research is generally limited because the companies cannot expect to recover their R&D costs with sales of those drugs.[84] If shorter development times significantly reduce such costs, the prospect of being able to recover costs from a more limited-market drug should increase. Coupled with the increase in precision in targeting diseases that is promised by these new techniques, research on such drugs could expand. Another benefit of shorter development time would likely be greater total revenues to the firm patenting the drug because less of the patent period would be taken up by drug development. It is possible that such an occurrence would also lower drug prices because the firm would have more time to make a return on its drug development investment.

There are factors, however, that may limit the extent to which application of these biomedical advances can result in lower drug development costs. First, as noted above, there is uncertainty about how well these advances will translate into more effective drug development with shorter development times. Second, application of these techniques is likely to require very large initial investments in equipment and facilities. The genetic profile process, for example, requires complex and extensive robotic systems that are not typically found in conventional drug discovery processes. Nevertheless, to the extent these new drug development techniques are successful, the promise of lower drug R&D costs and more specific drugs appears real.

Congressional Concerns

There are several issues associated with drug development (pharmaceutical R&D) that may be of interest to Congress. Three of the more important issues concern the cost of pharmaceutical R&D and its relation to prescription drug prices, the role of federally funded R&D (primarily NIH) in pharmaceutical development, and federal oversight of the drug development process.

Drug Development Costs

The options open to Congress to affect the cost of pharmaceutical R&D appear to be limited. It has taken steps, as noted above, to shorten the time of drug approval. Further shortening may not be acceptable to Congress or the public, however, and is not likely to affect costs very much while the rest of the development cycle remains as long as is now the case. Congress has also granted a general research and experimentation tax credit as well as a

[84] The Orphan Drug Act (see footnote 67) provides incentives to pharmaceutical manufacturers to develop drugs for diseases that afflict 200,000 people or fewer and may not otherwise generate sufficient returns to justify the necessary R&D.

specific R&D tax credit for the development of orphan drugs. As argued above, however, significant changes in those costs will probably require major advances in drug discovery that also permit much shorter clinical trial periods. These advances will be almost solely dependent on progress in science and technology. If a dramatic shortening of clinical trials appears scientifically feasible, however, drug approval regulations may have to be modified in order to accommodate those new conditions.

Federal Biomedical R&D Funding

One area where congressional action may significantly affect pharmaceutical R&D costs in the longer-run is through federal biomedical R&D funding. Congress has provided NIH with substantial year-to-year increases in its budget. From FY1998 to FY2001, the budget has grown from $13.6 billion to $20.3 billion, a 49% increase. For FY2002, the Administration is requesting $23.1 billion, a 13.8% increase over the current fiscal year. It is on track to double by 2003 to a level of about $27 billion, although it is not certain that doubling will happen by that time. The primary reason for this increase is to accelerate the push towards the development of effective therapies for the major diseases afflicting humankind. As noted above, there appears to be little overlap between the R&D funded by NIH and that funded by the pharmaceutical industry. Furthermore, the research sponsored and performed by NIH appears to be quite important to the industry.

As NIH funding grows, however, there is the possibility that a greater portion of it will be used in areas that are also being funded by the pharmaceutical industry, including biotechnology firms. This is true of the human genome project and is likely to be true of much of the followup work. In particular, both NIH and the industry are funding work in structural genomics,[85] which is an essential part of proteomics, the next step beyond mapping the human genome. NIH is funding pilot centers to develop methods of determining the structure of proteins, while industry has several projects underway. Because knowledge of protein structures is critical to drug discovery, it seems clear that it is important for industry to fund it. That does not imply that NIH should not fund any research in structural genomics – knowledge of protein structures is also important for the understanding of fundamental biological processes – but caution is needed to avoid unproductive duplication. It should be note that the synergy between federal and private funding of the human genome project has probably accelerated completion of that effort.

A related issue concerns ownership of the information generated by both public and private funding. The debate over whether human genome data generated by private companies should be made available to the public when the government is also funding such work is likely to be repeated with protein structure data. The fact that data generated by both efforts were complementary helped to smooth possible conflicts in the case of the genome. Because protein structure data is likely to be even more important to the pharmaceutical industry than genome data, however, data ownership issues may become more serious. If conflicts do emerge, NIH may end up duplicating much of the industry work to ensure broad public access. Congressional oversight of situations where both the industry and NIH independently pursue research related to drug development may be heightened.

[85] Service, "Structural Genomics", 1954.

Clinical Trial Practice

While Congress has direct oversight of clinical trials supported by NIH, congressional authority over trials supported by the pharmaceutical companies is more tenuous and indirect. It is primarily through its oversight of the FDA, which, as noted, has oversight and some regulatory responsibility over privately run clinical trials. Aside from the possibility of major changes in clinical trial practice resulting from scientific advances, there are some aspects of current practices that Congress may wish to examine. Two such topics are: patient protection and conflict of interest. While neither is likely to affect the length of time that clinical trials now take, they could have a significant effect on the quality and safety of such trials.

The death in September 1999, of a patient undergoing an experimental gene therapy treatment of the University of Pennsylvania has highlighted the possible dangers of participation in clinical research.[86] While trials are overseen by an Institutional Review Board and individuals must sign informed consent statements prior to participation in a trial, there are concerns that adequate protection for patient safety is not always present. Such protection is essential if trials are to continue to secure the numbers of patients needed to adequately test drug candidates. Currently, the Department of Health and Human Services, with the establishment of the Office for Human Research Protection, is significantly expanding its efforts in this area.[87]

Recently, concern about conflict of interest on the part of physician-researchers involved in clinical trials has grown.[88] The potential for conflict is a result of a growing number of academic researchers being involved in research funded by the pharmaceutical and biotechnology industries. Since the beginning of the modern pharmaceutical industry, there has been a close relationship between the industry and universities.[89] The last two decades have seen a growth of cooperative research between industry and NIH-funded academic researchers.[90] As a consequence, the linkage between academic scientists and the pharmaceutical industry has intensified substantially. Some have argued that this growing tie poses a risk to public confidence in the results of clinical trials performed by these researchers.[91]

Because industry contracts with universities for a significant fraction of the clinical trials it undertakes – about 40% of industry funding for clinical trials in 1998 went to universities[92] – it seems important that effective safeguards be in place to protect against abuses resulting from potential conflicts of interest. Currently, regulations from the Public Health Service (PHS), issued in 1995, deal with conflict of interest in federally funded clinical research. In addition, the FDA has regulations, issued in 1998, requiring financial disclosure from clinical investigators. They leave management of potential conflicts of interest up the individual institutions, and there is considerable variation among those institutions.[93] Some argue that

---

[86] Zivan, "Understanding Clinical Trials," 72.

[87] Bruce Agnew, "Koski takes over HHS Office for Human Research Protection, plans a tough approach on conflict of interest and overall human-subjects protections," *Washington Fax,* F-D-C Reports, Inc., September 7, 2000.

[88] See e.g., David Korn, "Conflicts of Interest in Biomedical Research," *JAMA,* 284 (Nov. 1, 2000), 2234-6.

[89] Ralph Landau, Basil Achilladelis, and Alexander Scriabine, *Pharmaceutical Innovation: Revolutionizing Human Health* (Philadelphia: Chemical Heritage Press, 1999), 38.

[90] CRS, *Rederal R&D, Drug Discovery and Pricing,* 4-7.

[91] Catherine D. DeAngelis, "Conflict of Interest and the Public Trust," *JAMA,* 282 (Nov. 1, 2000), 2238.

[92] Thomas Bodenheimer, "Uneasy Alliance: Clinical Investigators and the Pharmaceutical Industry," *The New England Journal of Medicine,* 342 (May 18, 2000), 1540.

[93] Mildred K. Cho, Ryo Shohara, and Anna Schissel, "Policies on Faculty Conflicts of Interest at US Universities," *JAMA,* 284 (Nov.1, 2000), 2204.

certain kinds of financial ties between academic researchers and the pharmaceutical industry should be prohibited altogether.[94] Others argue that such ties do not need to be banned, but a better job of managing financial conflicts of interest is needed by the institutions themselves.[95]

In 2000, the Department of Health and Human Services began consideration of new conflict-of-interest rules. The director of the then newly established Office for Human Research Protection (OHRP) announced that the office would seek to establish more stringent conflict of interest standards.[96] On January 10, 2001, the OHRP issued a "draft interim guidance document" on financial relationships in clinical research. The document also contained a request for comments due by March 2, 2001. The new guidelines are not meant to replace existing regulations of PHS agencies, including FDA, but to "help IRBs [Institutional Review Boards], Clinical Investigators, and Institutions in carrying out their responsibilities to protect human subjects" under existing regulations.[97] The draft guidelines recommend, among other things, that universities limit the direct participation in clinical research of scientists who could be influenced by financial ties to the sponsoring firm; that research institutions consider whether it is appropriate for its scientists to participate in research sponsored by firms in which the institution has investments; and that conflict-of-interest committees should be established by universities to review financial links of individual scientists.

In addition, the Association of American Medical Colleges (AAMC)established a task force to look at the issue. On February 13, 2001, a group of leaders of the nation's medical schools receiving the most federal research funds issued a set of recommendations for the AAMC task force to consider.[98] These recommendations include, among other things, that financial interests of researchers taking part in trials be disclosed to the IRBs and that they be reviewed periodically. The recommendations were endorsed by the AAMC. The group also recommended that responsibility for such disclosure be expanded to everyone directly involved in the clinical research.

While these recommendations appear to move towards better control of potential conflict-of-interest problems, they still would leave much of the management of those situations with the institutions. In addition, the contract research organizations (CROs) are only addressed to the extent academic researchers are involved in the trials managed by the CROs. It appears, therefor, that monitoring of both university and CRO efforts will be important to ensure that public confidence in clinical trials and in the academic biomedical research community does not suffer.

---

[94] Marcia Angell, "Is Academic Medicine for Sale?" *The New England Journal of Medicine, 342* (May 18, 2000) 1518.

[95] Jordan J. Cohen, "Trust Us to Make a Difference," *AAMC Annual Meeting,* October 29, 2000, Chicago, IL. [http://www.aamc.org/newsroom/speeches/00amspee.htm]

[96] Bruce Agnew, *Washington Fax,* September 7, 2000.

[97] Public Health Service, U.S. Department of Health and Human Services, *Financial relationships in Clinical Research: Issues for Institutions, Clinical Investigators, and IRBSs to Consider when Dealing with Issues of Financial Interest and Human Subject Protection,* January 10, 2001, [http://ohrp.osophs.dhhs.gov/nhrpac/mtg12-00/finguid.htm].

[98] Shirley Haley, "Leaders from top-funded medical schools release recommendations for managing financial conflicts of interest: principles will be basis of AAMC task force deliberations," *Washington Fax,* F-D-C Reports, Inc., February 14, 2001.

Conclusions

The debate about whether to include prescription drug benefits in Medicare has raised the visibility of pharmaceutical R&D. As noted in this report, pharmaceutical R&D is a complex, costly, and time-consuming process. It is also noted, however, that advances in molecular biology in recent years hold the promise of dramatically changing the way pharmaceutical R&D is carried out. These changes could shorten substantially the time it takes to bring a drug to market from initial research and therefore significantly affect the cost of drug development. How fast such changes may come about, however, could depend heavily on further research in molecular biology and the mechanisms of disease. Congress has strongly supported biomedical research in recent rears and there are calls for continuing to make it a high priority. In addition to biomedical research funding levels and priorities, issues related to human subject protection and conflict of interest are likely to affect the evolution of pharmaceutical R&D and, therefore, its costs.

APPENDIX A

A Brief History of Pharmaceutical Research and Development

Although substances have been used to treat disease for centuries, systematic pharmaceutical research did not begin until the late 19th century when chemistry had reached the point where its principles could be applied to medical problems and pharmacology became a scientific discipline. A major linkage occurred in the chemical dye industry when it was discovered that certain dyes have a chemical affinity for biological materials. German scientist, Paul Ehrlich (1854-1915), a pioneer in pharmaceutical research, determined that this "chemoreceptor" property would be different for certain organisms, such as parasites and cancer cells, than the host tissue, and this difference allowed the development of chemicals that could be used for therapeutic purposes.[99] He based this observation on experiments in which he synthesized a large number of compounds and testing each for its ability to destroy the organism without being toxic to the host. The basis for this process was Ehrlich's observation that certain chemicals would selectively attach themselves to proteins.[100]

At the same time, developments in chemistry permitted the isolation of active chemicals from plants that showed medicinal benefits. This was followed by efforts to standardize drug preparations. Medicinal chemistry also developed when it was discovered that coaltar could be used to create synthetic drugs. In addition, the science of pharmacology – the measurement and testing of the effectiveness of drugs – was being developed. These developments all combined to provide the impetus for the creation, from 1880 to about 1930, of the modern pharmaceutical industry.

The discovery of penicillin in 1929 led to the discovery of other antibiotics using the science of microbiology. The concepts of enzymes and receptors arising from the study of biochemistry began to play a role in drug discovery when they were found to be good targets for drug research. An important discovery was that receptors serve as switches to generate or

---

[99] Drews, "Drug Discovery: A Historical Perspective," 1960.

[100] Landau, et.al., *Pharmaceutical Innovation: Revolutionizing Human Health,* 39-40.

receive signals to the cell, and that these receptors could be either blocked or turned on by chemicals.[101] During World War II, the demand for penicillin and other antibiotics allowed the drug companies to develop the infrastructure and organization to undertake major R&D efforts. After the war, drug research accelerated because of the numerous opportunities and the large profits new drugs generated.[102]

Drug discovery, however, was still largely a trial and error process. That is, compounds were tried that were obtained somewhat haphazardly from libraries of molecules available to drug researchers. Those libraries were built up over the years because if was thought that the compounds, many of which were obtained from natural substances, might have some therapeutic value. In the 1960s and 1970s, advances in both life science research and chemistry greatly improved the drug research process, making it less random.[103] The focus of the life science research was the physiology of the cell, which allowed for design of specific drugs and greater understanding of how drugs worked than had been discovered through trial and error. In particular, as knowledge grew, drugs could be designed to inhibit well-defined proteins. Also, once the actions of certain drugs were understood, that knowledge was often used for greater understanding of the underlying disease, and, in turn, the design of new drugs. Advances in chemistry permitted systematic generation and testing of chemical compounds (combinational chemistry) as candidate drugs. The advances in both fields combined to make the drug discovery process more rational.

The 1960s also saw the development of the modern process for getting a drug to market. Beginning in 1938, drugs were required by the federal government to prove that they were safe.[104] It was not until the thalidomide episodes in the late 1950s, however, that the requirement for clinical evidence was established to gain approval to market a new drug. The Kefauver-Harris amendments passed by Congress in 1962 required a proof-of-efficacy and gave the FDA regulatory control over the necessary clinical trials.[105] At that time, the present-day process of elaborate clinical trials was established for determining the efficacy of candidate drugs.

Advances in molecular biology and biotechnology in the 1970s and 1980s have also contributed to drug research.[106] Biotechnology was first applied to drug development by bringing about dramatic increases in the production of certain drugs such as insulin whose efficacy was already established. Biotechnology was also used to enhance the search for new drugs. As molecular biology progressed, these two paths merged so that medical biotechnology is now primarily focused on the search for new drugs such as protease inhibitors used to treat AIDS, which must be produced by genetic engineering techniques.

Drug research over the last 120 years has evolved from a trial and error method, where many compounds were tried for their potential therapeutic value with only a little understanding of how they might work, to a much more rational approach that is based on a large body of knowledge about the origin of disease and workings of pharmaceuticals. Currently, drug discovery makes use of many disciplines, including chemistry, pharmacology,

---

[101] Drews, "Drug Discovery," 1961.

[102] National Research Council, "U.S. Industry in 2000: Studies in Competitive Performance", *Pharmaceuticals and Biotechnology,* (National Academy Press, Washington, DC, 1999), 368.

[103] Landau, et. al., *Pharmaceutical Innovation,* 91-92.

[104] This action resulted from a tragic situation when 107 people died while taking sulfanilamide in a liquid form. Drews, *In Quest of Tomorrow's Medicine,* 141.

[105] National Research Council, U.S. Industry in 2000, 375.

[106] Ibid., 378.

microbiology, and biochemistry. Sources for candidate drugs still include natural substances (such drugs are called biologics) as well as synthetic molecules created by chemical or biotechnology processes.

Chapter 10

HEALTH CARE REFORM AND INVESTMENT IN NEW DRUG DEVELOPMENT

Gary Guenther

One of the more contentious items on the legislative agenda of the 103rd Congress was health care reform. A multitude of bills was introduces; legislation was reported out of the House Ways and Means Committee and the Senate Finance Committee; and the leadership of the majority party in the House and Senate crafted comprehensive health care reform bills – amended versions of H.R. 3600 in the House and S. 2351 in the Senate.[1] Despite this activity, neither chamber voted on legislation to reform the Nation's health care system. Because the concerns that fueled the debate in the 103rd Congress are unlikely to disappear without significant changes in how health care is financed and delivered, the issue of health care reform could appear on the legislative agenda of the 104th Congress.

While the main proposals for reforming the health care system differ in scope, complexity, and approach, all seek to remedy what are widely seen as two major flaws in the current system: (1) the existence of millions of Americans without health insurance – in 1992, for example, 37 million Americans were uninsured on any given day, and (2) the high and spiraling cost of health care – from 1988 to 1993, for example, the average family premium for employer-based group health insurance more than doubled, rising from $2,500 to $5,200.[2]

An important policy issue in the debate over health care reform is the implications of reform for the incentives to invest in the development of new prescription drugs. Prescription drugs account for about 7 percent of U.S. spending on health care. Their role in treating diseases and other health problems can have substantial cost effects, and advances in drug therapy can bring about vast improvements in the quality of life or life expectancy of a large number of people.[3] The development of new drugs is a highly uncertain and lengthy process.

---

1 For more information on the health care debate in the 103rd Congress, see: U.S. Library of Congress. Congressional Research Service. *Health Care Reform: Overview*. Issue Brief No IB91093, by Mark Merlis, updated continually. Washington, August 30, 1994.

2 Rowland, Diane and Peter Long. Navigating the Health Swamp: A Primer. *New York Times*, June 12, 1994. p.F 3.

3 See: Boston Consulting Group. *The Contribution of Pharmaceutical Companies: What's at Stake for America*. September 1993. p.46-62.

As a result, investment in this process hinges on the prospects for earning returns that adequately compensate for the high costs and risks that must be incurred, especially in the period before a drug enters the market. Health care reform could affect the incentives for pharmaceutical innovation by fundamentally altering expected returns on pharmaceutical R&D, the lifeblood of new drug development. At the same time, health care reform presents an opportunity to reduce the cost to consumers and third-party payers of delivering health care by shrinking or eliminating whatever excess profits – if any – makers of branded drugs may be earning.

For pharmaceutical companies, who are the source of nearly every drug now in use in the United States, the impact of health care reform on their operations is no trivial matter. The U.S. market for leading brand-name drugs represents about half the world market. Thus, expected revenues from sales in the Unites States play a major role in decisions about which drug compounds to develop beyond the initial stages of discovery and animal testing.

This report examines the implications of health care reform for pharmaceutical innovation. More specifically, it discusses the elements of recent proposals for health care reform that are likely to have the biggest impact on the incentives to invest in the development of new drugs, and how those elements, individually and together, could affect those incentives. To set the stage for the discussion, the report first describes the dominant features of the drug development process and the forces shaping the current U.S. prescription drug market.

This discussion is based on several analyses of the Clinton Administration's proposed (and now defunct) health care reform plan, called the Health Security Act. The proposal served as the spark and the lodestar for the debate over health care reform in the 103rd Congress. Several studies have been done of how the plan might have affected pharmaceutical research and development (R&D). They are of interest because of the specific conclusions they arrive at about the Clinton plan, and because of the policy issues they highlight. One such issue lies at the heart of the debate over reforming the health care system: how to expand health insurance coverage, contain growth in spending on health care, improve efficiency in the drug development process, and not erode the incentives for investing in the development of new, cost-effective medical technologies, including some new breakthrough medicines?

NATURE OF THE DRUG DEVELOPMENT PROCESS

Even though the Federal Government is a major source of funding for pharmaceutical research and development (R&D), the vast share of prescription drugs approved for marketing in the United States have been discovered and developed by the private sector.[4]

[4] Some drugs originally were discovered through research funded by the Federal Government. In 1989, for example, Federal spending on preclinical and clinical pharmaceutical R&D totalled an estimated $704 million, or 12 percent of R&D spending in the United States by companies – both U.S. and foreign – who are members of the principal U.S. trade association for the pharmaceutical industry, Pharmaceutical Research and Manufacturers of America.
Of the 196 new drugs approved for marketing by the U.S. Food and Drug Administration from 1981 to 1990, the pharmaceutical industry was the source for 181, or 92 percent. See: Kaitin, Kenneth I., Natalie R. Bryant, and Louis Lasagna. The Role of the Research-Based Pharmaceutical Industry in Medical Progress in the United States. In: *Journal of Clinical Pharmacology*, Vol. 33, 1993. p.413-414.

The process of new drug development is lengthy, risky, and costly. Drug companies seeking to maximize profits will invest in such a process only if their managers expect to earn a return commensurate with expected risks and costs, including the cost of capital.

Risks and Costs of Pharmaceutical Innovation

It takes about 12 years for a new drug to proceed form initial synthesis in a research laboratory to final approval by the U.S. Food and Drug Administration (FDA).[5] This period has important implications for the profitability of investment in pharmaceutical R&D. During much of that period, the drug compound is protected by a 17-year patent, even though it is not earning revenues for the firm developing it. By the time, the drug gains marketing approval from the FDA, much of its patent protection has been used up, leaving the patent holder a relatively short period in which to exploit the monopoly power granted by the patent.[6]

Substantial risk is a hallmark of pharmaceutical innovation. Most drug compounds are discovered through a tedious process of trial and error where the odds of success, both clinical and commercial, are exceedingly slim. It is estimated that only 1 in 25,000 to 50,000 synthesized compounds ultimately gains FDA marketing approval. Moreover, only 1 in 83,000 to 167,000 synthesized compounds is likely to be a financial success.[7] Odds such as these make it likely that pharmaceutical industry executives would scrap a proposed R&D project if its expected returns only slightly exceed, match, or fall below the expected returns from investing the same amount of money in a virtually risk-free security such as 30-year U.S. Treasury bonds.

Not only is new drug development risky, but there is evidence that the risk of failure has increased considerably in the recent decades. One way to grasp the size of the increase is to examine recent trends in the estimated total cost of bringing a new drug to market.[8] A sharp rise in the average R&D cost of new drugs would imply that the threshold for commercial success for a new drug would also be much higher. As this threshold rises, the risk that a given drug compound will fail to attain it also grows, all other things being equal. Studies by Ronald Hansen (1979), Joseph DiMasi and group of colleagues (1991), the Congressional Office of Technology Assessment (OTA, 1993), and John Vernon and Henry Grabowski (1993) suggest that the average capitalized pretax R&D cost (in 1990 dollars) for new drugs

---

[5] See: Di Masi, Joseph A., et. al. Cost of Innovation in the Pharmaceutical Industry. *Journal of Health Economics*, vol. 10, 1991. p.124.

[6] As a result of the Drug Price Competition and Patent Term Restoration Act of 1984 (P.L. 98-417), owners of patents on drugs can extend the term of patents by a period of up to 5 years.

[7] According to a 1993 study by health economists John Vernon and Henry Grabowski, only 3 of every 10 drugs approved by the FDA between 1980 and 1984 can be expected to earn a stream of revenues over their product lifecycle that will exceed the average capitalized R&D cost. See: Grabowski, Henry G. and John M. Vernon. *Returns to R&D on New Drug Introductions in the 1980s*. Washington, American Enterprise Institute for Public Policy Research, September 1993. p.20-21.

[8] This cost covers all the expenses associated with bringing new drugs to market, including outlays for drug compounds that fail at one stage or another of the development process and the opportunity cost of the capital spent on drug development. The chief advantage of this approach is that it provides a reasonable way of determining how much money must be earned from drugs that reach the market to justify the amount spent on pharmaceutical R&D.

more than doubled from the late 1960s to the early 1980s.[9] Cost estimates for more recent periods are not available.

Returns to Pharmaceutical Innovation

The Formidable obstacles to commercial success in new drug development give rise to an obvious and important question: Do the returns to pharmaceutical innovation justify investing in an activity with such a long gestation period and such uncertain prospects for success?

Available evidence on the returns to pharmaceutical R&D suggests that they in fact do. Pharmaceutical firms invest in new drug development because it tends to be highly profitable over time. Studies by Vernon and Grabowski (1993) and OTA (1993) estimated that net returns on pharmaceutical R&D were positive, suggesting that the returns on new drug development are more than sufficient to recover the funds spent on it – including the cost of capital – and reward investors for the risks they incur.[10] What is more, for years the pharmaceutical industry has earned a much higher return on stockholders' equity than nearly every other U.S. industry. From 1980 to 1993, the median return for pharmaceutical companies included in Fortune magazine's annual ranking of the 500 largest U.S. industrial companies averaged 21.4 percent, compared to an average median return for all 500 companies of 12.4 percent. However, the actual gap in return on equity between the pharmaceutical industry and most other industries appears to be much smaller than these

---

[9] In a 1979 study of 67 new drug compounds first tested in humans between 1963 and 1975, Hansen found that the average pretax R&D cost capitalized to the date of FDA approval per successful drug was $54 million (1976 dollars), or $108 million in 1990 dollars. The DiMasi study was based on a random sample of 93 drugs which were first tested on humans between 1970 and 1982; it concluded that the average pretax R&D cost capitalized to the date of FDA approval per successful drug was $231 million (1987 dollars), or $259 million in 1990 dollars. OTA recalculated the DiMasi cost estimate using a range of capital costs to reflect the different levels of risk at each stage of the drug development process. It came to the conclusion that the DiMasi study underestimated the actual R&D cost of successful drugs. According to OTA's analysis, "a reasonable upper bound on the fully capitalized pretax R&D cost per successful drug at the time of market approval is $359 million (1990 dollars)"; the lower bound would be the $259 million from the DiMasi study. Vernon and Grabowski estimated the average pretax R&D cost capitalized to the date of marketing approval for new drugs introduced between 1980 and 1984 to be $280.5 million (1990 dollars), using a fixed cost of capital.

See: Hansen, Ronald W. The Pharmaceutical Development Process: Estimates of Development Costs and Times and the Effect of Proposed Regulatory Changes. In: Chien, Robert I. (ed.) *Issues in Pharmaceutical Economics.* Lexington, MA, D.C. Health and Co., 1979; DiMasi, Joseph A., et al. The cost of Innovation in the Pharmaceutical Industry. *Journal of Health Economics,* vol. 10, 1991; U.S. Congress. Office of Technology Assessment. *Pharmaceutical R&D: Costs, Risks, and Rewards.* Washington, U.S. Govt. Print. Off., February 1993. p.47-72; and, Grabowski and Vernon. *Returns to R&D on New Drug Introductions in the 1980s.* p.8.

[10] In a study of the returns to R&D investment for a group of drugs approved by the FDA between 1980 and 1984, John Vernon and Henry Grabowski concluded that the average drug in this group would earn a net return of $22.1 million (1990 dollars) over its assumed product lifecycle of 20 years. This amount represented about 11 percent of the estimated average after-tax capitalized R&D cost of $201.9 million (1990 dollars). In this analysis, a positive net return denotes an excess profit because the total expected return is greater than the minimum amount required to justify the investment in drug development, production, marketing, and distribution. Using a somewhat different set of assumptions, OTA analyzed the expected net returns on a group of drugs approved for marketing in the United States in 1981 to 1983. It concluded that the average drug would earn a net return of "at least 36 million" (1990 dollars), which represented 18.5 percent of the estimated average capitalized R&D cost. Both studies imply that the margin for error in government intervention to eliminate these excess profits is slim. The estimated average rates of return in both were within one percentage point of the assumed cost of capital for the pharmaceutical industry.

See: Grabowski, Henry G. and John M. Vernon. *Returns to R&D on New Drug Introductions in the 1980s.* p.15-17; and, Office of Technology Assessment. *Pharmaceutical R&D: Costs, Risks, and Rewards.* p.73-104.

accounting numbers suggest.[11] Perhaps the leading motive for investing in pharmaceutical innovation is to be the first company to introduce a new drug that offers superior or more cost-effective treatment for a prevalent chronic disease, such as high blood pressure, diabetes, or some kinds of cancer. A drug of this kind is known in the industry as a blockbuster. Companies that are the first to commercialize blockbuster drugs stand to reap lucrative rewards. By contrast, companies who lose the race but enter the market nonetheless typically earn much lower returns. For example, 1993 worldwide sales of Prozac, an antidepressant drug which was developed by Eli Lilly and represented a significant advance in drug therapy for depression when it first was introduced in the United States in 1988, totalled $1.2 billion; by contrast, combined 1993 worldwide sales of two substitute brand-name drugs – Zoloft (made by Pfizer) and Paxil (made by SmithKline Beecham) – which entered the market after Prozac came to $685 million.[12] However, few new drugs are likely to achieve the status of a blockbuster. The 1993 study by Vernon and Grabowski suggested that roughly 1 out of every 10 drugs approved by the FDA may achieve that status.[13] The same study found that 20 percent of the drugs in this group can be expected to account for 70 percent of total net returns for the group. It also found that only 3 of every 10 drugs in the group can be expected to earn revenues over their product lifecycles that equal or exceed the average capitalized R&D cost. Such a skewed pattern of commercial success has important implications for health care reform proposals that would contain spending on prescription drugs. These implications will be discussed in the concluding section of the report.

Spurred on by the prospect of earning high returns, pharmaceutical firms have invested heavily in R&D over the past 10 to 15 years. For example, companies that are members of the principal U.S. trade association for the pharmaceutical industry, Pharmaceutical Research and Manufacturers of America (or PHARMA, formerly known as the Pharmaceutical Manufacturers Association), spent an estimated $10.3 billion on R&D conducted in the United States in 1993, up from $6.8 billion in 1990, $3.4 billion in 1985, and $1.5 billion in 1980. At the same time, the industry's commitment to new drug development has deepened: in 1993, members of PHARMA spent an estimated 16.7 percent of their revenues from sales in the United States and U.S. exports on domestic R&D, up from 15.9 percent in 1990, 14.8 percent in 1985, and 11.7 percent in 1980.

---

[11] The explanation lies in current business accounting practice. According to this practice, spending on R&D and marketing is written off as a current business expense. Since spending on both affects a firm's revenues for many years to com, it makes sense to think of R&D and marketing spending as a capital asset and depreciate it over its useful life. Otherwise, the firm's rate of return on investment is calculated on an asset base that is smaller than it would be if it were to include the accumulated value of its R&D and marketing spending, which constitute an intangible asset. Under these conditions, it can be said that accounting rates of return on stockholders' equity overstate the true rate of return. This exaggeration is likely to be true of the pharmaceutical industry, which plows an unusually high share of its revenues into R&D and marketing.

A 1991 study that adjusted for this bias in accounting practice found that the average returns on investment for 88 drug companies between 1976 and 1987 were 2 to 3 percentage points higher than those for two control groups consisting of firms in other industries. This difference was about one-half of the difference yielded by standard accounting procedure. See: Office of Technology Assessment. *Pharmaceutical R&D: Costs, Risks, and Rewards.*

[12] Freudenheim, Milt. The Drug Makers Are Listening to Prozac. *New York Times,* January 9, p.F7.

[13] In the study, Henry Grabowski and John Vernon estimated that one of every ten drugs gaining marketing approval from the FDA between 1980 and 1984 can be expected to earn after-tax returns with a present value of $1 billion (1990 dollars). This amount, which covers the assumed lifecycle for each drug of 20 years from the date of FDA approval, was more than five times the present value of the estimated average after-tax capitalized R&D cost. See: Grabowski, Henry G. and John M. Vernon. *Returns to R&D on New Drug Introductions in the 1980s.* p.20.

In short, to quote economist F.M. Scherer, new drug development "resembles a risky lottery that throws out rich rewards to a few big winners while the majority of entrants lose money."[14] The entrants in this case are drug compounds.

THE CHANGING U.S. MARKET FOR PRESCRIPTION DRUGS

The decision to invest in the development of a new drug hinges on expected returns over its product lifecycle. Obviously, these returns would be affected by health care reform proposals that would fundamentally alter the demand for prescription drugs. This section describes the structure of the current market for these drugs and the forces shaping it. Together, they form the landscape that health care reform would take root in and inevitably reshape.

Structure of the Market

The U.S. market for prescription drugs, which is the largest market in the world and accounts for nearly one-half of world sales of leading brand-name drugs, has grown rapidly in recent years.[15] Drug manufacturers sell over 70 percent of their pharmaceutical products to wholesalers, who in turn distribute them to retail pharmacies, mail-order pharmacies, hospitals, health maintenance organizations (HMOs), and other buyers. Manufacturers also sell directly to pharmacies, HMOs, and hospitals. In 1991, retail pharmacies accounted for 61 percent of Pharmaceutical sales at the wholesale level; other leading buyers were hospitals (23 percent of wholesale sales), mail-order pharmacies (6 percent), and staff-model HMOs – which are HMOs that rely on salaried physicians – (2 percent).[16]

It also makes sense to view the market for prescription drugs from the standpoint of inpatient and outpatient demand. Inpatient demand refers to the use of prescription drugs in institutions like hospitals and nursing homes, and outpatient demand embraces all other uses. On the whole, health insurance in the United States covers a larger share of inpatient use than outpatient use.[17] Presently, outpatient demand accounts for about 77 percent of the volume of prescription drugs used in the United States.

The demand side of the market for prescription drugs departs from the model of a perfectly competitive market in a couple important ways. One is that consumers of these drugs generally do not directly bear the full cost of using them. In 1993, 50 percent of prescriptions filled by retail pharmacies were paid for out of pocket, compared to 59 percent in 1992. Insurance companies and other third-party payers covered the cost of 37 percent of prescriptions filled in 1993, up from 29 percent the previous year. And Medicaid, the Federal health insurance program for certain categories of low-income people, accounted for the

[14] Scherer, F.V. Pricing, Profits, and Technological Progress in the Pharmaceutical Industry. *Journal of Economic Perspectives*, Vol.7, No.3, Summer 1993. p.106.

[15] Grabowski and Vernon. *Returns to R&D on New Drug Introductions in the 1980s*. p.12.

[16] Office of Technology Assessment. *Pharmaceutical R&D; Costs, Risks, and Rewards*. p.238.

[17] A good case in point is Medicare, which is the primary Federal health insurance program for the elderly and disabled. Medicare covers the costs of treatment in a hospital, including use of medicines, but with only a few exceptions it does not cover outpatient use of prescription drugs.

remaining 13 percent, up from 12 percent in 1992.[18] An important economic implication of public and private insurance coverage of prescription drugs is that it makes consumers less inclined than they otherwise would be to base their purchasing decisions on actual market prices.

How much is spent on prescription drugs depends in part on the size of the elderly population. People 65 and older account for about one-third of U.S. spending on prescription drugs, even though they make up less than one-eighth of the U.S. population. In 1992, elderly Americans spent an estimated $503.89 per capita on prescription drugs (inpatient and outpatient use), compared to $149.59 per capita for the non-elderly population.[19] These figures imply that if the number of elderly were to increase faster than all other segments, per-capita spending on prescription drugs would rise, all other things being equal.

Push for Cost Containment

The supply side of the prescription drug market also has little in common with a perfectly competitive market. In fact, until the mid-1980s, the U.S. market for prescription drugs was characterized by a distinct lack of price competition. This condition flowed largely from three sources. One was the already mentioned insensitivity of most consumers to drug prices.[20] A second source was regulatory barriers to entering the market for generic drugs, which are lower-priced versions of brand-name drugs whose patents have expired. And a third source was patent protection of new drugs. A patent gives the holder a temporary monopoly over a product's commercial uses, including pricing and distribution. It serves as a formidable barrier to entry in the market for prescription drugs in that it prevents competitors from manufacturing a patented new chemical entity unless they first agree to pay some kind of licensing fee to the owner of the patent.

In a market dominated by these forces, makers of brandname (or patented) drugs had little incentive to compete on price. Rather, their main vehicle for generating sales growth tended to be heavy advertising and promotion directed at physicians.[21] Pharmaceutical firms faced few constraints on their ability to raise prices on existing products, and those that raised

---

[18] Standard & Poor's Corporation. Industry Surveys, Health Care Products & Services, Basic Analysis. New York, October 6, 1994. p.H19.

[19] New Directions for Policy. *Pharmaceutical Expenditures: Forecasts for the New Marketplace.* Washington, January, 1994, 1994. p.13.

[20] Historically, consumers have been insensitive to drug prices for two reasons. One is the role of health insurance in lowering the out-of-pocket cost to consumers of using prescription drugs, discussed briefly in the previous section. The second reason stems from the role of physicians in the consumption of prescription drugs. Since the enactment of the Food, Drug, and Cosmetic Act in 1938, which established the legal basis for the distinction between ethical drugs – which can be purchased only with a doctor's prescription – and proprietary drugs – which are sold over the counter, consumers have relied on physicians to decide when to take medicines and which ones to take. This reliance would not contribute to the price-insensitivity of consumers of drugs if physicians tended to behave like perfect economic agents for consumers, but such is not the case. In reality, physicians long have tended to pay little attention to differences in the prices of competing drugs, both generic and branded, when prescribing drugs. Typically, their top priority is to select what they see as the most appropriate drug therapy from the ones they are familiar with. And most consumers know too little about the tradeoffs between cost and benefit for alternative drug therapies to offer an effective counter to the tendency of physicians to overlook cost.

[21] Some analysts estimate that the typical pharmaceutical firm spends a higher share of revenues on advertising and promotion than on R&D. Stephen Schondelmeyer, a professor of pharmaceutical management and economics at the University of Minnesota, estimates that in 1989, the pharmaceutical industry spent 22 percent of revenues on marketing and promotion, compared to 16 percent to R&D.

prices could expect their sales revenues to increase proportionately, given that demand was relatively insensitive to price.

Since the mid-1980s, however, the marketplace for prescription drugs has undergone dramatic change, forcing pharmaceutical firms to alter their competitive strategies. Perhaps the most important consequence of this change bas been the emergence of significant price competition. The driving force behind this emergence been a mounting push for cost containment by public and private purchasers of (e.t., HMOs and the U.S. Veterans Administration) and public and private third-arty payers (e.g., Medicaid, health insurance companies, and employers) for prescription drugs. While the quest has its roots in the steep increase in health care costs over the past few decades, two recent and interrelated developments have made it a force in the current marketplace: (1) the rise of generic substitution, and (2) the rise of managed health care plans with restrictive formularies, which are lists of approved drugs that are the only ones participating physicians can prescribe. The push for drug cost containment is compelling an increasing number of makers of brand-name drugs to engage in the unfamiliar practice of price competition to spur growth in sales.[22]

Growing Use of Generic Drugs

An important tool of drug cost containment has been generic substitution. This is the practice of substituting a lower-priced generic drug for the brand-name version. Generic drugs are the biochemical equivalents of brand-name drugs whose patents have expired. Typically, they are introduced at substantial discounts from the prices of the branded versions, and within two years of entering the market the average generic price is about half the branded price. Generic drugs are made by makers of brand-name drugs as well as by smaller firms dedicated to the business of generic drug production; in recent years the former have made significant inroads in the U.S. generic drug market. As a result of a major change in Federal regulation of generic drugs in 1984, the number of different generic drugs on the market has skyrocketed in recent years.[23] This increase in choice in turn has encouraged greater generic substitution by third-party payers and institutional purchasers.

Nowadays, many health insurance companies either offer incentives for policyholders to use generic drugs or require generic substitution if a generic version of a prescribe branded drug is available. Mail-ordered pharmacies, hospitals, and HMO's with restrictive formularies also put considerable pressure on physicians to prescribe generic versions of drugs. And the

[22] According to a 1993 study by the Boston Consulting Group, the growing clout of managed-care organizations in the market for prescription drugs is compelling producers of brand-name and generic drugs to raise the size of the discounts from list price they traditionally have offered. The study estimated that the average weighted discount jumped form 4 percent in 1987 to 16 percent in 1992. See: The Boston Consulting Group. *The Changing Environment for U.S. Pharmaceuticals.* April 1993. p.10.

[23] The Drug Price Competition and Patent Term Restoration Act (P.L. 98-417), better known as the Waxman-Hatch Act of 1984, made two important changes in Federal regulation of prescription drugs. First, the Act shortened and simplified the process of gaining FDA marketing approval for new generic drugs. Second, it made it possible for owners of patents on brand-name drugs to extend the original patents for a period of up to 5 years. The Act effectively lowered the barriers to entry in the market for generic drugs because it substantially reduced the time and cost of meeting FDA requirements for marketing approval. Makers of generic drugs no longer have to prove independently that their products are safe and effective; they only need to demonstrate that their versions of brand-name drugs contain roughly the same dose of the active ingredients, are absorbed by the body at roughly the same rate, and are manufactured according to FDA standards of purity and sanitation.

Medicaid program required generic substitution unless a physician expressly forbids it on the prescription form.[24]

From 1980 to 1993, the share of prescriptions filled by generic drugs rose from 23 percent to 40 percent. This share is expected to continue to grow in coming years as additional branded drugs with $27 billion in current annual U.S. sales are scheduled to lose their patent protection in the United States by 2005.[25] As these figures suggest, the potential for further cost saving through generic substitution remains considerable.

Rising Influence of Managed-Care Organizations

The drive for drug cost containment has been spearheaded by managed-care organizations. Experts disagree on how these organizations should be defined and what share of the prescription drug market they control. Nonetheless, there is reason to believe that increasing numbers of prescriptions are being dispensed by managed-care health plans.[26] Total enrollment in HMOs, perhaps the prototype of a managed-care organization, increased from 3 percent to 14 percent of the U.S. population between the early 1980s and early 1990s.[27]

HMOs were the pioneers in managed care. They provide comprehensive medical care for a fixed annual fee, either through salaried physicians or a network of affiliated physicians. Thus, HMOs' profits hinge on keeping their per capita costs of providing inpatient and outpatient health care below annual enrollment fees. Most health care experts would agree that HMOs have developed the cost-control techniques that today are synonymous with managed care. Because HMOs strive to minimize the cost of keeping their subscribers in good health, their use of prescription drugs increasingly is tailored to managing the total cost of treatment over the course of a patient's illness with the aim of achieving a desirable health outcome.

Managed-care organizations – including pharmaceutical benefit management companies (or PBMs), which manage prescription drug benefits for many large employers and health insurers – use a variety of tools to contain the cost of the drug benefits they provide. The chief ones are mandatory substitution of generic drugs, restrictive formularies, drug utilization reviews, and mail-order pharmacies.

Restrictive formularies, which are lists of approved drugs chosen for cost and efficacy that physicians may prescribe without special permission, are proving especially effective in engendering substantial price reductions by makers of selected brand-name drugs.[28] They are

---

[24] U.S. Congress. Senate. Special Committee on Aging. *Pharmaceutical Marketplace Reform: Is Competition the Right Prescription?* Hearing, 103rd Cong., 1st Sess., November 16, 1993. Washington, U.S. Govt. Print. Off., 1994. p.92.

[25] Green, Daniel. Price Wars Over Name-Dropping. *Financial Times,* May 18, 1994. p.12.

[26] According to a 1993 report by the Boston Consulting Group, in 1981 about 5 percent of Americans with health insurance were enrolled in some kind of managed care program (defined as an HMO, preferred provider organization, or managed indemnity insurance plan); but by 1991 these programs covered 80 percent of all Americans with health insurance. The report also found that in 1991 about half of the volume of prescription drugs dispensed were covered by these programs, and it noted that "some projections suggest that 90 percent of the drug market will be under the influence of managed care by the year 2000. See: The Boston Consulting Group. *The Changing Environment for U.S. Pharmaceuticals.* p.17.

[27] Office of Technology Assessment. *Pharmaceutical R&D: Costs, Risks, and Rewards.* p.245.

[28] For more information on drug formularies, see: U.S. Library of Congress. Congressional Research Service. *Prescription Drug Prices: The Effects of Generics, Formularies, and Other Market Changes.* Report No. 93-740 E. by Sylvia Morrison. Washington, August 17, 1993. p.4-6.

most effective in reining in costs in therapeutic categories with many close branded substitutes. In these categories, operators of formularies such as hospitals or HMOs can use access to the formulary as a powerful bargaining chip to gain price concessions from makers of competing branded drugs. Such a practice is known as therapeutic substitution. Most major hospitals and about half of all HMOs make use of restrictive formularies.[29]

Drug utilization reviews (DURs) involve monitoring what drugs are prescribed and how often. They serve many purposes. One is to enable managers at managed-care organizations and PBMs with formularies to make sure that physicians are adhering to the prescribing guidelines. DURs are also used to reduce the inappropriate use of drugs, to ensure that patients comply with recommended drug regimens, and to coordinate the use of multiple drugs to minimize or prevent adverse side effects.

Managed-care organizations that rely more on mail-order pharmacies than community pharmacies to fill prescriptions can save money for a couple reasons. First, mail-order pharmacies typically have greater operational efficiencies than community pharmacies; for example, mail-order pharmacies tend to purchase in larger volumes and to have lower operating costs.[30] And second, mail-order pharmacies are more likely to practice generic substitution.[31]

Implications for Pharmaceutical Innovation

The mounting drive for cost containment in the market for prescription drugs has important implications for the development of new drugs. In a significant break with longstanding practice, the drive is forcing pharmaceutical firms to compete on price in selected therapeutic categories. Not surprisingly, this increase in price competition, which is reflected in a slowdown in prescription drug price increases, has contributed to recent declines in the growth of revenues and profits for some major drug companies (see Figure 1).[32] As their growth is profits has slackened, pharmaceutical firms have felt increasing pressure to alter their R&D strategies. In fact, some major firms have already done so by becoming more selective in the R&D projects they are pursuing, cutting their growth in R&D spending in the process.[33] These cutbacks can be seen as a response to the squeeze that the spread of managed-care cost-control techniques has put on expected returns to new drug development.

Continued expansion in the share of the prescription drug market influenced by managed care organizations could pave the way for broader declines in pharmaceutical R&D. Health economist Uwe Reinhardt has stated that managers of managed health care plans tend to be more concerned about squeezing the profit margins of providers of health care products and services to bolster their own than they are about ensuring that these same providers earn an adequate return on their investment in new technologies.[34]

---

[29] Boston Consulting Group. *The Changing Environment for U.S. Pharmaceuticals.* p.18.
[30] Standard & Poor's Corporation. *Industry Surveys. Retailing: Basic analysis.* New York, May 5, 1994. p.R95.
[31] Office of Technology Assessment. *Pharmaceutical R&D: Costs, Risks, and Rewards.* p.244.
[32] Part of the slowdown in drug price inflation since 1990 reflects well-publicized decisions by a number of leading pharmaceutical firms to hold increases in their average prices for brand-name drugs to one or two percentage points above the rate of general inflation as measured by the Consumer Price Index.
[33] See: Drugmakers Are Discovering the High Cost of Cutting Costs. *Business Week,* October 17, 1994. P.204-10.
[34] See: Reinhardt, Uwe E. *Managed Competition and Technical Innovation.* Unpublished manuscript, April 1994.

However, a lasting decline in pharmaceutical R&D driven by widespread use of managed-care cost-cutting techniques would not necessarily translate into a slower rate of development for breakthrough drugs. The current push for drug cost containment is built on efforts by buyers and third-party payers to encourage generic and therapeutic substitution. A key element in these efforts is the availability of close substitutes – also known as me-too or imitative drugs – for drugs still protected by patents. To the extent that the push for cost containment forces the prices of me-too drugs down, or that it forces makers of these drugs to set lower initial prices than they otherwise would, expected returns on me-too drugs would likely fall relative to expected returns on breakthrough drugs, especially those that lower the net costs to health insurers and managed-care organizations of treating of particular illnesses. By definition, during some indeterminate period there are no close substitutes for breakthrough drugs. Thus, in a market dominated by managed-care organizations, producers of new breakthrough drugs would gave more latitude in setting and raising prices than producers of me-too drugs. Such a situation appears to prevail today.[35] A fall in expected returns on investment in the development of me-too drugs would give pharmaceutical firms a strong incentive to channel a larger share of their R&D budget into the development of cost-effective breakthrough drugs.[36]

From the standpoint of public policy, a sharp decrease in the rate of imitative drug development would have an undesirable and unintended effect. Such a decrease could erode a key pillar of the emerging price competition in the pharmaceutical market. Me-too drugs, derided by some as a wasteful use of resources, often serve as the bargaining chips that enable buyers and third-party payers to extract price concessions from suppliers of brand-name drugs before they face generic competition.[37] A decline in their rate of development conceivably could reduce price competition in the market for brand-name drugs, bolstering the monopoly power of the makers of original breakthrough drugs.

---

[35] See: Standard & Poor's Corporation. *Industry Surveys: Health Care Products and Services.* p.H25; and Grabowski, Henry. *Health Reform and Pharmaceutical Innovation.* p.18.

[36] For a pharmaceutical firm, the choice between investing in the development of a breakthrough drug and investing in the development of a close substitute for a patented drug already on the market is not necessarily clear-cut. In many cases, the first firm to exploit new biomedical knowledge is merely the winner of a race to the market involving several firms. In such a rivalry, at least some of the losing firms could be expected to bring their patented versions of the breakthrough drug to the market in the hope of recouping some – if not all – of their R&D investments. New imitative drugs often are introduced at prices below those of the original breakthrough products. See: Congressional Budget office. *How Health Care Reform Affects Pharmaceutical Research and Development.* p.7-8.

[37] Testimony of Judith Wagner. *Pharmaceutical Marketplace Reform: Is Competition the right Prescription?* p.94.

Figure 1. Changes from Previous Year in Pharmaceutical Industry Revenues and Profits and Prescription Drug Prices, 1987-1993

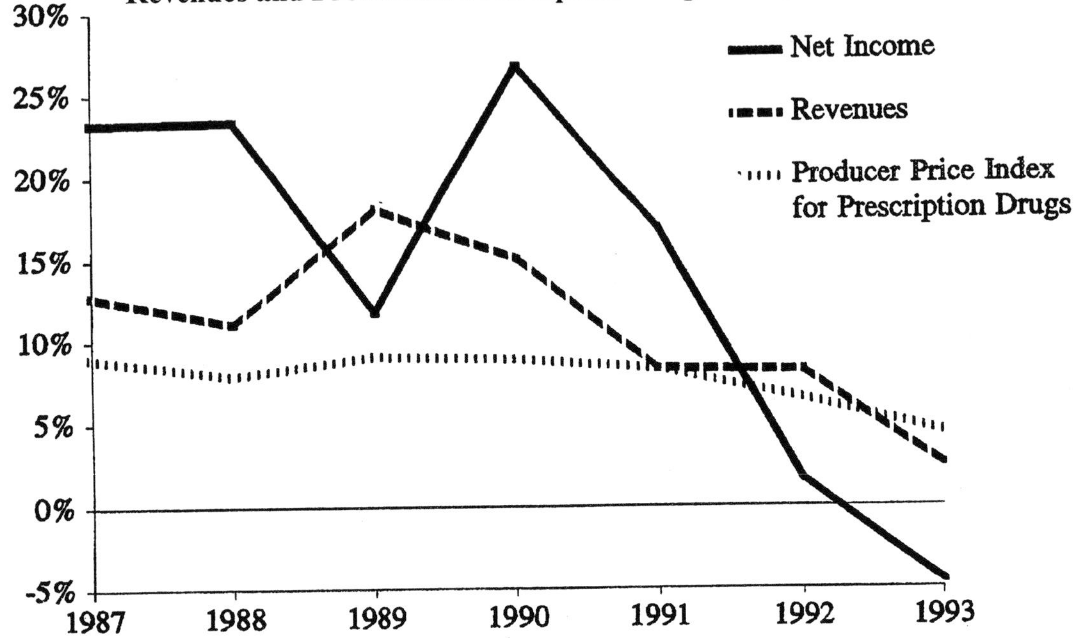

Note: Revenue and net income figures are for the top 13 sellers of prescription drugs in the United States, based on 1992 rankings. The companies in descending order were Merck, Glaxo, Eli Lilly, American Home Products, Marion Merrell Dow, Pfizer, Bristol-Myers Squibb, SmithKline Beecham, Upjohn, Ciba-Geigy, Johnson&Johnson, Schering-Plough, and Syntex. All but Glaxo, SmithKline Beecham, and Ciba-Geigy are based in the United States. The figures for net income and revenues relate to the worldwide operations of each company.

Sources: U.S. Department of Labor, Bureau of Labor Statistics; Standard and Poor's Corporation; and Moody's Investors Service, *Moody's Handbook of Common Stocks: Summer 1994.i*

HEALTH CARE REFORM PROPOSALS AND THE 103RD CONGRESS

Much of the debate on health care reform in the 103rd Congress centered on two widespread concerns: (1) the millions of Americans without health insurance at any given moment, and (2) the spiraling cost of health care. Many of the 50 or so proposals to reform the U.S. health care system introduced in that Congress sought to remedy these problems.[38] They differed in scope, complexity, and approach. The range of proposed solutions suggested there was no consensus in the 103rd Congress on what role the Federal Government should play in expanding health insurance coverage or curbing growth in spending on health care.

Despite their differences, most of the proposals can be place in one of three broad categories: single-player plans, managed-competition plans, and insurance-market reform plans. Although all three types of plans seek to expand health insurance coverage while reining in growth in spending on health care, they take strikingly divergent approaches.

[38] For an overview of the debate on health care reform in the 103rd Congress, see: U.S. Library of Congress. Congressional Research Service. *Health Care Reform: Overview*. Issue Brief IB91093, by Mark Merlis, updated continually. Washington, august 30, 1994. p. 16.

Single-Payer Plans

In general, single-payer plans would create a system of universal health insurance that would be administered by the Federal Government – or by the States under Federal guidelines. Most would abolish existing Federal health insurance programs (e.g., Medicare and Medicaid) and fold their beneficiaries into a national insurance program. Under such a program, the Federal Government (or the States) would establish universal coverage for a package of standard health benefits. The Federal Government also would set reimbursement levels for most health products and services, including outpatient prescription drugs. Single-payer plans would finance such coverage by increases in broad-based taxes, with minimal or no premiums or cost sharing by patients. In the 103rd Congress, health-care reform proposals by Representative McDermott (H.R. 1200) and Senator Wellstone (S. 491) would have created a single-payer system.

Managed-Competition Plans

By contrast, managed-competition plans would focus on using the powers of the Federal Government (or States acting under Federal Guidelines) to foster more competition among providers of health services and products. The central aim of such a policy measure would be to contain or lower costs by giving providers of health services powerful incentives to become more efficient in delivering high-quality care, thereby restraining inflation in health care costs. Under a managed-competition plan, the process of certifying health insurance plans and enrolling consumers in them would be controlled by regional health plan purchasing cooperatives. Each certified plan would have to offer a standard benefits package, issue periodic reports on the quality of care given by participating providers, and accept anyone who wishes to enroll, regardless of health status. Consumers would bear part of the cost of receiving health care. In the 103rd Congress, proposals that embodied such an approach included bills introduced by Representative Cooper (H.R. 3222) and Senator Breaux (S.1579).

Health-Insurance-Market-Reform Plans

On the whole plans to reform the market for health insurance would entail less government intervention than the other two kinds of plans. Moreover, their primary goals would be more limited. For example, many insurance-market-reform plans would create small, voluntary purchasing pools for health insurance, and these pools would make available standard health benefits packages to small business and individuals who currently lack health insurance. Many plans also would take one or more of the following steps: (1) limit the ability of health insurance companies to deny coverage to persons with pre-existing health problems; (2) offer subsidies to low-income people for the purchase of health insurance; (3) restrict the growth of Federal health insurance programs without imposing caps on private health spending; (4) permit the creation of medical savings accounts; and (5) limit the deductibility of employer-provided health insurance premiums from Federal Taxes. A number of proposals to reform the health insurance market were introduced in the 103rd Congress, including bills introduced by Representative Santorum (H.R. 3918), Senator Gramm ((S. 1807), and Senator Dole (S.2374).

Proposed Health Security Act

One proposal sparked and set the tone for the debate on health care reform in the 103rd Congress: the Clinton Administration's plan for reforming the U.S. health care system, known as the Health Security Act.[39] Under this plan, which combined elements of a single-payer plan and a managed-competition plan, all Americans would have been entitled to health insurance by 1998. Most people would have received coverage through a regional health alliance; an exception would have been made for people who work for firms that self-insure and employ more than 5,000 workers. Through regional or corporate alliances, people would have been able to choose among three types of health plans: HMOs, preferred provider plans, and traditional fee-for-service plans. Each plan would have been required to offer the same standard package of health benefits, including coverage of outpatient prescription drugs. Participating health insurers would have had to charge a community rate and accept anyone who wanted to enroll or renew, regardless of health status. Costs would have been controlled in part thorough federally mandated caps on annual premium increases; after the year 2000 premiums could have risen no faster than the growth rate of gross domestic product per person, adjusted for inflation.

The Clinton plan was mired in controversy from the time it was unveiled in October 1993 until the 103rd Congress drew to a close. As the legislative process in the 103rd Congress unfolded, the plan, along with a few other leading proposals, was modified so that the final versions under discussion in the House and Senate resembled hybrids of two (or in some cases all three) generic approaches to health care reform. Two notable examples were the health care reform bills introduced by the leadership of the House and Senate in August 1994.[40] In both cases, a chief motive for combining elements of different approaches was to craft legislation that had the potential for attracting sufficient bipartisan support to pass in each chamber. It appears doubtful that the Clinton Administration will push for the enactment of a similar plan in the 104th Congress.[41]

---

[39] For a detailed description of the contents of the President's plan, see: Library of Congress. Congressional Research Service. *Health Care Reform: President Clinton's Health Security Act.* Report No. 93-101 EPW, by Beth C. Fuchs and Mark Merlis. Washington, November 22, 1993. p.73.

[40] The House leadership bill contained elements of a single-payer approach and a managed-competition approach. By contrast, the Senate leadership bill seemed to be a hybrid of the managed-competition and insurance market reform approaches. See: U.S. Library of Congress. Congressional research Service. *Summary of Senator Mitchell's Substitute to the Health Security Act.* Memorandum, Education and Public Welfare Division. Washington, August 18, 1994. p.29; and: U.S. Library of Congress. Congressional Research Service. *Summary of Representative Richard Gephardt's Substitute Health Care Reform Bill.* Memorandum, Education and Public Welfare Division. Washington, August 26, 1994. p.39.

[41] See: McGinley, Laurie. Minor Health-Care Steps, Such as Reforming Insurance, May Face Hard Time in New Congress. *Wall Street Journal,* January 12, 1995, p.A16.

MAJOR HEALTH CARE REFORM PROPOSALS AND NEW DRUG DEVELOPMENT

Federal Efforts to reform the U.S. health care system could affect industry incentives to invest in the development of new drugs. Insights into the possible effects are provided by several studies of the Clinton plan's implications for the development of new drugs. Of all the health care reform proposals with significant ramifications for the market for prescription drugs introduced in the 103rd Congress, the Clinton plan appears to have drawn the most scrutiny of this sort. The hybrid nature of the plan makes it well-suited to the difficult task of analyzing the implications of health care reform for pharmaceutical R&D. In the remainder of this section the provisions in the Clinton plan related to prescription drugs and the main findings of the studies are briefly summarized.

Prescription Drug Provisions of the Proposed Health Security Act

The provisions in the Clinton plan that would have affected the market for prescription drugs fall into two broad categories: those that would have increased demand, and those that would have contained costs.

Provisions to Boost Demand

The plan would have increased the demand for prescription drugs in two ways. First, it would have created a universal entitlement to a comprehensive package of health benefits thatincluded coverage of outpatient prescription drugs. Second, it would have added an outpatient prescription drug benefit to Medicare, which is the primary source of health insurance for Americans 65 and older.[42] Together, these provisions would have extended insurance coverage of outpatient prescription drugs to the 70 or so million Americans who now lack it, either because they are uninsured or their health insurance does not provide such coverage.

The Congressional Budget Office (CBO) estimated that the plan would raise domestic spending on prescription drugs by 4 to 6 percent in its first full year, compared to a scenario based on a continuation of the status quo.[43] Most of this increase (3 to 5 of the 4 to 6 percentage points) would result from extending an outpatient drug benefit to all Americans under the age 65, who account for about two-thirds of spending on prescription drugs. Other analyses of the impact of the Health Security Act on demand for prescription drugs have arrived at similar estimates, despite using different analytical methods.[44]

---

[42] For more details on the proposed Medicare outpatient drug benefit in the Clinton plan, see: Library of Congress. Congressional Research Service. *Health Care Reform: Proposed Medicare Drug Coverage.* Report No.94-363 EPW, by Jennifer O'Sullivan. Washington, April 19, 1994. p.32.

[43] Congressional Budget Office. *How Health Care Reform Affects Pharmaceutical Research and Development.* p.x.

[44] Donald Muse of the Policy Research Group estimated that the Clinton plan would have raised spending on prescription drugs from 4.7 percent to 6.9 percent; the lower increase assumes a high shift to managed care plans, whereas the higher increase assumes the opposite. See: Muse, Donald N. *Costs Estimates of Prescription Drug Benefits Contained in the Health Security Act.* Washington, Policy Research Group, December 17, 1993. p.4.
In another analysis, Lewin-VHI Inc. estimated that during the first year that the health Security Act was in effect, revenues of the average pharmaceutical firm would have risen by 6.1 percent.

Provisions to Contain Costs

A number of provisions in the Clinton plan would have sought to contain total spending on prescription drugs. Some would have operated indirectly, making their effects on pharmaceutical industry revenues difficult to assess. Perhaps the most important indirect constraint on prescription drug spending would have been the caps that the Clinton plan would impose on increases in the premiums for health plans offered by regional and corporate alliances. Mandated limits of this sort could intensify the current push for cost containment in the prescription drug market by giving third-party payers, HMOs, PBMs, and managed-care organizations even more of an incentive to extract price concessions from suppliers of brand-name drugs, and to increase their use of generic drugs. Moreover, several features of the Clinton plan would have augmented existing incentives for people to enroll in less costly health plans like HMOs.[45] If it were to significantly boost enrollment in such plans, it could have the effect of enhancing the bargaining power of third-party payers and managed-care organizations in the market for brand-name drugs.

Another provision in the Clinton plan that would have indirectly restrained spending on prescription drugs sparked considerable controversy. This was the creation of an Advisory Council on Breakthrough Drugs. The Council's principal purpose would gave been to assess the "reasonableness" of initial or "launch" prices for new breakthrough drugs, which the plan defined as drugs that represented "a significant advance over existing therapies." Depending on how narrowly the Council interpreted this definition, it would consider only a handful of drugs each year; according to FDA data, breakthrough drugs accounted for only one-seventh of all the new drugs it approved for marketing from 1975 to 1991. Although the Council's rulings would not have been legally binding on manufacturers, they would have been made public, with incalculable but potentially powerful consequences for the pricing policies of pharmaceutical firms.

Other provisions in the Clinton plan would have directly sought to contain spending on prescription drugs, mainly through Medicare. The principal vehicle would have been mandatory manufacturer rebates on drugs dispensed to Medicare beneficiaries. Under the plan, manufacturers who wanted their brand-name drugs covered by the Medicare outpatient drug benefit would have had to agree to pay the Federal Government a basic rebate equal to 17 percent of the average prices they received for the same drugs from wholesalers or retail pharmacies – or their buying groups (In the plan, these prices were referred to as "average manufacturer retail prices."). The rebates would have been paid on all brand-name drugs dispensed to Medicare beneficiaries, but they would not have applied to drugs dispensed to non-Medicare beneficiaries. Makers of generic drugs would be exempt from the rebates. The basic rebate would have been larger if the difference between the average manufacturer retail price for a drug and the average price received from institutional buyers (e.g., hospitals and HMOs) for the drug exceeded 17 percent. In that case, the rebate would have equalled the average discount from list price given institutional buyers. The basic rebate also would have been larger if the average manufacturer retail price rose faster than the rate of inflation as measured by the Consumer Price Index.

---

[45] Some of the features that would do this are requiring a choice of plans through regional or corporate alliances, standardizing benefit packages, and increasing the availability of price and quality information about health plans and providers. See: Cutler, David M. A Guide to Health Care Reform. in: Journal of Economic Perspectives, Vol. 8, No.3, Summer 1994. p.22-23.

To contain spending on new drugs under Medicare, especially high-priced breakthrough drugs, the Clinton plan would have given the Secretary of Health and Human Services (HHS) the authority to negotiate special rebates for these drugs, which were defined as drugs first marketed in the United States after June 30, 1993. Under the plan, the Secretary could have negotiated a special rebate for a new drug if he or she had reason to believe that its price was excessive, or that it was being sold in one or more specified developed countries at a much lower price than in the United States. If an acceptable rebate could not have been negotiated with the supplier, the Secretary could have excluded the drug from coverage by Medicare.

Possible Impact of the Proposed Health Security Action Pharmaceutical R&D

Given that the Health Security Act would have both increased demand for prescription drugs and contained spending on them, what would have been its net effect on incentives to invest in the development of new drugs, especially those that represent significant therapeutic advances?

The question is important for two reasons. First, new drugs can have substantial short-term and long-term cost effects, and they can bring unprecedented health benefits, enhancing social welfare. Second, the Act would have sent mixed signals to pharmaceutical firms. On the one hand, the Act would have enlarged the potential market for branded drugs. On the other hand, it would have imposed mandatory rebates on all branded drugs dispensed under the Medicare program, which could account for one-third or more of the total market, and it would have strengthened the climate for drug cost containment among health plans serving those under 65 who would not have been eligible for Medicare.

A few studies examined the question of how the Act would likely affect the domestic climate for new drug development. One was by the Congressional Budget Office (CBO), and another by Henry Grabowski, a health economist and director of Duke University's Program in Pharmaceuticals and Health Economics.[46] In addition, the Clinton Administration prepared a partial assessment of how the Health Security Act would have affected the domestic climate for pharmaceutical innovation.[47] The main findings of each analysis are summarized below.

CBO Study

To evaluate the impact of the Health Security Act on the incentives for investing in new drug development, CBO divided the U.S. market for prescription drugs into two unequal segments: the under-65 market, and the 65-and-over market. The rationale for this approach was simple and straightforward. The Act would have established a special set of conditions for selling outpatient branded drugs to Medicare beneficiaries, who as a group account for roughly one-third of U.S. spending on prescription drugs. CBO gave separate estimates of

[46] See: Congressional Budget Office. *How Health Care Reform Affects Pharmaceutical Research and Development.* p. 65; and, Grabowski, Henry. *Health Reform and Pharmaceutical Innovation.* Washington, American Enterprise Institute for Public Policy Research, 1994. p.39.

[47] For a summary of this assessment, see: U.S. Congress. House of Representatives. Committee on Science, Space, and Technology. Subcommittee on Technology, Environment and Aviation. *Health Care Reform and the Role of Medical Technologies – Views of the Administration and of Industry Representatives.* Hearing, March 17, 1994. Washington, U.S. Govt. Print. Off., 1994. p.20-25.

how the Act would have affected demand for outpatient drugs and net sales of prescription drugs in the two segments.

CBO them estimated how the Act would have affected the returns from developing a new drug in a base case. An increase in returns would have suggested that the Act could spur pharmaceutical firms to spend more on such development. In this case, the returns on a drug are the present (or discounted) value of profits (i.e., sales revenues less production, marketing, distribution, and administrative costs) it generates over its product life. The base case came from a 1993 study by Henry Grabowski and John Vernon, which estimated that average returns from new drugs first marketed in the United States from 1980 to 1984 would total $210 million (1990 dollars) and would exceed average R&D costs (including the opportunity cost of capital) by $22 million (1990 dollars), or by a margin of 11.7 percent.[48] These results implied that as recently as the early 1980s pharmaceutical firms were modestly better of investing a given sum of money in new drug development rather than in a virtually risk-free security such as a 30-year U.S. Treasury bond.

For the under-65 population, CBO estimated that the Health Security Act would have raised the present value of average returns on a *drug developed exclusively for it* by $26 million (1990 dollars), which would have represented a 12 percent increase in the average returns in the base case ($210 million). This added profit reflected the combined effect of establishing universal coverage for a standard package of health benefits and abolishing the existing manufacturer drug rebates under the Medicaid program.

For the 65-and-over population, CBO estimated that the Act would have reduced the present value of returns on *drugs developed exclusively for it* by an average of $39 million (1990 dollars). This decline resulted from combining a Medicare outpatient prescription drug benefit with the mandatory rebates on drugs dispensed to Medicare enrollees. The estimate also assumed that makers of brand-name drugs who entered Medicare rebate agreements did not raise prices to offset some or all of the revenue lost because of the rebates.

What was CBO's view of the Act's overall effect on incentives to invest in new drug development? This question needed to be addressed because many drugs are used by people in both age groups. For the entire market for prescription drugs, CBO estimated that the Health Security Act would have boosted the present value of average returns on new drug development by $6 million (1990 dollars), which represented about a 3 percent increase in the average returns in the base case ($210 million). It should be kept in mind that a good deal of uncertainty surrounded this estimate. The main reason was that it did not take into account any changes in per capita drug use that would have been caused by an increase in enrollment in managed-care health plans. Many experts believed that the Act would have triggered such an increase, but its extent was a matter of speculation. As CBO maintained, a gain of 3 percent suggested that on the whole the Act would have imparted a modest stimulus to investment in pharmaceutical R&D.[49]

Moreover, CBO pointed out that the markedly different results for the population under 65 and the population 65 and over suggested that the Act would have given pharmaceutical firms a robust incentive to plow more of their R&D budgets into developing drugs that are used to treat or prevent health problems that are common among younger people. More

[48] See: Grabowski, Henry G. and John M. Vernon. *Returns to R&D on New Drug Introductions in the 1980s*. p.50.

[49] Congressional Budget Office. *How Health Care Reform Affects Pharmaceutical Research and Development*. p.55.

specifically, the mandatory Medicare rebates would have weakened the incentives for developing drugs that are used mostly by elderly people, assuming Medicare administrators forced producers of branded drugs to absorb the cost of the rebates. By contrast, if these administrators had little or no success in making these firms absorb the rebate, then the firms could try to shift some or all of the cost of the rebates to consumers under 65 by raising branded drug prices.[50]

Grabowski Study

A somewhat less rigorous perspective on the implications of the Health Security Act for new drug development emerges from a recent report by health economist Henry Grabowski. Unlike the CBO, he sketched what could be described as a worst-case scenario on the questionable premise that the drug cost-containment provisions of the Act would have acted in practice as price controls.

While acknowledging that the Act would increase domestic demand for prescription drugs, Grabowski claimed that its "most important... provisions for pharmaceutical innovation are the cost-control measures that directly impinge on new drug returns."[51] It is not wholly clear why he thought these measures would have had more of an impact on new drug development than the provisions that would have boosted outpatient demand for drugs. In Grabowski's view, the most important cost-control measures were the "negotiated rebates and related authority to exclude new drugs under Medicare, the Advisory Council on Breakthrough Drugs, and the premium caps on the growth of health care expenditures." To Grabowski, they "constitute an incipient system of price controls over new drugs."

To evaluate the implications of these cost-containment measures for the development of breakthrough drugs, Grabowski imposed a set of "public utility-type cost controls" on the results of a 1993 study he did with John Vernon on expected returns from pharmaceutical R&D for 67 drugs first marketed in the United States in the early 1980s. The results of the 1993 study served as the base case. Grabowski contended that such an analytical approach was plausible because under the Clinton plan the Secretary of HHS would have ended up using a "cost-based standard similar to what is employed by regulatory agencies for electricity and other public utilities" in negotiating special rebates on new drugs for Medicare beneficiaries.[52] Such an argument seemed at odds with the language of the Act, which required that the Secretary consider all relevant costs in determining what an appropriate rebate would be for a given new drug.[53]

Grabowski analyzed the effects of three separate cost-control scenarios on expected returns from pharmaceutical innovation. In one scenario, he assumed that the Federal Government imposed rebates on domestic sales of the drugs that fell in the top 10 percent of returns in the base case. The rebates were structured to permit manufacturers to earn a return that equalled the average capitalized R&D cost in the base case and nothing more; in other

[50] Ibid., p.58.

[51] Grabowski, Henry. *Health Reform and Pharmaceutical Innovation.* p.20.

[52] Grabowski, Henry. *Health Reform and Pharmaceutical Innovation.* p.22.

[53] The Act specified that in determining whether or not the launch price of a new drug was excessive, the Secretary of HHS must consider the following factors: "the prices of other drugs in the same therapeutic class, cost information requested by the Secretary and supplied by the manufacturer or estimated by the secretary, prescription volumes, economies of scale, product stability, special manufacturing requirements, prices of the drug in countries specified in subparagraph (A)(i), and other relevant factors."

works, the rebates eliminated all net returns or "excess profits" for these drugs. The net return here was the difference between the present value of total expected returns and the present value of average R&D cost, including the cost of capital. A positive net return would represent excess profits because it would be greater then the total return required to recoup all relevant costs, including the cost of capital – which in this case constitutes normal profits. As a result of the rebates in Grabowski's analysis, the average net returns in the base case dropped form $22.2 million (1990 dollars) to -$60.2 million. Such a result implied that investing a certain sum of money in new drug development would yield a lower rate of return than investing the same amount in 30-year U.S. Treasury bonds.

Grabowski also assessed the effects of two other cost-control scenarios. In one, the Federal Government got rid of excess profits on drugs in the top 20 percent of returns in the base case; and in the other, excess profits were eliminated for drugs whose returns fell in the top 30 percent of all the drugs in the base case. The results in each case were worse than the first scenario. In the former scenario, average net returns dropped to -$91 million (1990 dollars), and in the latter scenario, they fell to -$94 million.

Perhaps it would make sense to view these results as a cautionary tale rather than a realistic appraisal of the implications of the Act for pharmaceutical innovation. Even if one were to grant that Grabowski was correct in asserting that the drug cost containment provisions of the Act would have functioned as a system of government price controls, the provisions he found most deleterious to new drug development would have applied only to outpatient drugs dispensed to Medicare beneficiaries, who account for about one-third of total spending on prescription drugs. Nevertheless, the results suggested that stringent price controls on the most profitable drugs could lead to steep declines in spending on pharmaceutical R&D. These drugs are thought to account for the vast share of returns for all brand-name drugs. Government price controls that would limit returns for the most profitable drugs to the level of average R&D cost (including the opportunity cost of capital) could carry a significant risk of pushing the average return for all new drugs below average total R&D cost. Such a development, if sustained would lead some pharmaceutical firms to cut their spending on pharmaceutical R&D.

View of the Clinton Administration

The Clinton Administration maintained that the Health Security Act would lead to a substantial expansion in domestic demand for prescription drugs. For example it cited an estimate by actuaries at the Health Care Financing Administration that, after taking into account payment of the required rebates, the proposed Medicare outpatient drug benefit alone would boost total revenues for the pharmaceutical industry by approximately $24 billion over the first five years.[54] This increase would stem from a projected 35 percent rise in spending for outpatient drugs by the elderly, a rise which the Administration believed the benefit would induce. By its own admission, the Administration did not estimate the overall effect of the Act on industry revenues.[55] Nevertheless, it contended that the added demand induced by the Medicare drug benefit alone would be sufficient to stimulate increased industry investment in new drug development.

---

[54] U.S. Congress. House of Representatives. *Health Care Reform and the Role of Medical Technologies – Views of the Administration and of Industry Representatives.* p.24.

Contrary to the views of Henry Grabowski – among others, the Administration argued that the drug cost containment provisions in the Act would not have deterred pharmaceutical firms from continuing to spend heavily on pharmaceutical R&D. In written testimony delivered to the House Science, Space and Technology Subcommittee on Technology, Environment, and Aviation on March 17, 1994, Helen Smits, the Deputy Administrator of the Health Care Financing Administration at the Department of Health and Human Services, stated that the policy goal in establishing an Advisory Council on Breakthrough Drugs was to "create an environment in which drug companies have an incentive to charge a price that is fair but still adequate for them to continue developing... vital medicines." Smits went on to state that the required Medicare rebates were intended to contain the cost of the proposed benefit to taxpayers "without stifling incentives for research and development." To back her claim she pointed out that the Act did not "specify a particular formula for calculating an appropriate rebate for new drugs", but it did require the Secretary of HHS to weigh a number of factors in making such a calculation, including all the costs incurred by the manufacturer. Smits also stated that "the exclusion of a new drug – particularly a breakthrough drug – from the Medicare program is expected to be a rare occurrence."

SUMMARY AND CONCLUSIONS

Public policy has profound and myriad effects on the incentives for the private sector to invest in new drug development. Federal regulation of the development of new drugs adds to the cost of bringing new drugs to the market. But Federal support for pharmaceutical R&D through tax policy and Federal grants for biomedical research can bring down this cost. Federal health insurance programs such as Medicare and Medicaid also help shape the incentives for developing new drugs. Together, they represent between 35 and 40 percent to the domestic market for prescription drugs. And Federal patent laws make it possible for companies that develop widely used breakthrough drugs to reap huge returns on their investments. Furthermore, efforts at the Federal level to improve equity and efficiency in the delivery of health care can affect industry incentives for investing in new drug development. In the 103rd Congress, this issue surfaced repeatedly in the lively debate over reforming the U.S. health care system.

The development of new drugs, especially those representing significant therapeutic advances, is a time-consuming, risky, and costly process. On average, it takes 12 years for a new drug to make the highly uncertain journey from synthesis in a research laboratory to approval by the FDA. The odds of developing a new drug that will earn a positive net return on investment have been estimated to range from 1 in 83,000 to 167,000. Obviously, pharmaceutical firms are likely to invest in the development of new drugs only if their senior executives expect to earn returns that adequately compensate for such high costs and risks.

In recent years, the competitive dynamics of the U.S. market for prescription drugs have changed dramatically. The impetus for this change has been a mounting push for cost containment on the part of major buyers of and third-party payers for prescription drugs. Health maintenance organizations (HMOs) have spearheaded this push. To control growth in their spending on prescription drugs, they employ a number of tools, including mandatory

---

[55] Ibid., p.49.

generic substitution, therapeutic substitution, restrictive formularies, drug utilization reviews, and mail-order pharmacies. Other managed-care organizations, including pharmaceutical benefit management companies and preferred provider health plans, have adopted these cost-control techniques. Furthermore, the bargaining clout of managed-care organizations in the market for prescription drugs is growing. No longer is it true that the decision to use medicines is completely in the control of independent physicians treating patients covered by traditional fee-for-service insurance plans.

The growing push for cost containment is forcing an increasing number of major producers of branded drugs to engage in an unfamiliar practice to spur sales growth: price competition. This is reflected in an estimated fourfold increase in recent years in the discounts from list price offered by producers of branded and generic drugs. The emergence of price competition explains much of the slowdown in the rate of growth in pharmaceutical industry profits and prescription drug prices since the late 1980s.

In the midst of this change in the prescription drug marketplace, the 103rd Congress turned its attention to health care reform. A variety of reform proposals was introduced. While they differed in scope, complexity, and approach, most addressed two major problems with the current health care system: (1) a persistent lack of universal access to adequate health insurance, and (2) persistent rapid inflation in health care costs. Many of the proposals fell into one of three generic approaches to reform: single-payer plans, managed-competition plans, and health-insurance-market-reform plans. Single-payer plans would entail the most government intervention in the delivery and financing of health care, and insurance-market-reform plans the least.

One proposal both launched and dominated the debate in the 103rd Congress over health care reform. This was the reform proposal crafted by the Clinton Administration, known as the Health Security Act. It combined key elements of a single-payer plan and a managed competition plan. In essence, the Act would have achieved universal health insurance coverage and contained growth in spending on health care through a form of managed competition backed by a system of federally mandated caps on annual increases in health insurance premiums and on overall health care spending. The Act was mired in controversy from its unveiling in October 1993. As the legislative process in the 103rd Congress unfolded, the Act was modified in numerous ways in both the House and the Senate. Neither chamber noted on the last versions under consideration, the health care reform bills introduced by the House and Senate leadership in early August 1994.

What are the potential effects of health care reform on the development of new drugs, especially breakthrough drug therapies? The analyses of the drug provisions of the Health Security Act discussed in the previous section offer some guidance.

As the analyses show, the answer hinges in part on the scope and content of whatever health care reform plan the Congress might adopt. Reform plans that would increase the demand for prescription drugs by extending health insurance coverage of physician services and outpatient drugs to some or all of the 70 or so million Americans who currently lack such coverage could be expected to raise expected returns on investing in new drug development. A rise in expected returns in turn would bolster industry incentives for investing in such development.

By contrast, reform plans that would seek to contain spending on prescription drugs could lower expected returns on new drug development, depending on the nature and mix of the measures used to control spending. For example, reform plans that would regulate the prices of highly profitable branded drugs to restrain growth in profits without allowing for the negative net returns earned by the vast majority of approved drugs would surely reduce industry incentives to invest in new drug development. A sizable fall in expected returns in turn would eventually lead to a decline in the rate of technological progress in the pharmaceutical industry, with possibly adverse consequences for consumer welfare.

Plans that would attempt to accomplish both goals at once, such as the Health Security Act and the health care reform bills introduced by the House and Senate leadership in the 103rd Congress, would have an uncertain effect on industry incentives to invest in new drug development. Whether or not a hybrid plan of this sort would boost average expected returns from new drug development would depend on the relative strength of the demand-enhancing provisions and the cost-containing provisions on the scale of expected revenues from commercializing new drugs.

How health care reform would affect the incentives for investing in new drug development also depends in part on the structure and competitive dynamics of the market for prescription drugs at the time a reform plan were implemented. As recent trends in the U.S. pharmaceutical market show, conditions in the demand- and supply-sides of the market can and do change dramatically. Unlike 20 or even 10 years ago, many buyers and third-party payers now have the clout to negotiate significant price concessions from makers of some brand-name drugs. Reform plans that would reinforce these features and reform plans that would weaken them would be unlikely to have similar effects on expected returns from new drug development.

For instance, a health care reform plan that would achieve universal coverage but would accelerate the ongoing shift of Americans with health insurance into HMOs could lead to a smaller increase in expected returns than a plan that would achieve universal coverage but would encourage Americans to enroll in fee-for-service plans, making it likely that pharmaceutical industry profits would be large under a health care system dominated by fee-for-service health insurance.

By the same token, health care reform plans that seek to contain drug costs by encouraging increased generic and therapeutic substitution could give more of a stimulus to industry investment in new breakthrough drugs than plans that seek to contain drug costs by imposing across-the-board controls on prices. Plans of the former type would alter the relative risks of R&D strategies available to pharmaceutical firms by increasing the potential cost of failing to be the first to bring a new breakthrough drug to the market; in such a situation, firms would have a powerful incentive to divert more of their available R&D resource from developing imitative or me-too drugs to developing breakthrough drugs. It should be noted that such a choice may not apply to drug firms who are racing to be the first to market a particular breakthrough drug. In this case, even the losers would be likely to seek approval from the FDA to market their branded versions in order to maximize their return on investment.

Health care reform may not receive the same priority as a legislative issue in the 104th Congress as it did in the 103rd Congress. Nevertheless, those Members who want to make significant changes in how health care in the United States is financed and delivered face numerous formidable challenges in devising a feasible plan. A key one is to expand access to outpatient prescription drugs, especially those which represent significant therapeutic advances, without impairing the pharmaceutical industry's incentives to invest in new drug development so that the rate of technological progress in the industry suffers a major decline.

Chapter 11

DRUG PRICES AND THE CPI

David J. Cantor

SUMMARY

The effect of drug prices on inflation has significant implications not only for the consumer's access to medications, but also for the cost of government programs that are indexed to the Consumer Price Index (CPI). In turn, this could affect the achievement of public policy goals of balanced budgets for the Federal Government Whatever else may be asserted about the pricing of prescription drugs, the date indicate increases in their prices in the 1980s and 1990s did not add greatly to the rise in the overall CPI for urban consumers.

CONSUMER PRICE INDEXES FOR ALL ITEMS AND ALL ITEMS *LESS* PRESCRIPTION DRUGS AND MEDICAL CARE, 1980-1994

Consumer prices – as measured by the Consumer Price Index for All Urban Consumers (CPI – rose by about 75.4 percent from December 1980 through December 1994, or at an annual rate of about 4.1 percent. In varying degrees, most expenditure categories included in the CPI contributed to this increase. Among them are prescription drugs as well as the broad grouping of all medical care categories. If only prescription drug prices had been excluded, the CPI-U would have risen by about 74.8 percent, or nearly as much as with drug prices included in the CPI-U. Excluding prescription drug prices, the annual rate of growth of th CPI-U was also about 4.1 percent. But, if all medical care prices paid by consumers were excluded form the expenditure categories used to calculate the CPI-U throughout this period, all consumer prices would have risen not by 75.4 percent, but by the noticeably smaller percentage of about 70.2 percent; the annual rate of growth of consumer prices *less* medical care averaged about 3.9 percent.[1] Table 1 presents the changes in the CPI-U for of all medical care prices on the CPI-U from December 1980 through December 1994.[2]

[1] In addition to calculating the CPI-U for all items, the Bureau of Labor Statistics calculates and publishes the CPI *less* medical care. It does not publish the CPI *less* prescription drugs. To show the effect of eliminating the

Table 1. Changes in the Consumer Price Indexes for All Items and for All Items Less Prescription Drugs and Medical Care, December 1980 – December 1994

Expenditure Category	Percent Change
All Items	75.37
All Items Less Prescription Drugs	74.76
All Items Less Medical Care	70.17

Compiled by CRS, using as sources published data of the Bureau of Labor Statistics

Figure 1. The Consumer Price Index for All Urban Consumers (CPI-U) for All Items, All Items *Less* Prescription Drugs, and All Items *Less* All Medical Care, December 1980 – December 1994.

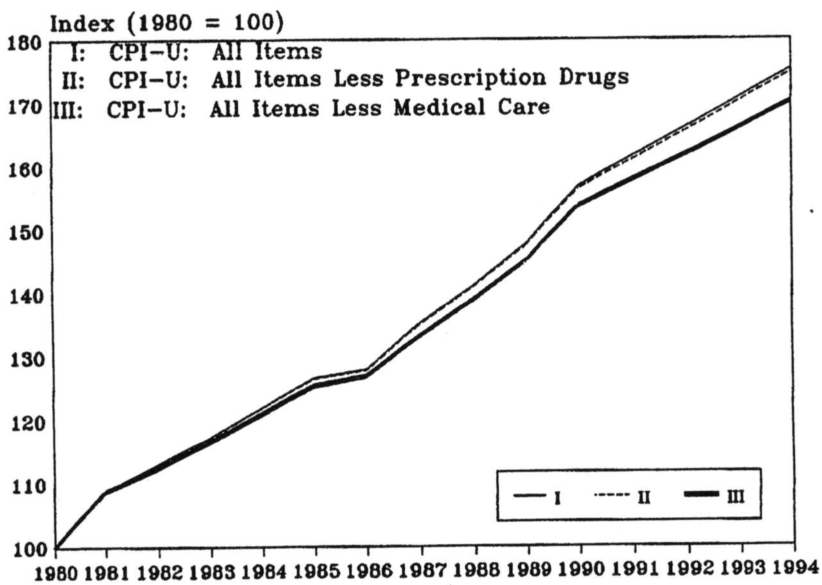

Note: This figure uses 1980 as a base year to illustrate the trends in the indexes. The underlying indexes complied by BLS have the period, 1982-1984 = 100, as their base.

Source: Compiled by CRS, using as sources published data of the Bureau of Labor Statistics.

---

inclusion of any item in the CPI-U, three steps are required. First, the change in its price weighted by its relative importance in the overall index is subtracted from the percentage change in the CPI-U from one period to another. Second, the relative importance of all items also has to be revised to reflect the change in the composition of the market basket used to develop the CPI-U. This is done by subtracting from the relative importance of all items in the initial market basket – which, by definition, is equal to 100 – the weight of the item(s) to be excluded. Third, the percentage change in the rebased CPI-U is then obtained by dividing the result of the first step in this process by the result of the second operation. This set of procedures to rebase and recalculate the CPI-U less some component is really no different from calculating the percentage change in the all items index. The third step – namely, dividing the percentage change in prices by the relative importance of all items in the index – is explicitly or implicitly performed. The difference is that the percentage change in prices in the overall index is divided by 1 or 100.

[2] The one-eighth share of drug prices of the total influence of all medical care prices on the overall CPI-U is simply its effect divided by the effect of all medical care; that is, 0.61/5.2.

Figure 1 provides an illustration of the impact of prescription drugs on the overall rate of inflation as compared with the impact of all medical care expenditures. The movement of the all items *less* all medical care expenditures deviates noticeably from the CPI-U for all items. The inflation rate would have been markedly lower, if medical care prices had not risen over this period. Prescription drug prices represented less than one-eighth of the total influence in the CPI-U indexes for all items, all items less prescription drugs, and all items less medical care in the period from December 1980 through December 1994.[3]

CONCLUDING OBSERVATIONS

This analysis indicates that drug prices have really had only a small impact on the trend in overall consumer prices. What drove the medical care component of the CPI-U were the price increases of Physicians' services and hospitals and related services. Had prices of Physicans' services been excluded from the index in the review period, the CPI-U would have risen by 72.68 percent. Physicians' services accounted for nearly half the impact of all medical care prices on the CPI-U. If prices of hospital and related services were excluded, the increase in the CPI-U would have been 73.83 percent. These services represented somewhat more than one-fourth of the effect of medical care prices on the CPI-U for all items.

The results of this analysis are somewhat surprising, because both the relative importance[4] of prescription drugs rose by a factor of about 2.5, from 0.385 percent in December 1980 to 0.896 in December 1994. The relative importance of the entire medical care expenditure category rose by a factor of about 1.5 in the same period, from 4.717 in December 1980 to 7.266 in December 1994. The consumer price index for prescription drugs rose more than threefold from 75.2 to 233.2. The consumer price index for the entire medical care category rose by a factor of about 2.8, from 77.6 to 215.3. The CPI-U for all items rose by a factor of about 1.7 in this period, from 86.3 in December 1980 to 149.7 in December 1994.[5] The increasing importance of prescription drugs and the rise in its price index relative to both medical care and all items suggest that prescription drugs should have had a greater impact on the overall increase in consumer prices than they did. The trends in drug prices notwithstanding, the relative impacts of other medical care components and of other expenditure categories in the overall index tended to diminish the influence of prescription drugs on the overall movement of consumer prices.

One reason that prescription drug prices might not have had a greater effect on the overall CPI-U is the competition among sellers in the retail market. Although the CPI-U is calculated on the movement of prices of a specific group of items, often referred to as the so-called

---

[3] The years covered were selected solely to have a relatively long period of time to assess the effects of prescription drugs and the broader category of medical care on the CPI-U.

[4] A critical element of the process of assessing the influence of price changes in any given expenditure category is the relative importance of that item. The greater the relative importance of an item, the more likely that changes in the price of the item will have a noticeable impact on the overall CPI-U. The estimates of the relative importance of an item changes monthly based not only on changes in its price, but also on changes in its price *relative* to all other price changes. For a more detailed explanation of the concept of relative importance in the CPI-U, see: U.S. Department of Labor. Bureau of Labor Statistics. *Relative Importance of Components in the Consumer Price Index, 1994.* Bulletin 2463. June 1995. Washington, 1995. p.1.

[5] These index numbers reflect a base of 1982-1984 = 100. As noted previously, the base year in figure 1 is set at 1980 = 100 solely to illustrate the trends in the indexes after excluding prescription drug and all medical care component prices.

market basket, BLS has made efforts at least in recent years to capture changes in the competitive forces in the market for any component. Monthly, BLS asks a sample group of consumers where they purchase a given item, not what they pay for the item. Using this "point-of-sale" information, BLS then has been surveying vendors in the various kinds of retail outlets on the prices they charge for the item.

In the case of pharmaceuticals, the kinds of retail outlets are several: the so-called traditional stand-alone pharmacy, the chain pharmacies, general merchandize stores (e.g., K-Mart), and food stores. The competition among these kinds of stores could suppress increases in prices over time. In addition, price competition between name brand and generic drugs was credited with holding down medical care prices in 1994.[6] Although generic drug substitutes for name brand drugs were *not* included in the market basket of goods and services on which the CPI-U was based in 1994, the indirect influence of lower generic drug prices was considered to be a factor holding down the rate of price increase of the prescription drugs that were included.[7, 8]

One factor that does not come into play in assessing the influence of prescription drug prices on the inflation rate is their prices in the base period. The CPI-U measures trends in prices. If the price of a good or service in the base period is high, a low annual rate of change would result in only a small change in the index. For example, if some product is priced at, say, $50 per unit in the base period, but only increases at a hypothetical rate of 0.25 percent annually, in 10 years, its price would be about $51.26. The impact of a particular good or service on the overall rate of inflation it's the *change* in its relative value rather than its absolute price in the services in the base year.

---

[6] Pavalone, Joseph. Consumer Prices in 1994. *Monthly Labor Review,* v. 118, June 1995. p.33.

[7] criticism has been levelled at the CPI that focuses upon issues of product quality, substitution, and point of sale. For a full discussion of the issues surrounding the usefulness of the CPI, see: U.S. Library of Congress. Congressional Research Service. *The Consumer Price Index: Is It Biased?* Report No. 95-654E, by Brian W. Cashell. Washington, 1995, p.14.

[8] Beginning in 1995, the Bureau of labor Statistics is obtaining prices of both name brand drugs and generic substitutes. This information was obtained in a telephone communication with BLS staff, October 26, 1995.

Chapter 12

GATT AND THE PHARMACEUTICAL INDUSTRY: PROSPECTIVE EFFECTS OF THE URUGUAY ROUND ON THE INDUSTRY

Sylvia Morrison

SUMMARY

If Congress approves the bill to implement the package of agreements produced by the Uruguay Round of negotiations on the General Agreement on Tariffs and Trade (GATT), the effect on the U.S. Pharmaceutical industry will be slight in the short run, but in the long run may be significant. First, repeal of tariffs on pharmaceuticals by the three nations that make up 75 percent of the U.S. export market could increase revenues and employment in the U.S. industry[1] even though exports account for only about 10.4 percent of the value of shipments of U.S. pharmaceutical manufacturers.[2] Second, the intellectual property portion of the agreement requires signatory nations to close, or seek licenses for, unlicensed laboratories that manufacture and sell medications that secure patents after the agreement comes into effect. At the same time, however, it allows developing nations at least *10 years* to put the intellectual property portion of the agreement into effect. Third, the agreement on subsidies permits the transfer of basic research information from U.S. Federal and federally funded laboratories to private manufacturers under the U.S. technology transfer program to continue without the pharmaceutical products being subject to countervailing.[3]

---

1 U.S. International Trade Commission. *Potential Impact of the U.S. Economy and Industries of the GATT Uruguay Round Agreements,* Vol.1. Publication 2790. Washington, D.C. June 1994, p.III-21.

2 U.S. Department of Commerce. *U.S. Industrial Outlook for 1994.* Washington, D.C. 1994. p.43-1. These data are for 1992.

3 To *countervail,* in international trade law, is to levy a compensatory duty on an imported article that is equal to the subsidy the product received, or sufficient to eliminate injury that could result from the importation of the subsidized article.

Characteristics of the Market for U.S. Prescription Drugs

"The U.S. market for prescription drugs is the largest national market in the world, accounting for about one-half of the world market for brand-name drugs."[4] U.S. companies are the main suppliers of the domestic market, which consumes nearly 90 percent of their output. American manufacturers also make nearly half of the major pharmaceuticals manufactured worldwide.[5] In 1993, total shipments by the U.S. pharmaceutical industry (including products manufactured outside the United States) reached $69 billion, compared with $39 billion only six years earlier.[6] The overall U.S. balance of trade in pharmaceuticals has been consistently positive. Still, competition from the pharmaceutical manufacturers of other nations is growing steadily.[7]

How would the Uruguay Round Help the Pharmaceutical Industry?

The most immediate advantage the Uruguay Round would offer the American Pharmaceutical industry is the all-at-once reciprocal elimination of tariffs on pharmaceuticals by Canada, the European Union, and Japan.[8] These nations make up more than 75 percent of the overseas market for U.S. pharmaceuticals. However, exports account for only about 10.4 percent of the value of shipments of U.S. pharmaceuticals. Therefor, the tariff elimination by America's main trading partners in pharmaceuticals will probably increase revenues and employment in the U.S. industry[9] over time (as reduces tariffs stimulate trade), but the short-run effect will probably not be dramatic.

A second benefit to the pharmaceutical industry from the Uruguay Round is found in the subsides segment of the agreement. This agreement allows substantial government subsides for industrial research without subjecting the article to countervailing by the importing country. In effect, it permits the current American practice of transferring basic research data on promising compounds from Federal laboratories and federally funded laboratories to private manufacturers who complete research and development to create marketable products. This technology transfer program was established by Congress in the form of

- *The Stevenson-Wydler Technology Innovation Act (P.L. 96-480),* which made technology transfer (to private manufacturing companies) a primary goal of Government-owned and Government-funded laboratories, and required each Federal laboratory to establish an Office of Research and Technology Applications to facilitate technology transfer; and,
- *The Bayh-Dole University and Small Business Patent Act (P.L. 96-517),* which provided research support and allowed small businesses and nonprofit institutions

---

[4] U.S. Congress. Congressional Budget Office. *How Health Care Reform Affects Pharmaceutical Research and Development.* Washington, D.C., June 1994, p.3.

[5] *Ibid.*

[6] U.S. Department of Commerce. *U.S. Industrial Outlook for 1994.* Washington, D.C. 1994. p.43-1.

[7] *Ibid.*

[8] Tariffs on pharmaceuticals have also been eliminated by Singapore and the Czech and Korean Republics.

[9] U.S. International Trade Commission. *Op. Cit.* p.III-21.

(mainly universities) to retain title to the patents for their Government-funded inventions.

The Uruguay round agreement defines the term "subsidy" for the first time in GATT, and enumerates the various kinds of national subsidies, classifying them as prohibited, permissible, and those subject to countervailing.

> Government subsidies for research assistance are permitted for up to 75 percent of the costs of industrial research and up to 50 percent of the costs of pre-competitive development activity. Industrial research is defined as [generating] new knowledge for developing new products, processes or services, or for bringing about a significant improvement to existing products, processes or services. Pre-competitive development activity is defined as the application of industrial research for new or improved products, processes or services, up to creation of a first prototype that would not be capable of commercial use.[10]

The benefit to the industry may be only temporary, however. The subsidies agreement requires a review of the R&D provision in six months, and the provision will expire in five years unless it is reconfirmed.

How Would the Uruguay Round Fail the Industry?

While the Uruguay Round agreement offers certain advantages to the American pharmaceutical industry, it delays for ten years corrective action for the most serious international trade problem the industry faces. This problem is that pirate laboratories, located for the most part in less developed nations, copy and sell products that brand-name research companies of the United States (and other developed nations) have developed and patented at a reported average cost of more than $300 million per drug.[11]

According to the Pharmaceutical Research and Manufacturers of America (PhRMA), the most serious offenders are located in Argentina, Brazil, Colombia, Egypt, India Thailand, Turkey and Venezuela. Frequently, these nations, and certain others to a lesser degree, not only fail to pass and/or enforce patent protection laws, but actually protect their indigenous pirates by charging high tariffs on imported patented medications. The reasons offered for breaching the patent rights of U.S. companies are that the developing nations cannot pay full price for patented medications, that their citizens should not have to do without medication because they are poor, and that they lack the trained personnel and budget to establish patent protection services.

The segment of the Uruguay Round agreement that addresses this issue, the *Agreement of Trade-Related Aspects of Intellectual Property Rights (TRIPs),* is designed to protect holders of patents and copyrights against infringement, and it will apply to the developed world as soon as the agreement takes effect. For "developing" nations, however, the agreement delays

[10] U.S. Library of Congress. Congressional Research Service. *Research and Development Subsidies and the GATT* by Lennard Kruger. May 6, 1994. p.4.

[11] Testimony by Gerald J. Mossinghoff, President, Pharmaceutical Manufacturers Association, before the Subcommittee on Trade of the Committee on Ways and Means, U.S. House of Representatives, February 22, 1994.

the requirement to protect pharmaceutical patents for at least ten years. The agreement requires that patents granted at any time after the Uruguay Round goes into effect shall be held in a pending status by developing countries until those countries pass patent protection laws. While in a pending status in a given country, medications may be marketed in that country only by their originators. When patent laws are passed, patents granted after the Uruguay Round has gone into effect are to be observed.

Since new U.S. pharmaceutical products are usually patented at least a decade before the FDA clears them for sale (i.e., they are "in the pipeline"), in some cases, as in the past, they may be copied overseas before they are cleared for sale in the United States despite their pending status. In February 1994, a pharmaceutical industry spokesman testified that "patent piracy by developing countries costs the international pharmaceutical industry as much as $5 billion annually."[12] Given the American share of the world market, a large portion of the losses can be assumed to be losses to American companies, which sell just over $7 billion in pharmaceutical products abroad. It can therefore be argued that the United States may now be losing one-third as much in dollars to pirates as it ships to overseas customers.

The practice by some developing nations by assessing high tariffs will be somewhat mitigated by the fact that the Uruguay Round agreement "binds" the pharmaceutical tariffs of a number of developing countries. That is, it freezes the tariffs at a specific level. The new agreement raises the percentage of pharmaceutical tariffs that are "bound" by developing countries from 32 to 85 percent.[13] The Uruguay Round agreement also forbids nations to compel foreign patent holders to license production of their products, unless negotiations to obtain a license have proved unsuccessful, the license will be non-exclusive, the goods will be made mainly for domestic consumption, and the patent-holder is compensated fairly.

The Link between R&D and Intellectual Property

The core of the pharmaceutical industry is the intellectual prowess and creativity of the scientists who perform research. Their work creates invaluable intellectual property that the Constitution protects by patent in the United States so that its creators may be rewarded. The fact that intellectual property cannot be protected in nations that lack either the will or the mechanisms to provide that protection is an economic threat to the United States at a time when much of its comparative advantage lies in the high technology fields where intellectual property is a fundamental element.

The U.S. pharmaceutical industry, which reports that it will spend nearly $14 billion in 1994 on R&D, endorses the Uruguay Round agreement with several recommendations. The industry requests that the United States intensify its efforts to conclude bilateral intellectual property agreements with the nations not now providing patent protection to U.S. Pharmaceuticals, and failing that, make use of "Section 301" of the Trade Law.

---

[12] *Ibid.*

[13] U.S. Department of Commerce, International Trade Administration. *Uruguay Round Opportunities:* Pharmaceuticals. Undated. p.2.

Section 301 and the Uruguay Round

The Congress defined intellectual property infringement as an unfair trade practice in the Trade and Tariff Act of 1984.[14] The 1988 Trade Act included a section referred to as Special 301 (actually section 1303), which placed upon the U.S. Trade Representative (USTR) the responsibility for annually identifying those countries that violate U.S. intellectual property rights (IPR). Under the Act, the USTR must place on a "watch list" those countries against whom trade sanctions are being considered. If a watch-listed nation does not respond, the President may activate Super 301 (section 1302 of the 1988 Trade Act) to identify and investigate "priority practices" of "priority countries," and if necessary to retaliate against such practices.[15]

The Unites States will be committed under the TRIPs agreement, if Congress endorses it, to deal with infringers on U.S. intellectual property rights by submitting complaints to the Dispute Settlement Body of the World Trade Organization. The pending American implementing legislation (H.R. 5110) currently states that "Nothing in this Act shall be construed... to limit any authority conferred under any law of the United States, including section 301 of the Trade Act of 1974, unless specifically provided for in this Act."[16]

Other Associated Issues

The pharmaceutical industry has suggested use of the Generalized System of Preferences (GSP), mandated by Title V of the Trade Act of 1974, as an incentive to developing countries to protect intellectual property rights. The GSP is intended to help developing countries participate in world trade by providing duty-free treatment for certain of their dutiable exports to the United States.[17] The industry advocates a change in law that would require the President expressly to consider intellectual property protection in designating eligible countries. This proposal would likely meet opposition from those who would view it as a detriment to GSP's original purpose.

The pharmaceutical industry also recommends that discussion with South and Central American nations of their possible accession to the North American Free Trade Agreement (NAFTA) be conditional upon their establishing at least TRIPs-style patent protection. The industry would prefer that any agreements granting accession to NAFTA improve upon

[14] Testimony by Gerald J. Mossinghoff, full citation in footnote 11.

[15] For more detailed information on section 301, see Congressional Research Service Issue Brief IB92030, *Responding to Foreign Trade Barriers to U.S. Exports: Section 301* by Wayne Morrison. Updated regularly.

[16] U.S. Congress, (103rd) H.R. 5110, Sec. 102 (2) (B), p.14.

[17] In 1991, the program "provided duty-free treatment on imports valued at about $13.7 billion from about 140 designated developing countries and territories." U.S. Congress. House of Representatives. Committee on Ways and Means. *Overview and Compilation of U.S. Trade Statutes.* 1993 Ed.

TRIPs by covering all medications under patent in the United States, especially those not as yet cleared for sale by the FDA. The obvious benefit of this to the pharmaceutical industry might come at the price of some countries refusing to joint any expansion of NAFTA.

Chapter 13

BACKGROUND*

THE GERM THEORY

In the second half of the 19th century, scientists such as Louis Pasteur and Robert Koch laid the groundwork for a revolutionary theory: specific micro-organisms, or germs, cause disease. Pasteur learned that some cultures of bacteria lose their lethal character and become "attenuated," knowledge that led him to vaccinate with attenuated rabies microbes a nine-year-old boy who had been bitten by a rabid dog. The boy survived unharmed.[1] On Christmas day 1891, Emil von Behring successfully treated a sick child with diphtheria antitoxin, signaling the eventual end of this disease.[2]

In 1894, a young chemist named Felix Hoffman joined the pharmaceutical division of the German chemical company Bayer and began searching for compounds to ease the pain of his arthritic father. He came upon salicylic acid, originally derived from willow bark, and made a chemical derivative to reduce the gastric distress it caused, tested it, and developed a commercial method of producing it. The result was aspirin.[3]

In 1910, German bacteriologist Paul Ehrlich formulated the first "magic bullet," an arsenic compound effective against syphilis. The medicine, called Salvarsan, was developed and marketed by a German pharmaceutical and chemical company.[4]

THE ROLE OF PHARMACEUTICAL COMPANIES

As discoveries were made, pharmaceutical companies rose to the task of developing these compounds, ensuring safety and efficacy and mass-producing and marketing the medicines. This is well illustrated by the discovery and development of insulin.

Diabetes mellitus is caused by a malfunctioning pancreas, which fails to produce insulin, the hormone that regulates blood sugar. For most of human history, diabetes meant death. In the late 19th century, scientists figured out the relationship of the pancreas to diabetes and

---

* Excepted from Pharmaceutical Research Association and related websites.

1 J.N. Hays, The Burdens of Disease: Epidemics and Human Response in Western History, New Brunswick, N.J., Rutgers University Press, 1998, p. 232 ff.

2 Ibid., p. 251.

3 History of Pharmacy, Bayer A.G. Leverkusen (Germany) p. 217.

4 American Chemical Society, The Pharmaceutical Century, "1800s to 1919: Patents & Potions."

attempted to isolate the hormone. All experiments failed until 1921, when Canadian physician Frederick Banting isolated the hormone. A U.S.-based company, which had a research affiliation with the University of Toronto where Banting did his research, won the right to manufacture the drug. Overcoming technical problems, Lilly perfected methods of large-scale collection of raw material, extraction, purification, and mass production. Lilly introduced insulin commercially in 1923 and, within a few years, enough insulin was being produced to meet the needs of diabetes patients around the world.[5]

Vaccines began to be commercially produced during World War I, and, together with rising living standards, helped curb some infectious diseases. But the major onslaught against infection began in the late 1920s, when the German chemical giant I.G. Farben hired a young scientist named Gerhard Domagk. In 1933, experimenting with dyes, Domagk found that an orange-red dye called Prontosil killed bacteria in mice. A few weeks later, the substance saved the life of a baby dying of a bloodstream staph infection. Called "sulfa drugs" after the active ingredient in the dye, these medicines were found to halt the growth and proliferation of bacteria while the body's natural defenses fought off the infection.[6]

The Magic Mold

Penicillin, the great breakthrough against infection of the 20th century, had actually been discovered — but not developed — in 1928. Returning from vacation, Dr. Alexander Fleming, a bacteriologist at London's St. Mary's Hospital, found that a mysterious mold had sprouted in a petri dish. Bacteria covered the entire dish — except where the mold was. Fleming noted the mold's anti–bacterial action and named it penicillin, but failed to develop it. In 1940, Oxford University scientists Howard Florey and Ernst Chain developed penicillin into a therapeutic agent, but, in 1941, could not produce enough of the compound to cure a policeman with severe septicemia. The patient improved when the drug was administered, but died when the meager supply was exhausted. By 1943, several U.S.–based pharmaceutical companies were mass–producing purified penicillin. By 1944, sufficient penicillin was available to treat all of the severe battle wounds suffered by U.S. troops in the D-Day battles. In the 1950s, known as the decade of antibiotics, new breakthroughs - to treat tuberculosis and other infections — followed swiftly.[7]

Progress against Cancer

Cancer has been known and studied since antiquity, but in the words of one scholar: "Before the twentieth century, the main institutions dealing with cancer were hospitals to die in.[8]

Early hopes for treating cancer focused on the mustard gas used in the First World War, the first chemotherapy agent for cancer. Unfortunately, the gas killed healthy cells as well as cancer cells and, at best, delayed death for a short time. Similarly, children with leukemia

---

[5] American Chemical Society, The Pharmaceutical Century, "1920s & 1930s, Salving with Science."
[6] Ibid.
[7] Ibid.
[8] Porter, op. cit., p. 577.

were treated with cortisone drugs, which prolonged remissions for only a short time.[9] In 1948, Lederle Laboratories developed methotrexate, one of the earliest anticancer agents and an anti–metabolite that destroys cancer cells. George Hitchings and Gertrude Elion developed anti–metabolites for acute leukemia in the late 1940s and early 1950s, while working at the Burroughs Wellcome Co.[10]

This and other early work formed the basis for the remarkable progress made against cancer in recent decades. According to the National Cancer Institute, deaths from all cancers combined (as well as for the top 10 cancer sites) declined in the United States between 1990 and 1997, and eight out of 10 children now survive leukemia. Said John R. Selfrin, Ph.D., CEO of the American Cancer Society: "Cancer death rates have been falling since 1991, and since 1995 that decline has been even more rapid. This gives us great hope that in the new millennium, our dreams of conquering cancer are closer than ever to becoming a reality."[11]

A March 2001 survey by the Pharmaceutical Research and Manufacturers of America (PhRMA) found 402 new medicines in development for cancer.

THE #1 KILLER — HEART DISEASE

Heart disease has topped the list of killer diseases of Americans for decades, but, thanks in large part to new medicines, deaths from heart disease have been cut by more than half since 1950.[12]

The first known heart medicine was discovered in an English garden in 1799, when physician John Ferriar noted the effect of dried leaves of the common foxglove plant, Digitalis purpura, on heart action. Still used in heart medications, digitalis slows the force of heart contractions and increases the amount of blood pumped per heartbeat. In 1867, nitroglycerin, a key ingredient of dynamite, joined the armamentarium against heart disease, to relieve angina. In 1901, drug company and university scientists isolated adrenaline from the glands of cattle and used it in medicines to stimulate the heart.

Until relatively recently, however, there were few medicines to treat some of the underlying causes of heart disease, such as high blood pressure and high cholesterol. When President Franklin D. Roosevelt developed high blood pressure in the early 1940s, all his doctors prescribed were sedatives and a low–salt diet. In 1949, Indian physician Rostom Jal Vakil wrote in a British medical journal about using the powdered root of the tropical plant Rauwolfia serpentina to lower blood pressure. Three years later, drug company chemists isolated the active ingredient of the plant and made the drug resezione for high blood pressure.

The first diuretic to treat high blood pressure was approved in 1950. The first clinically used beta–blocker appeared in 1967. The first ACE inhibitor and the first calcium channel blocker were approved in 1981.[13]

---

[9] Ibid., pp. 576-577.
[10] American Chemical Society, The Pharmaceutical Century, "1940s Antibiotics and Isotopes."
[11] PhRMA, "Researchers Are Testing 402 New Medicines for Cancer," March 2001.
[12] Health, United States, 2000, Centers for Disease Control and Prevention, U.S. Department of Health and Human Services, July 2000.
[13] "Brands of the Century," Med Ad News, January 2000.

In the early 1970s, drug company scientists looking for a drug for a poultry disease discovered an organism that inhibits an enzyme required for the synthesis of one of the building blocks of cholesterol. This serendipitous discovery led to a new class of drugs called statins, which can cut the risk of coronary death by more than 40 percent. Clot-dissolving drugs, pioneered in the 1980s, can actually stop heart attacks in mid–stream before permanent damage to the heart is done.

Despite the progress, nearly 61 million Americans — more than one in five — suffer from at least one type of cardiovascular disease, and nearly a million Americans a year die of these diseases — more than 2,600 every day. Pharmaceutical companies are currently developing 122 new medicines for cardiovascular diseases, many of which use 21st century technologies.[14]

The American Heart Association projects that, if all major forms of heart and blood vessel disease were eliminated, U.S. life expectancy would rise by almost seven years and the economic savings would total more than $300 billion a year. Cardiovascular disease claimed about 950,000 lives in the U.S. in 1998, which is 40.6 percent of all deaths.[15]

CONCLUSION

In the past 100 years, pharmaceutical research has helped transform health care from a largely palliative practice to a science–based endeavor. Due in part to this transformation and in part to improvements in sanitation, average life expectancy in the U.S. has increased from 47 years in 1900 to more than 76.5 years today.

In addition to longer lives, pharmaceutical progress has brought better lives to millions of people. It has consigned many infectious scourges of the past to history books; it has transformed mental illness from a misunderstood cause of shame and fear into a highly treatable condition. It has helped make old age a time of active independence, rather than disability, for many. It has made impressive inroads against cancer, heart disease, stroke, and many other diseases.

As the 21st century begins, pharmaceutical companies are continuing the battle against humankind's ancient enemies and meeting new challenges, including seeking better treatments and cures for AIDS and Alzheimer's disease.

[14] PhRMA, "122 Medicines in the Pipeline Offer Hope of More Powerful Weapons Against Heart Disease and Stroke," February 2001.

[15] American Heart Association, "Cardiovascular Disease and Life Expectancy," 2001 Heart and Stroke Statistical Update, 2000.

Chapter 14

GROWTH IN R&D INVESTMENT

Research and development (R&D) is the key to innovation and, thus, the discovery of new medicines and cures. Increasing investment in pharmaceutical R&D since the end of World War II greatly contributed to improved life expectancy and health during the second half of the 20th Century.

In 2001, research-based pharmaceutical companies will invest $30.5 billion in R&D. This represents an 18.7 percent increase over expenditures in 2000 and more than triple the investment in 1990. This year, $23.6 billion in R&D will be spent within the United States by both U.S.-owned and foreign-owned companies. An additional $6.8 billion in R&D will be conducted by U.S.-owned firms abroad.

Over the past three decades, the amount of sales allocated to R&D has increased from 11.4 percent in 1970 to 17.4 percent in 1999. In 2001, it is estimated to be 18.5 percent.

The percent of sales allocated to R&D by the Drugs & Medicine sector of the Standard & Poor's Compustat database (which includes the research-based pharmaceutical industry and non-research-based companies) is 12.8 percent, which compares to 3.9 percent invested in R&D for all U.S. industries.[1] Based on corporate tax data compiled by S&P's Compustat, pharmaceutical manufacturers invest a higher percentage of sales revenue in R&D than virtually any other U.S. industry, including high-tech industries such as electronics, aerospace, computers, and automobiles.[2]

THE PROCESS OF DISCOVERY: BASIC, TRANSLATIONAL AND APPLIED RESEARCH

The process of drug discovery begins with knowledge about disease. This knowledge is developed through basic research, primarily supported by research-based pharmaceutical companies and funds from the National Institutes of Health (NIH). Basic research — conducted in government, university, and industry laboratories — reveals disease mechanisms or processes that may become the target of pharmaceutical intervention.

Excepted from Pharmaceutical Research Association and related websites.

[1] Standard & Poor's Compustat, a division of McGraw-Hill.

[2] *Ibid.*

Translational research is a transition between basic research and applied pharmaceutical research. Funded by research-based pharmaceutical companies and, in some areas, by the NIH, academia, and private foundations, this research connects basic research with clinical practice. Translational research takes basic research into the first phases of product development and initial human trials, producing new findings that answer questions about safety and efficacy. This research may increase scientists' knowledge about disease.

Applied research, or the development and testing of medicines, is conducted primarily by pharmaceutical companies. This process includes large-scale clinical trials, dosage testing, and research to determine information that should be included in product labeling. Applied research is conducted in the laboratories of pharmaceutical firms, universities, and contract research organizations hired by pharmaceutical companies.

Allocation of R&D Investment

Approximately one-third of company-financed R&D in the United States is devoted to the evaluation of promising new drug compounds in human clinical trials. Phase I, II, and III trials, required for drug approval, account for 29.1 percent of R&D. An additional 11.7 percent of R&D is allocated to Phase IV clinical trials, which occur after a product has been approved by FDA. In addition, 8.3 percent of R&D is for process-development and quality-control functions required to meet stringent manufacturing standards.[3]

Companies allocate approximately 36 percent of R&D expenditures to preclinical functions. Ten percent is spent on synthesizing and extracting compounds for evaluation; 14.2 percent is for biological screening and pharmacological testing, in which thousands of compounds are evaluated for every one that continues in the development process; 4.5 percent is for continued testing in the areas of toxicology and safety; and 7.3 percent is spent for dosage formulation and stability testing.[4] This year, 78.5 percent of pharmaceutical R&D expenditures is dedicated to new products. The remaining 21.5 percent is devoted to significant improvements in, and/or modifications of, existing products.

Research Targets

It is difficult to determine exactly how much R&D is dedicated to specific diseases due to the nature of the R&D process and of disease. A product may be under investigation to treat several conditions or diseases — such as HIV/AIDS — that require numerous treatments within numerous therapeutic areas. Generally speaking, the majority of R&D is invested in products falling into 12 major classes

- Approximately $7.3 billion of R&D in 2001 will be spent on products acting on the central nervous system and sense organs, which include such diseases as Alzheimer's, schizophrenia, depression, epilepsy, and Parkinson's.[5]

---

[3] PhRMA, *PhRMA Annual Survey*, 2001.

[4] *Ibid.*

[5] *Ibid.*

- Approximately $7.4 billion will be spent on products affecting neoplasms, the endocrine system, and metabolic diseases, including cancer, osteoporosis, and diabetes.[6]
- Approximately $3.9 billion will be spent on products dedicated to cardiovascular disease.[7]
- Approximately $4.1 billion will be spent on products acting on parasitic and infectious diseases, including anti-viral and antibiotic compounds.[8]
- Approximately $1.3 billion will be spent on medicines acting on the respiratory system, including asthma and tuberculosis.[9]

COLLABORATION BETWEEN THE NATIONAL INSTITUTES OF HEALTH AND INDUSTRY

In 1950, NIH consisted of six component research institutes with a total appropriation of $43 million.[10] Today, the NIH comprises 25 separate Institutes and Centers and is one of eight health agencies of the Public Health Service, with an appropriation of $20.4 billion.[11] The NIH budget has more than doubled in the past 10 years.

About 75 percent of the NIH budget is awarded to scientists and doctors at research centers and universities throughout the country who compete for NIH grants. The core research programs conducted at NIH itself only account for about 10 percent of its total budget.

According to NIH, public-private research collaboration has been a critical component of NIH's core research efforts. Cooperative Research and Development Agreements (CRADAs), authorized by the 1986 Federal Technology Transfer Act, enhance and facilitate this collaboration by providing a mechanism through which NIH scientists and pharmaceutical companies can more rapidly translate NIH research findings into new medicines for patients. Although they represent only a small fraction of NIH's research activities, CRADAs "significantly advance biomedical research by allowing the exchange and use of experimental compounds, proprietary research materials, reagents, scientific advice, and private financial resources between government and industry scientists," according to NIH. Typically, CRADAs result in new scientific knowledge, but not new products.

NIH is currently engaged in 325 active CRADAs. Examples include research into retroviral-mediated gene transfer for AIDS therapy and gene therapy for pulmonary diseases. In FY 1997, NIH executed a total of 153 new CRADAs.[12]

The unprecedented pace of development of new drugs to treat AIDS illustrates the productive relationship between government and industry research. NIH scientists identified the AIDS virus in 1983. A pharmaceutical company brought the first drug treatment for AIDS

---

[6] *Ibid.*
[7] *Ibid.*
[8] *Ibid.*
[9] *Ibid.*
[10] Varmus, H., "Special Report: Shattuck Lecture-Biomedical Research Enters the Steady State," *The New England Journal of Medicine*, Vol. 333, No. 12, 1995.
[11] National Institutes of Health, Office of Financial Management, www.nih.gov/ofm.
[12] National Institutes of Health, Office of Financial Management, www.od.nih.gov/ofm/PRIMER97/index.stm.

to market just four years later. Today, there are 64 approved medicines to treat AIDS and associated opportunistic infection, and another 103 products are in development.

The Centers for Disease Control and Prevention (CDC) recently issued its 24th report on the health status of the nation and national trends in health statistics. The report confirmed that the U.S. death rate for HIV infection declined more than 70 percent during 1993-1996. This sharp decline is due in large part to combination drug therapy.[13]

NIH Return-on-Investment Proposal

Along with efforts to encourage public-private research collaboration has come pressure from some in Congress to impose a return-on-investment tax on successful FDA-approved drugs. Such a measure is intended to allow NIH to "recoup" some of its funding of research that contributes to pharmaceutical innovation.

In the fall of 2000, the Labor-HHS Appropriations Conference Report incorporated language charging the Director of NIH to provide the Chairman and Ranking Member of the Senate Committees on Appropriations and Health, Education, Labor, and Pensions a "proposal to require a reasonable return on investment" on both intramural and extramural research by March 31, 2001. As of May, the NIH response was still being developed, and any impact on NIH-industry collaboration remains unclear.

What is clear, however, is that there is already solid existing federal statutory protection for NIH intellectual property rights; under the Bayh-Dole Act, NIH and other federal agencies are authorized to obtain patents for their inventions, to grant licenses and charge royalties, and to "undertake all other suitable and necessary steps to protect and administer rights to federally owned inventions on behalf of the Federal Government either directly or through contact..."[14] Tax proposals can only serve to chill the utilization of federally sponsored inventions, contrary to the intent of Bayh-Dole.

Cost of Drug Development

The discovery and development of new medicines is an expensive and time-consuming process. Estimates by The Boston Consulting Group indicate that the pre-tax cost of developing a medicine introduced in 1990 was $500 million.[15] This estimate takes into account the cost of research failures as well as the cost of interest over the period of the investment.

The precise cost of drug development today is difficult to determine. Since the late 1970s, major drivers of development costs, such as the number of required clinical trials and patients per trial, have more than doubled.[16] New, increasingly more expensive technology that has

---

[13] *Health, United States, 2000*, Centers for Disease Control and Prevention, U.S. Department of Health and Human Services, July 2000.

[14] 35 U.S.C. § 207(a).

[15] The Boston Consulting Group analysis based on J.A. DiMasi et al. (1991) as quoted by the Office of Technology Assessment in *Pharmaceutical R&D: Costs, Risks, and Rewards*, February 1993.

[16] The Boston Consulting Group, *The Contribution of Pharmaceutical Companies: What's at Stake for America*, September 1993.

aided in the discovery and development of more effective medicines has also increased the cost of R&D.

The Tufts University Center for the Study of Drug Development found that the time from synthesis of a new drug to U.S. marketing approval has increased over time.[17] The Tufts data indicate that this period has increased from approximately eight years for approvals in the 1960s to approximately 14.2 years for approvals in the 1990s.[18] Lengthening development times dramatically increase the cost of bringing a new drug to market by increasing the cost of capital needed for R&D. The cost of capital increases as companies are exposed to economic risks and uncertainties over a longer period of development time.

While larger companies are often able to diversify their product portfolios to minimize the risks that a single product will fail to gain market approval, the different risks associated with increasing capital costs are determined by the economy and are not diversifiable.[19] Due to the large and increasing costs of bringing a new medicine to market, full commercial success is possible only for a small number of products.

A 1994 study conducted by economists at Duke University found that only three of every 10 drug products, or new chemical entities, introduced from 1980 to 1984 had returns higher than average after-tax R&D costs.[20] The study indicated that the top 20 percent of the products with the highest revenues generated 70 percent of the returns during the period of analysis.[21] Thus, given the costs and risks of drug research, companies must rely on a limited number of highly successful products to finance their continuing R&D.

PHARMACEUTICAL PROFITS

Standard accounting measures of profitability, such as those quoted in Fortune magazine, are not an accurate reflection of the profitability of research-based pharmaceutical companies. Economists have found that, when properly measured, pharmaceutical company profits are not out of line with other industries that deal in intellectual property or other patentable or copyrighted products.[22]

Harvard University economist F.M. Scherer explains: "Under standard accounting practice, R&D and new product marketing outlays, both of which are atypically high in pharmaceuticals, are written off as current expenses. Since both, and especially R&D, affect revenue for many years to come, it would be more accurate in principle to capitalize the outlays and then depreciate them over appropriate time periods. Otherwise, the rate of return on 'investment' is calculated using an asset base that improperly excludes accumulated

[17] Testimony before the House Committee on Commerce, Subcommittee on Health and the Environment, 105th Cong., 1st Sess. (April 23, 1997) (Statement of Joseph A. DiMasi, Director of Economic Analysis, Tufts Center for the Study of Drug Development, Tufts University, Boston, Massachusetts).

[18] *Ibid.*

[19] Congress of the United States, Office of Technology Assessment, *Pharmaceutical R&D: Costs, Risks, and Rewards*, February 1993.

[20] Henry G. Grabowski and John M. Vernon, "Returns to R&D on New Drug Introductions in the 1980s," *Journal of Health Economics* 13 (1994) 383-406.

[21] *Ibid.*

[22] Merrill Matthews Jr., "Prices, Profits and Prescriptions: The Pharmatech Industry in the New Economy," Institute for Policy Innovation, Policy Report 157 (September 2000)

intangible R&D and marketing capital. Accounting figures tend to overstate the true rate of return on investment under these conditions."[23]

The development of thousands of new medicines over the past half-century has been fueled by growing R&D expenditures by the pharmaceutical industry. Drug innovation is both high-cost and high-risk, and only a small percentage of new medicines ever recover average development costs. Companies rely on a few highly successful products to fund R&D. Without reasonable returns on R&D investments, companies will not attract the capital or generate the revenues needed to fund ongoing research to discover and develop new life-saving, cost-effective medicines.

[23] F.M. Scherer, "Pricing, Profits, and Technological Progress in the Pharmaceutical Industry," *Journal of Economic Perspectives*, Vol. 7, No. 3, Summer 1993, 97-115.

Chapter 15

DISCOVERY AND DEVELOPMENT*

Drug discovery and development is a long and complex process. Only one of every 5,000-10,000 molecules screened in the laboratory ever makes it to market as a new drug.[1]

Once a process of trial-and-error and serendipity, drug discovery has become more rational and systematic through the use of sophisticated technology and as a result of continuing advances in knowledge. Safety continues to be the paramount concern at every stage of drug discovery and development.

BENEFIT AND RISK ASSESSMENT

Research-based pharmaceutical companies and FDA take extraordinary measures to ensure the safety and efficacy of all approved prescription medicines in the United States.

Currently, the drug development and approval process takes an average of 14.2 years due, in large part, to the careful and methodical measures taken by pharmaceutical companies and FDA to ensure that drug benefits outweigh any risks. Pharmaceutical researchers are conducting more clinical trials with more patients than ever before. This means that more information about the benefits and risks of new chemical entities is being developed than in the past.

Pharmaceutical companies and FDA know, however, that no medicine is ever risk-free. Drugs are chemical substances that have benefits and potential risks, but FDA does not approve a new medicine without determining that the health benefits for the vast majority of patients outweigh any potential risks. Unfortunately, in spite of all of the determined efforts of pharmaceutical companies and FDA to ensure the safety of each new product, there will always be the possibility of risk for patients. FDA and the pharmaceutical industry follow careful scientific procedures to ensure patient safety in four distinct stages:

1. Preclinical safety assessment,
2. Pre-approval safety assessment in humans,
3. Safety assessment during FDA regulatory review, and

---

* Excepted from Pharmaceutical Research Association and related websites.

[1] DiMasi, J.A., "Risks in New Drug Development: Approval Success Rates for Investigational Drugs," *Clinical Pharmacology & Therapeutics*, May 2001.

4. Post-marketing safety surveillance.

Preclinical Safety Assessment

The relative safety of newly synthesized compounds is initially evaluated in both in vitro and in vivo tests. If a compound appears to have important biological activity with the possibility of providing useful medicinal qualities, special tests are conducted to evaluate its safety in the major organ systems (for example, the liver; the central nervous, cardiovascular, and respiratory systems). Other organ systems are evaluated when potential problems appear. These pharmacology studies are conducted in animals to ensure that a drug is safe enough to be tested in humans.

The goal of preclinical animal studies is to characterize any relationship between increased doses of a drug and toxic effects in the animals. The development of a drug is terminated when tests suggest that it poses a significant risk for humans — especially organ damage, genetic defects, birth defects, or cancer.

Pre-Approval Safety Assessment in Humans

A drug sponsor can begin clinical trials in humans once FDA is satisfied that the preclinical animal data do not show an unacceptable safety risk to humans. It usually takes many additional years for a clinical development program to gather sufficient data to prepare a New Drug Application (NDA) seeking FDA regulatory review to market a new product.

Each clinical trial evaluates safety regardless of the stated objective of the trial. During each stage of clinical study, including quality-of-life and pharmacoeconomic studies, patients are observed for adverse events. All harmful reactions are reported to FDA and, when appropriate, the information is incorporated in a drug's package labeling. The average NDA for a novel prescription medicine is based on approximately 70 clinical trials involving over 4,000 patients — more than twice the number of trials and patients for the NDAs submitted in the early 1980s. Clinical trials are conducted in three stages:

- Phase I: Drugs are evaluated for safety in healthy volunteers in small initial trials. The first trial is conducted with a single dose of the drug. If the drug is shown to be safe, multiple doses of the product are evaluated for safety in other clinical trials.
- Phase II: The primary focus of Phase II clinical trials is to evaluate the safety and efficacy of a drug. Second-stage trials are conducted with patients instead of healthy volunteers. Data are collected to determine if the drug is safe for the patient population intended for treatment.
- Phase III: These large trials evaluate safety and efficacy in groups of patients with the disease to be treated, including the elderly, patients with multiple diseases, those who take other drugs, and patients whose organs are impaired.

Cumulatively, these several thousand patients may be studied during the clinical phase. Numerous medical procedures are performed on the patients to acquire the necessary safety and efficacy data to support the marketing application.

Sponsors and investigators follow federal regulations to ensure safety at every stage of clinical trials. An Institutional Review Board (IRB) — customarily located where clinical trials are conducted — reviews and approves a research plan before a trial begins and exercises continuing oversight of the research. According to the IRB regulations, at least one member of the Board is to have training in science, one is to be trained in an area outside of science, and one member is not to be affiliated with the institution where the IRB is located.

Investigators must promptly report all unanticipated adverse events that are moderate or severe to the IRB and the drug sponsor. In addition, investigators are required to notify a sponsor of all adverse events that occur during a trial. A sponsor must report an adverse event that is unexpected, serious, and possibly drug-related to FDA within 15 days. Each adverse event that is fatal or life-threatening must be reported within seven days. A sponsor has a special obligation to ensure that FDA, the IRB, and all participating investigators are promptly notified of any significant new adverse effects or risks associated with a drug.

Beyond these federal requirements, sponsors often take additional steps to ensure their products can be used safely. For example, they may use independent safety-monitoring boards to monitor specific areas of concern so that, if a significant problem arises, a trial can be terminated at the earliest possible time. In addition, they conduct specific safety trials such as drug interaction trials or trials in special patient populations and provide medical information concerning the safety and efficacy of their products to other health-care professionals after their products are marketed.

Safety Assessment during FDA Regulatory Review

A sponsor submits an NDA to FDA for approval to manufacture, distribute, and market a drug in the U.S. based on the safety and efficacy data obtained during the clinical trials. In addition to written reports of each individual trial, an NDA must contain an integrated summary of all available information *received from any source* concerning the safety and efficacy of the drug.

FDA usually completes its review of a "standard" drug in 10 to 12 months. One hundred and twenty days prior to a drug's anticipated approval, a sponsor must provide the agency with a summary of all safety information in the NDA, along with any additional safety information obtained during the review period.

The addition of 600 new reviewers made possible by the user fees paid by pharmaceutical companies has enabled FDA to approve new drugs more expeditiously than in the past while maintaining high safety standards. Over the years, the percentage of applications approved and rejected by FDA has remained essentially the same. Two decades ago, 10 to 15 percent of the NDAs were rejected — the same as today.

Post-Marketing Safety Surveillance

Monitoring and evaluating a drug's safety become more complex after it is approved and marketed. Once on the market, a drug will be taken by many more patients than in the clinical trials and physicians are free to use it in different doses, different dosing regimens, different patient populations, and in other ways that they believe will benefit patients. This wider use expands the safety information about a drug.

Adverse reactions that occur in fewer than 1 in 3,000 to 5,000 patients are unlikely to be detected in pre-approval investigational clinical trials, and may be unknown at the time a drug is approved. These rare adverse reactions are more likely to be detected when large numbers of patients use a drug after it has been approved.

Safety monitoring continues throughout the life of a medicine. Post-marketing surveillance is a highly regulated and labor-intensive global activity. Even before a drug is approved, multinational pharmaceutical companies establish large global systems to track, investigate, evaluate, and report adverse drug reactions (ADRs) for that product on a continuing basis to regulatory authorities around the world.

Pharmaceutical companies must inform regulatory agencies of reports of serious and unexpected ADRs they receive from anywhere in the world within 15 days. They report less serious ADRs at regular intervals. Companies also voluntarily take corrective safety steps as appropriate, such as changing a package insert or, if necessary, withdrawing a drug from the market.

As a condition of approval, FDA may require a company to conduct a post-marketing study or a company on its own may decide to undertake such a study to gather more safety information. A company also may undertake a study if it believes that the reports of ADRs it has received require such action. These studies may consist of new clinical trials or they may be evaluations of existing databases.

For its part, FDA sponsors a MedWatch Partners program to solicit, monitor, and assess reports of ADRs. Supported by more than 140 organizations, including health professionals and industry, MedWatch Partners help to ensure that safety information is promptly collected and communicated to the medical community.

FDA collects reports of ADRs from companies (which submit more than 90 percent of the reports), physicians, and other health-care professionals. The agency evaluates the reports for trends and implications and may require a company to provide more data, undertake a new clinical trial, revise a drug's labeling, notify health-care professionals, or even remove a product from the market.

Pharmaceutical companies and FDA take as a primary responsibility the duty to ensure the safe use of all approved medicines in the United States. Throughout the long and careful process — from discovery and development through approval and post-marketing surveillance — the principal concern of both the agency and the industry is that patients receive medicines that have been demonstrated in every reasonable medical, scientific, and practicable way to provide more benefits than risks when used appropriately in accordance with label instructions.

PRIVACY REGULATION

Virtually all research necessary to develop new medicines and demonstrate their safety and effectiveness depends on data from patients and their health-care providers. It is therefore essential that, in protecting a patient's right to privacy, the government also protect the public interest in research.

In April 2001, the Secretary of the Department of Health and Human Services (HHS) announced the Administration's decision not to delay the effective date of a new federal privacy regulation pursuant to the Health Insurance Portability and Accountability Act of 1996. This means that affected entities under the regulation (primarily health-care providers, health plans and data clearinghouses) have essentially two years to establish internal systems to ensure full compliance. The Secretary's statement also indicated that HHS intends to address some of the concerns raised in the 26,000 comments it received on the final privacy rule through implementation guidances and additional proposed rulemaking.

Many health-care organizations, as well as PhRMA, suggested modifications to ensure that quality patient care would not suffer as a result of any unintended consequences of the regulation. PhRMA emphasized the industry's underlying concern that parts of the final rule would make doctors, hospitals, and health plans reluctant to participate in company-sponsored research because of the complex, burdensome, and costly compliance requirements and legal ambiguities. PhRMA's comments include specific recommendations that address both research and post-marketing surveillance activities.

THE FDA MODERNIZATION ACT

The FDA Modernization Act of 1997 (FDAMA) reauthorized for five more years the 1992 Prescription Drug User Fee Act (PDUFA). Under the original legislation, the industry agreed to pay $329 million during 1993-1997 to enable FDA to hire 696 additional reviewers to improve the drug-approval process without compromising safety standards. The law also made other improvements in the agency's procedures. In 2000, FDA approved 33 important new medicines that were developed by pharmaceutical companies.

During the five-year extension of the user fee law, companies will pay an estimated $690 million in fees so FDA can hire additional reviewers and invest in other resources to continue to reduce approval times.[2] As with the earlier law, FDA has agreed to a number of specific performance goals to streamline the development and approval of new drugs. For example, FDA has agreed to review "standard" NDAs, applications for biologics, and efficacy supplements in an average of 10 months by the end of five years, down from the current average of 12 months (representing further progress toward the long-standing statutory six-month review deadline).

FDAMA also established time periods for holding meetings, ending clinical holds, and resolving disputes on procedural and scientific issues. In addition, FDA agreed to establish a paperless, electronic filing system by 2002 for NDAs, Investigational New Drug (IND) applications, and other regulatory submissions. The agency must also submit an annual report to Congress on its performance in meeting its goals and its use of user-fee funds.

Other major provisions of FDAMA:

- **The FDA Mission:** FDA has a legislatively established mission — to promote public health by the timely review of applications for new products, and to protect

[2] Department of Health and Human Services, Food and Drug Administration, PDUFA II Five Year Plan FY 2000 Update, Attachment 2, www.fda.gov/oc/pdufa2/2000update.htm.

public health by ensuring that regulated products are safe, effective, and properly labeled.

- **Drugs for Children:** To encourage the provision of more information about how drugs should be used for children, six months of additional market exclusivity is provided for the study of drugs for which FDA believes pediatric information would be beneficial.
- **Fast-Track Drugs:** Fast-track approval review is granted to medicines that provide for the unmet medical needs of patients with serious or life-threatening conditions.
- **Expanded Access:** Expanded access to investigational medicines is allowed for those patients with serious diseases and conditions.
- **Data Bank:** NIH is to maintain a public data bank on clinical trials for drugs in development to treat serious or life-threatening diseases.
- **Substantial Evidence:** Data from one adequate and well-controlled clinical study, together with confirmatory evidence, may — at the discretion of FDA — be sufficient to prove substantial evidence of effectiveness. Previously, two such studies were routinely required. The House Report emphasized that "the quality of the data and information about a drug, rather than the number of studies performed" should determine whether a drug is approvable.
- **Health-Care Economic Information:** Health-care economic information that, for example, compares the cost of a course of treatment for one drug to another can be provided to managed-care organizations and other such groups to help them make informed decisions about putting a drug on their formulary. The information is to be based on "competent and reliable scientific evidence."
- **Off-Label Information:** Copies of peer-reviewed medical journal articles and other validated scientific information about unapproved uses of approved drugs can be distributed to physicians and other health-care professionals, under strict conditions and supervision by FDA. Thus, physicians will have more up-to-date product information and will be better able to meet their patients' medical needs.
- **IND Application:** The size and burden of IND applications are reduced.
- **NDA Applications:** FDA is to describe when abbreviated reports may be submitted in lieu of full reports for clinical and nonclinical studies required in an NDA or biologics-license application.
- **Outside Experts:** To improve the timelines and/or quality of a review, FDA is authorized at its discretion to use outside experts to help review or evaluate any application or submission. FDA will always make the final decision when outside experts are to be used.
- **Standards for Review:** FDA is to issue guidance for all internal and external reviewers relating to "promptness in conducting the review, technical excellence, lack of bias and conflict of interest, and knowledge of regulatory and scientific standards."
- **Scientific Advisory Committees:** Scientific advisory committees provide expert scientific advice and recommendations to FDA on the clinical investigation and approval for marketing of new drugs and biological products. The House Report states that this provision is intended "not merely to create additional administrative requirements for either FDA or its scientific advisors, but to make the advisory

system more responsive to the needs of FDA, sponsors and manufacturers, and patients."

- **Dispute Resolution:** FDA must resolve scientific disputes through review by an appropriate scientific advisory committee.
- **Supplemental Applications:** FDA follows standards for the prompt review of supplemental applications for new indications for approved products.
- **Harmonization of Drugs and Biologicals:** The review and approval requirements for biological products and drugs are to be harmonized. All provisions of the new law are to apply both to drugs and biologics.
- **Annual Report:** The agency is to publish an annual report in the Federal Register and seek public comment on its performance in carrying out its statutory obligations.
- **International Harmonization:** FDA is to cooperate with other governments to harmonize regulatory requirements, as discussed below.

Overall, FDA has done a good job of meeting its goals under the FDAMA legislation.

REGULATION OF PHARMACEUTICAL MANUFACTURING

In addition to meeting regulatory requirements necessary to prove drug safety and efficacy, manufacturers also must comply with FDA regulations to ensure the quality of pharmaceutical manufacturing. These "Good Manufacturing Practice" (GMP) requirements govern quality management and control for all aspects of drug manufacturing. To enforce GMP requirements, FDA conducts field inspections during which trained investigators periodically visit manufacturing sites to ensure that a facility is in compliance with U.S. regulations.

The FDA Modernization Act of 1997 was enacted to reduce the number of post-marketing manufacturing changes that require approval from FDA. Under the new law, a company must obtain prior approval from FDA before implementing any "major" changes in the manufacturing procedure. Such changes may adversely affect the identity, strength, quality, purity, or potency of a drug.

Other changes may be implemented either with or without the submission of a supplemental NDA. Those changes not requiring a supplemental NDA or other data required by the agency are to be reported in an annual report filed with FDA.

Manufacturers also are required to ensure pharmaceutical quality by adherence to enforceable drug standards developed by the United States Pharmacopeia (USP). Drug products marketed in the United States are required to meet all appropriate USP standards or their labels must indicate that they do not comply with these standards.

REGULATION OF PHARMACEUTICAL MARKETING

FDA also regulates pharmaceutical marketing. These regulations are to ensure that health-care professionals and the public are provided with adequate, balanced, and truthful information and that all promotional claims are based on scientifically proven clinical evidence. Key aspects of marketing regulations include:

- **Labeling:** Labels and other written, printed, or graphic matter on a drug or its packaging (including all other promotional material, such as brochures, slides, videotapes, and other sales aids) must not be false or misleading in any way. The labeling must include adequate directions for use of a product; warnings when needed against use in children or people with certain conditions; dosage information; and methods and duration of use. Labeling must include a brief summary of a drug's side effects, contraindications, and effectiveness. Any deviation from labeling regulations is considered "misbranding," a serious violation of federal law.
- **Promotional Claims and Comparisons:** Claims of safety relate to the nature and degree of side effects and adverse reactions associated with a drug or the overall risk-benefit rationale of the drug. Claims of effectiveness relate to the ability of a drug to achieve its indicated therapeutic effect. Any product claims relating to safety and effectiveness must be supported by "adequate and well-controlled" studies. The FDA Modernization Act allows promotion of economic claims to HMOs based on "competent and reliable scientific evidence."
- **Investigational New Drugs:** Unapproved drugs under clinical development or approved drugs under investigation for a new indication can be discussed in scientific literature and at medical conferences, but cannot be promoted as safe or effective. FDA may authorize distribution of an unapproved investigational new drug to seriously ill patients who are not participating in clinical trials. In these cases, FDA may allow manufacturers to advertise the availability of these drugs to physicians.
- **Direct-to-Consumer (DTC) Advertising:** In 1962, FDA began regulating prescription drug advertising. For the following two decades, prescription drug advertising was directed only at physicians and health-care organizations. In the early 1980s, a few pharmaceutical advertisers experimented with advertising to consumers. In response, FDA asked in September 1982 for a moratorium on DTC advertising by pharmaceutical manufacturers. The moratorium was lifted in 1985. However, several constraints were placed upon the advertising, including a requirement that the ads must meet the same standards as those aimed at professionals. That is, the broadcast ads would have to contain a somewhat lengthy "major statement" of risks and would have to make "adequate provision" to allow consumers an opportunity to get labeling information.

Manufacturers were prohibited from identifying both the drug and the disease, or the condition it was approved to treat, in the same advertisement unless a manufacturer provided extensive information about contraindications, side effects, and other matters. Given these constraints, it was nearly impossible for the requirements to be met in television or radio ads, which meant either the name of the brand or the condition to be treated had to be excluded from the ad. The result was that ads mentioned that treatment existed for a condition, with no mention of a brand-name. Or, a brand-name was listed, with no mention of its use.

In 1997, FDA issued a proposed guidance intended to clarify the requirements for prescription drug advertisements for television and radio. The guidance was designed in part to make the ads more understandable to consumers. Pursuant to the draft guidance, pharmaceutical manufacturers that advertise prescription drugs must disclose certain information about a product's uses and risks. Under the new guidelines, broadcast ads are required to present a fair balance between effectiveness and risk information. In addition, a major statement conveying the risks and product indications in a consumer-friendly, understandable way must be included. The new guidance made clear that radio and television ads could satisfy FDA standards by including something simpler than the "major statement" required previously.

In lieu of providing a "brief summary" of all important information about a drug, an advertiser must provide an "adequate provision" mechanism to ensure that consumers can easily obtain product labeling. For example, an advertiser can include in the ad a toll-free number for consumers to call for the approved package labeling. Another acceptable mechanism is for the ad to state that additional product information is provided with print advertisements appearing concurrently with the broadcast ad. Other means also include a statement in the broadcast that pharmacists and/or physicians as well as an Internet web address and a toll-free number may provide additional product information to the consumer. In order to evaluate the effects of the draft guidance, FDA asked that sponsors that use this "adequate provision" mechanism collect relevant data and make their findings known to the agency.

The draft guidance issued in 1997 stated that, within two years of publication of the final guidance, FDA would evaluate the guidance, including the effect on public health of DTC promotion and specifically of consumer-directed broadcast advertising. At the end of the evaluation, FDA would determine whether the guidance should be withdrawn, continued, or modified to reflect the agency's current thinking.

In August 1999, FDA issued a final guidance on DTC advertising. The requirements as specified in the 1997 draft guidance remained basically unchanged. "FDA is unaware of any data supporting the assertion that the public health is harmed or likely to be harmed, by the Agency's actions in facilitating consumer-directed broadcast advertising," the agency stated. Survey research, including FDA's own survey of consumers in 1999, supports this position.

As a follow-up to its 1999 survey, FDA announced on March 19, 2001, that it would be conducting another survey of patients, as well as a survey of physicians regarding "their reactions to, and behaviors that stem from, DTC prescription drug advertising in order to develop a policy on appropriate requirements for regulating drug product promotional materials."

FDA's labeling and advertising requirements apply uniformly to all promotional materials, regardless of the medium in which they occur. As a result, communications on the Internet are subject to the same restrictions as communications in general circulation magazines.

R&D Tax Credit

The establishment of the research and experimentation (R&D) tax credit as a permanent rule in the tax code was included in the $1.6 trillion ten-year tax relief plan proposed by President Bush early in 2001. Original bills, by Senators Orrin Hatch (R-UT) and Max Baucus (D-MT), and by Representatives Nancy Johnson (R-CT) and Robert Matsui (D-CA), with a number of both Republican and Democratic Senators and Congressmen as respective cosponsors, have been introduced to achieve this objective and also provide for a one-percent increase in the alternative incremental research credit (AIRC) rates. PhRMA strongly supports these bills.

Although the R&D tax credit, which will expire on June 30, 2004, has received broad congressional support, it is uncertain whether the credit will be made permanent.

The credit provides tax incentives for companies that increase R&D spending in the U.S. over a base amount. Since its inception in 1981, the R&D credit has provided a critical and proven incentive for companies to increase their investment in U.S.-based research and development. Because the credit is targeted primarily at salaries and wages related to direct U.S. R&D activities, it provides an effective incentive for companies to create and sustain valuable new high-skilled jobs for American workers. The credit supports the development of new and innovative medicines, technologies, products, and services, which benefit all Americans. Moreover, the continued encouragement of private-sector R&D is particularly important in light of the substantial tax and other financial incentives offered by many foreign trade competitors of the U.S.

Experts agree that the R&D credit represents a very sound investment in U.S. economic growth, through strengthening the foundation for technological innovation and thereby improving the productivity of capital and labor. Because pharmaceutical R&D is expensive, time-consuming, and high-risk, the R&D tax credit can be an effective incentive for research at the margin.

A 1995 Congressional Research Service study of all high-technology industries found that every dollar of tax benefit generates as much as one dollar of additional R&D spending in the short term, and as much as two dollars of long-term investment in R&D. Moreover, a 1998 study by Coopers and Lybrand (now part of PricewaterhouseCoopers) found that R&D spending drives productivity growth, adding to the nation's productive capacity, increasing personal income, and ultimately paying for itself in increased tax revenue.

The R&D tax credit's history of repeated temporary, sporadic extensions has prevented it from completely fulfilling its intended purpose of maximizing U.S. research. Corporate research projects generally require five to 15 years from planning to completion. To be most effective, the credit should apply consistently and without interruption for many years.

Pediatric Exclusivity

As part of FDAMA, Congress created an incentive — six months of additional marketing exclusivity — for pharmaceutical companies to conduct studies of drugs in children when requested by FDA. The provision, which sunsets on January 1, 2002, has been highly successful and should be renewed. The new law is working just as intended: it is producing a significant amount of new knowledge about the safety and effectiveness of drugs commonly used to treat children. In just over three years, nearly 60 pediatric studies were performed under the new law, 28 drugs were awarded exclusivity, and labeling changes were made for 16 of these drugs (all are expected to have new pediatric labeling once FDA has completed its review of each drug). "Superior drug treatment information will permit quicker recoveries from childhood illnesses, with few attendant hospital stays and physician visits," FDA has stated. "These improved health outcomes should produce significant health care cost savings for the United States economy."

ORPHAN DRUG ACT

The Orphan Drug Act was passed to spur the development of "orphan drugs" to treat diseases that affect fewer than 200,000 patients. Ten to 20 million Americans suffer from about 5,000 orphan diseases for which there are no effective cures or treatments. The law was enacted temporarily in 1983 and reenacted periodically thereafter. It expired in 1994 and was made permanent in 1997. One difficulty in developing orphan products is that not many patients are available for clinical trials, and the patients who are available often live far apart.

To help these patients, the law provides two principal incentives to try to make it commercially feasible to develop orphan drugs:

- A seven-year period of market exclusivity following approval of an orphan drug by FDA.
- A 50 percent tax credit for certain clinical research expenses involved in developing an orphan product.

Although orphan exclusivity generally is regarded as the key incentive, there are certain issues that are often discussed. A 1997 study noted that the exclusivity applies only to the approved orphan indication.[3] Thus, one or more versions of the same drug may be approved for different indications, and these versions can then be prescribed off-label for the original orphan indication. In addition, any number of different drugs may be approved for an already approved orphan indication prior to the expiration of the seven-year exclusivity period.

Nevertheless, the law has been highly effective. Since the Orphan Drug Act was passed, more than 220 drugs and biological products for rare diseases have been brought to market.[4] In contrast, fewer than 10 such products came to market in the decade prior to 1983.[5]

The U.S. orphan drug program has influenced other countries. It served as the prototype for programs adopted in Japan in 1993and by the European Commission in 1998. In 1997, the Australian government announced that it would facilitate the approval of a drug for the same indication when the prevalence of the condition is no more than 1 per 5,000 following U.S. approval of the orphan drug.

In the last five years, FDA has approved 96 orphan drugs.[6]

Examples of conditions treated by orphan drugs include the following:

---

[3] Pharmacoeconomics, Sheila R. Shulman of the Tufts University Center for Drug Development and Michael Manocchia of the Health Institute of the New England Medical Center, September 1997.

[4] U.S. Food and Drug Administration, Office of Orphan Products Development, www.fda.gov/orphan.

[5] *Ibid.*

[6] *Ibid.*

- A genetic sucrase deficiency, a rare condition in which a patient's body lacks the enzymes necessary to properly digest and absorb table sugar and a type of starch from the gastrointestinal tract.
- Crohn's disease.
- Essential thrombocythemia, a life-threatening condition characterized by elevated blood-platelet counts.
- Hemophilia B, an inherited disorder that affects some 3,300 patients, most of whom are men, in the U.S.
- Homocystinuria, a rare genetic disorder affecting approximately 1,000 patients in the U.S.
- Interstitial cystitis, which causes a sharp pain in the pelvic area and the need to urinate 50 to 60 times a day.
- Malignant pleural effusions, an accumulation of fluid in the space between a layer lining the chest cavity and the membrane covering the lungs.
- Narcolepsy, a chronic neurological sleep disorder afflicting an estimated 125,000 Americans.
- Orthostatic hypotension, a drop in blood pressure when a person is standing.
- Pulmonary tuberculosis, a highly contagious lung infection.
- Transplant rejection prevention.
- Urea cycle disorders, which are characterized by the body's inability to process waste nitrogen and which affect fewer than 400 patients around the world.

PHARMACEUTICAL LIABILITY

State health-care liability systems have an impact on the R&D decisions made by pharmaceutical companies. Currently, health-care liability in the U.S. is governed by a patchwork of different laws in each state and separate rules in the federal court system. Cases heard in different jurisdictions may operate under different theories and standards for establishing a pharmaceutical manufacturer's liability.[7]

Under the current liability system, damage awards can vary widely and may or may not be commensurate with the severity of the injury or degree of liability. Two common provisions of state law are particularly troubling — punitive damages, and joint and several liability.

Punitive Damages: In most states, a pharmaceutical company can be held liable for huge punitive-damage awards even though all drugs must meet FDA's stringent approval standards. Punitive damages are intended to *punish* a defendant for acting *willfully, flagrantly, or maliciously,* for conduct that shocks the conscience of the community. Nonetheless, juries have held manufacturers responsible for punitive damages even though they have scrupulously followed FDA's requirements in developing and testing their products, provided all required warnings, reported patients' adverse reactions, and sought the approval from FDA to modify warnings when they learned of additional risks posed by a product. In Kansas, for example, punitive damages of $2.75 million were awarded for kidney damage allegedly

[7] Congress of the United States, Office of Technology Assessment, *Pharmaceutical R&D: Costs, Risks and Rewards*, 1993.

caused by an oral contraceptive, even though FDA had previously refused to allow a warning for that condition to be added to the product's labeling.[8] Currently, only eight states recognize a defense to punitive damages for products approved by FDA: Arizona, Colorado, Illinois, New Jersey, North Dakota, Ohio, Oregon, and Utah. In addition, four states do not allow claims for punitive damages: Massachusetts, Nebraska, New Hampshire, and Washington.

Joint and Several Liability: Another common provision in state laws is that all defendants in a product-liability case are jointly and severally liable for the damages. Under these provisions, it is possible for a manufacturer to pay most of the damages even if other parties in the litigation are found more at fault.

Experts have concluded that there is "evidence that the willingness of pharmaceutical firms to undertake research and development for new products has been adversely affected by product liability concerns."[9] Some areas of health care have been most affected by the fear of law-suits.[10] As a result of these concerns, products that could benefit large numbers of people may not be developed because a medicine might harm a small fraction of those who would use it.

Vaccines provide a dramatic example of the chilling effect liability concerns can have on investment decisions. Because vaccines are administered to large numbers of healthy people, adverse reactions are both more likely and less tolerated than reactions to therapeutic drugs. In the case of childhood vaccines, the potential for many decades of lost productivity results in greater lia-bility exposure than from products administered to adults.

Between 1966 and 1977, half of all private vaccine manufacturers stopped manufacturing and distributing vaccines. In 1986, the Vaccine Injury Compensation Program was created as a no-fault compensation system for children adversely affected by vaccines. Although lawsuits have decreased significantly under the program, manufacturers still have liability concerns because the program does not cover all vaccines.

General liability reforms that could serve to reduce uncertainties surrounding the drug-development process include:

- A uniform federal law to replace the current patchwork system of state laws.
- A government-standards defense to punitive damages for medicines approved by FDA as safe and effective.
- A system of proportionate liability, under which a defendant is responsible only for the damage it causes, instead of joint and several liability.
- Caps on non-economic damages, such as pain and suffering.
- A provision to allow defendants to inform a jury when plaintiffs receive payment from a third party for all or some of their medical expenses and lost wages.

---

[8] *Wooderson v. Ortho Pharmaceutical Co., 235 Kan. 387, 681 P.2nd 1038, cert. denied, 469 U.S. 965 (1984).*

[9] Huber, P., and Litan, R., *The Liability Maze: The Impact of Liability Law on Safety and Innovation,* 1991, p. 360.

[10] Institute of Medicine, *"Contraceptive Research and Development: Looking to the Future,"* 1996.

International Harmonization and Mutual Recognition Agreements

Drug regulators and representatives of the pharmaceutical industry from the United States, Europe, and Japan have been participating for 10 years in the International Conference on Harmonization (ICH). The purpose is to eliminate duplicative requirements for drug development and approval in the three regions, thus providing all patients with more timely access to new medicines. The most recent focus of ICH was the development of a Common Technical Document (CTD) that would form the basis for drug submission to regulatory authorities in the three regions. The CTD report was finalized at the fifth international meeting of the ICH on November 9-11, 2000.

In 1997, the United States and the European Union negotiated a pharmaceutical Mutual Recognition Agreement (MRA) with the intent of eliminating regulatory barriers and promoting trade between the two regions. Once the MRA is fully implemented, the regions will recognize each other's inspections of manufacturing facilities for human drugs and biologics in their respective regions. Previously, inspectors from each area had to inspect every factory where a drug imported into that area was manufactured. This wasted time and money, and often caused delays in the availability of medicines.

Chapter 16

PHARMACEUTICAL EXPENDITURES IN PERSPECTIVE

According to the Health Care Financing Administration (HCFA), total national health expenditures in 1999 amounted to $1.2 trillion — 13 percent of gross domestic product (GDP).[1] Total national health expenditures are projected to reach $1.3 trillion in 2000 — 13.1 percent of GDP.[2] The national health expenditures for 2001, as projected by HCFA, are expected to reach $1.4 trillion. The share of GDP allocated to health has nearly doubled over the past three decades, from 7.0 percent in 1970 to 12 percent in 1990.

Furthermore, the health-care dollar is spent on a number of key components, including hospital care ($0.32), physician and clinical services ($0.22), nursing homes ($.07), and prescription drugs ($.08).

The U.S. currently devotes a higher percentage of GDP to health expenditures than any other major industrialized country. Since 1980, the gap has widened between this country and other industrialized countries in the share of GDP allocated to health. However, the share of GDP devoted to pharmaceuticals in the U.S. is about average among major industrialized countries. Although these trends indicate rapidly growing health-care costs, they also indicate that pharmaceuticals are not the main driver of the increases.

IMS Health reports that, in 2000, drug expenditures increased 14.7 percent: 2.1 percent from increased prices, 3.9 percent from the mix of prescription products (new elements/new medicines) that were used, and 8.7 percent from increased usage of prescription medicines. These data also suggest that pharmaceutical expenditures do not contribute to higher than average health expenditures in the U.S.

Over time, expenditures on outpatient prescription drugs in the U.S. have varied. In 1960, 10 percent of national health-care expenditures was on prescription drugs. In the 1980s, 5.0 percent of health-care expenditures was for prescription drugs, and that figure steadily increased in the 1990s. In 1999, the percentage was 8.2 percent, or 1.07 percent of GDP.[3] It is estimated to be 8.6 percent in 2000 and projected to be 9.0 percent in 2001.

In relation to consumer spending on other items, expenditures on prescription drugs are relatively small. In 1999, Americans spent less per capita on prescription drugs ($358) than

---

Excepted from Pharmaceutical Research Association and related websites.

[1] Health Care Financing Administration, Office of the Actuary, National Health Statistics Group; U.S. Department of Commerce, Bureau of Economic Analysis; and U.S. Bureau of the Census.

[2] *Ibid.*

[3] *Ibid.*

they did on alcohol, tobacco, and admissions for entertainment ($413).[4] In terms of personal consumption, prescription drugs represent $1.19 a day compared to $8.69 for food and $3.75 for clothing.

CONTRIBUTING FACTORS TO RISING PRESCRIPTION DRUG COSTS

Spending for health care rose 8.3 percent in 2000 from a year earlier and was expected to reach $1.3 trillion in that year.[5] HCFA actuaries anticipate a slight decrease in spending of 7.7 percent in 2001, with a moderation in growth of 6.5 percent in 2010.[6] Health spending is expected to account for 15.9 percent of GDP by 2010, the result of more rapid growth in health spending and slightly slower GDP growth.

The increase in pharmaceutical spending can be attributed to several factors. The main reason is that more people are using new and better medicines. People are using more medicines to treat and prevent disease and improve their quality of life for obvious reasons. First, patients and physicians are better informed about the benefits of using medicines to prevent serious conditions and reduce the need for more costly treatments. People know that modern medicines can keep them healthy and independent, on the job and at home with their families instead of in a nursing home. Second, medicines are the least invasive — and most preferred — form of treatment for many diseases. In many cases, drug therapies have replaced more traditional treatments such as hospitalization and surgery. For example, hospital expenditures accounted for 37 percent of Medicare spending in 1999, down from 41 percent in 1993.

The least significant factor contributing to the increase in pharmaceutical spending is price increases. In 2000, price inflation was approximately one-fifth of the growth.[7]

The impact of higher prices on prescription-drug spending is actually less today than it has been during the past decade. From 1987 to 1994, about half of the 11.9 percent average annual rate of spending growth for pharmaceuticals reflected increased prices, while the other half was attributed to utilization growth. During 1994-1999, the growth rate remained in the double digits, but only about one-fifth was directly attributable to increased prices and the remaining 80 percent of increased drug spending was attributable to growth in utilization, including the use of newer medications.[8]

These new medicines have enabled patients to live longer, healthier, and more productive lives, as exemplified by the falling disability rates among the elderly and declining death rates from heart disease, cancer, and many other diseases.

---

[4] Uwe E. Reinhardt, Ph.D., "The Market for Prescription Drugs: Waking Up the Demand Side," presented to the Council on the Economic Impact of Health System Change, Washington, D.C., March 28, 2001.

[5] Health Care Financing Administration, Office of the Actuary, National Health Statistics Group; U.S. Department of Commerce, Bureau of Economic Analysis; and U.S. Census Bureau.

[6] *Ibid.*

[7] *IMS Health, Pharmaceutical Pricing Update*, 2001.

[8] R.W. Dubois et al., "Explaining Drug Spending Trends: Does Perception Match Reality?" *Health Affairs* (Mar/Apr 2000): 231-239.

The Cost-Effectiveness of Pharmaceuticals

The use of prescription medicines has proven to be one of the most cost-effective forms of medical therapy. Surgery, hospitalization, physician visits, and nursing care are typically time-consuming and expensive. Prescription-drug therapy, however, often eliminates the need for these costly interventions. Recent examples of the cost-effectiveness of prescription drugs include:

AIDS:

- During the 16 months after the introduction of antiretroviral therapy for HIV, a 43 percent drop occurred in hospital inpatient care as reported by a recent study published in *The New England Journal of Medicine.* According to Samuel A. Bozzette, a physician with the Veterans Affairs San Diego Healthcare System who headed the study, "The drugs are almost a perfect substitute for hospital care. We can afford them because, in fact, we are already spending the money on HIV care" in the form of hospitalization.[9]
- Protease "cocktail" therapies found to lower hospital costs. Data from medical centers that treat large numbers of AIDS-infected patients indicate that protease "cocktail" therapies for AIDS might generate long-term savings, enabling many to return to work and reducing the need for hospitalization. Nine months after the introduction of the therapies, use of expensive in-patient health services by AIDS patients appeared to be declining. The combination therapies cost approximately $16,000 a year per patient; a federal study estimated that, before the therapies were available, AIDS patients generated $100,000 a year in hospital costs.[10]
- Full access to new AIDS drugs helped realize a net savings of $18 million. According to a study presented at the 12th World AIDS Conference in 1998, the Department of Veterans Affairs found that providing patients full access to new AIDS drugs helped to realize a savings of $18 million in AIDS treatment costs in 1997.[11]

Migraines:

- **New drug for migraines lowering the total cost of care.** A study published in the *American Journal of Managed Care* shows that a new drug for migraine headaches is lowering the total cost of caring for patients with this disease. Although drug expenditures for patients in the study increased, the total costs of treating these patients for migraine headaches declined 41 percent as a result of treatment with the new drug.[12] Another study showed that the drug lowered labor costs and reduced employees' lost productivity due to migraines. The benefit to

---

[9] "Providing Antiretroviral Therapy for HIV Infection," *The New England Journal of Medicine*, Vol. 344, No. 11, March 15, 2001.

[10] Michael Waldholz, "But Success in Many Others is Cutting Hospital Costs," *The Wall Street Journal*, October 10, 1996.

[11] Abid Rahman *et al.*, "Inversion of Inpatient/Outpatient HIV Service Utilization: Impact of Improved Therapies, Clinician Education and Case Management in the U.S. Department of Veterans Affairs," AIDS Service Department of Veterans Affairs, International Conference on AIDS, July 1998.

[12] Legg, R.F., et al., "Cost-Effectiveness of Sumatriptan in a Managed Care Population," *The American Journal of Managed Care*, Vol. 3, No. 1, January 1997.

employers of this reduction in lost productivity was valued at $435 per month per employee. In contrast, the cost of the drug was $43.78 per month. The benefit-to-cost ratio was 10 to 1.[13]

Asthma:

- **For asthma patients, increased drug spending kept patients out of the hospital.** A program for Medicaid asthma patients resulted in an average 42 percent decline in the rate of emergency room and urgent hospital visits. In a little more than one year after the program was implemented, it saved Medicaid about $285,000 in Virginia. Had the program been in effect throughout the state — rather than in just seven counties — it is estimated that the savings could have topped $2 million.[14]
- Total health-care costs reduced nearly 25 percent and hospitalization rates dropped by 50 percent for asthma patients using new inhaled corticosteroid therapy. A study that reviewed patient records in the North Carolina Medicaid program for one year before and one year after the introduction of inhaled corticosteroid therapy found that, for those patients using the inhaled steroid therapy for asthma, there was a 50 percent decrease in hospitalization rates and a 26 percent decrease in outpatient visits. The comparison group had a 23 percent increase in hospitalization rates and a 36 percent increase in outpatient visits. According to a cost analysis, use of the inhaled corticosteroid therapy reduced total health-care costs by 24 percent per asthma patient per month.[15]
- Hospitalization rates for children with asthma significantly decreased with the addition of ipratropium bromide to albuterol and corticosteroid therapy. A study of children between the ages of 2 and 18 with an acute exacerbation of asthma found that, when treated with ipratropium bromide in combination with albuterol and corticosteroid therapy, they experienced a significant decrease in hospitalization. Since the average per-child cost of hospitalization at the hospital where the study was conducted was $3,267, and the cost of the drug was $3 per 500-µg dose, the savings were substantial.[16]

Cancer:

- **Growth colony stimulating factor treatment saves $30,000 per patient in hospitalization costs for bone-marrow transplants.** A study of cancer patients whose immune systems were weakened by high-dose chemotherapy found that they were helped by a pharmaceutical known as colony-stimulating factor. The

---

[13] Legg, R.F., et al., "Cost Benefit of Sumatriptan to an Employer," *Journal of Occupational and Environmental Medicine*, Vol. 39, No. 7, July 1997.

[14] Results from the Virginia Health Outcomes Partnership Program for Medicaid Patients.

[15] R. Balkrishnan MS (Pharm), *et al.*, "Outcomes and Cost Benefits Associated With the Introduction of Inhaled Corticosteroid Therapy in a Medicaid Population of Asthmatic Patients," *Clinical Therapeutics*, Vol. 20, No. 3, 1998.

[16] Faiqa Qureshi, M.D., *et al.*, "Effect of Nebulized Ipratropium on the Hospitalization Rates of Children With Asthma," *The New England Journal of Medicine*, Vol. 339, No. 15, October 8, 1998.

treatment saved $30,000 per patient in hospitalization costs for bone-marrow transplants.[17]

Cardiovascular Disease:

- Use of ACE inhibitor drugs for patients with congestive heart failure helped avoid $9,000 in hospital costs per patient over a three-year period. A study published in the *The New England Journal of Medicine* showed that patients on ACE inhibitors avoided nearly $9,000 each in hospitalization costs over a three-year period — and that the drugs reduced deaths by 16 percent. The potential savings for Americans with heart failure amounts to $2 billion a year.[18]
- A beta blocker used to treat high blood pressure and congestive heart failure was found to sharply reduce hospital admissions. A recent study of patients' severely weakened hearts due to heart failure found that use of the drug carvedilol, a beta blocker, not only reduced death rates by 35 percent compared with patients given a placebo, it also sharply reduced hospital admissions, hospital stays, and the use of tests and procedures in the hospital.[19]
- Disease-management program achieves net savings of $9.3 million for 1,100 patients with congestive heart failure. In a year-long disease-management program for about 1,100 patients with congestive heart failure run by Humana Hospitals, pharmacy costs increased by 60 percent, while hospital costs declined by 78 percent. The net savings were $9.3 million.[20]
- Cholesterol-lowering drug shown to increase life expectancy and save costs. Use of a cholesterol-lowering drug in patients with angina or who have had a heart attack increases life expectancy in men and women of various ages and varying cholesterol levels, according to a Scandinavian study. The researchers analyzed the direct costs saved by this therapy for people of different ages and cholesterol levels. They found that savings ranged from $3,800 per year of life for 70-year-old men with cholesterol levels over 300, to $27,400 per year of life for 35-year-old women with cholesterol levels in the lower 200s.[21]
- Use of a new cardiovascular drug reduced hospitalizations and led to a reduction in overall health-care costs. A study analyzing the effects of simvastation, a pill that lowers cholesterol, was found to reduce hospital admissions by a third during five years of treatment. It also reduced the number of days that patients had to spend in the hospital when they were admitted, and reduced the need for bypass surgery and angioplasty. Dr. Sanford Schwartz, a physician and economist at the University of Pennsylvania, stated, "This is both good medicine

[17] Peters, W.P., "Comparative Effects of Granulocyte-Macrophage Colony-Stimulating Factor (GM-CSF) and Granulocyte Colony-Stimulating Factor (G-CSF) on Priming Peripheral Blood Progenitor Cells For Use With Autologous Bone Marrow After High-Dose Chemotherapy," *Blood*, Vol. 81, No. 7, pp. 1709-19, April 1, 1993.

[18] The SOLVD Investigators, "Effect of Enalapril on Survival With Reduced Left Ventricular Ejection Fractions and Congestive Heart Failure," *The New England Journal of Medicine*, Vol. 325, No. 5, pp. 293-302, 1991.

[19] Ron Winslow, "GlaxoSmithKline's Coreg Benefits Heart Patients in Two Big Studies," *The Wall Street Journal*, March 21, 2001.

[20] "Provide Education About Congestive Heart Failure and Pump Up Your Savings," *Managed Healthcare*, April 1998, Vol. 8, No. 4, pp. 42-44.

[21] Johannesson, M., Johnson, B., *et al.*, "Cost Effectiveness of Simvastation Treatment to Lower Cholesterol Levels in Patients with Coronary Heart Disease," *New England Journal of Medicine*, Vol. 336, pp. 332-336, 1997.

and good economics." Dr. Schwartz said the treatment was highly "cost-effective" compared with other widely accepted therapies and tests.[22]

Mental Health:

- **Cost-effectiveness of prescription drugs highlighted by a decline in the aggregate price of treating acute major depression.** Researchers at the National Bureau of Economic Research examined the overall costs of treating heart attacks and depression. The researchers found that the cost of treating major depression in the U.S. fell by 25 percent during 1991-1995. This trend highlights the cost-effectiveness of prescription drugs.[23]
- **Overall health-care costs dropped with the use of new treatments for schizophrenia.** A study examining the costs of schizophrenia to a state Medicaid program, including pharmacy, medical, hospital, and outpatient mental-health claims over a five-year period, revealed that total cost per patient was $2,458 lower for the group treated with new antipsychotic medications.[24] Another study, which examined the employment rates of schizophrenia patients using a new antipsychotic medication, found that employment rates doubled with its use.[25]

Organ Transplants:

- **Immunosuppressive drug was found to shorten average hospital stays and reduce hospitalization after kidney transplants.** Immunosuppressive drugs have dramatically improved the success rate of organ-transplant surgery by preventing patients' immune systems from destroying the new tissue. One of these drugs was found to shorten average hospital stays by as much as 10 days and reduce hospitalization after kidney transplants. The cost for postoperative hospitalization may be nearly $10,000 less for patients treated with the immunosuppressive drug.[26]

Stroke:

- **Clot-busting drug nets an average savings of $4,400 per patient per year.** A study sponsored by NIH found that treating stroke patients promptly with a clot-busting drug nets an average savings of $4,400 per patient per year by reducing the need for hospitalization, rehabilitation, and nursing-home care. According to NIH, use of this medicine could save the health-care system more than $100 million per year.[27]
- **Use of a blood-thinning drug would prevent 40,000 strokes a year and save the health-care system $600 million per year.** A study by the Agency for Healthcare Research and Quality concluded that increased use of a blood-

---

[22] "Cholesterol Pill Linked to Lower Hospital Costs," *The New York Times*, March 27, 1995.
[23] Frank, R.G., *et al.*, "Price Indexes for the Treatment of Depression," American Enterprise Institute/Brookings Institution, December 1997.
[24] *Psychopharmacol Bull* 34:373, 1998.
[25] *Journal of Clinical Psychiatry* 59:23, 1998.
[26] Showstack, J., *et al.*, "The Effect of Cyclosporine on the Use of Hospital Resources for Kidney Transplantation," *The New England Journal of Medicine*, Vol. 321, No. 16, 1989.
[27] S.C. Fagan, *et al.*, "Cost-effectiveness of Tissue Plasminogen Activator for Acute Ischemic Stroke," *Neurology*, Vol. 50, pp. 883-889, 1998.

thinning drug would prevent 40,000 strokes annually, saving $600 million a year. The lifetime cost of a stroke for a single patient exceeds $100,000, while the average annual cost of treatment with the blood-thinning drug, including monitoring, is $1,025.[28]

Vaccines:

- **Routine annual influenza vaccination of all working adults could save the nation as much as $1.3 billion each year.** Traditionally, only high-risk groups such as the elderly have been targeted for vaccination. According to a recent study by the Department of Veterans Affairs, average health costs would be reduced $13.66 per person vaccinated if all of the nation's 94 million full-time workers, ages 18 to 64, also received the vaccination. These savings would total $14 million annually. Among the general, non-elderly population, the flu causes up to 75 million lost workdays and 22 million doctors' visits each year. Half of the flu cases result in a visit to a primary-care physician. Lead author of the study, Kristin L. Nichol, M.D., M.P.H., M.B.A., of the Center for Chronic Disease Outcomes Research at the VA Medical Center in Minneapolis, stated, "The results show that substantial health and economic benefits could be realized from vaccinating all working adults against influenza, especially when immunization takes place at the work site or another site that would be efficient and low-cost.[29]
- **Routine chicken pox vaccination program could save an estimated $391 million.** A 1994 study published in the *Journal of the American Medical Association* estimated that a routine chicken pox vaccination program in the U.S. would save $391 million annually in work-loss costs. Work-loss costs include the value of work missed by adults with chicken pox and the value of work parents miss when their children are sick.

Cystic Fibrosis:

- **Cystic fibrosis treatment reduces risk of infection, which often leads to more costly hospitalization.** Bronchial-mucolytic therapy for cystic fibrosis, when used in conjunction with standard therapies, was proven in clinical trials to reduce the risk of respiratory-tract infections requiring IV antibiotic therapy by 27 percent, reducing costly hospitalizations and other related medical costs.[30]

---

[28] Matchar DB, Samsa GP, Secondary and Tertiary Prevention of Stroke, Patient Outcomes Research Team (PORT) Final Report - Phase 1, AHRQ Pub. No. 00-N001, Rockville, MD: Agency for Healthcare Research and Quality, June 2000.

[29] Kristin L. Nichol, MD, MPH, MBA, "Cost-Benefit Analysis of a Strategy to Vaccinate Healthy Working Adults Against Influenza," *The Archives of Internal Medicine*, Vol. 161, March 12, 2001.

[30] Cystic Fibrosis Foundation, "Rationale for the Use of Human Deoxyribonuclease 1 (rhDNase-Pulmozyme) in Patients with Cystic Fibrosis," *Consensus Conferences*, Volume IV, Section 1, September 22, 1993.

From the Manufacturer to the Patient

The cost-effectiveness of prescription drugs — combined with a steady stream of new-product introductions — has contributed to healthy industry growth. In 1997, sales amounted to $1.1 billion. Sales by research-based pharmaceutical companies were projected to reach $164.7 billion in 2000, an 8.2 percent increase from $153.3 billion in 1999. Sales within the United States by both U.S.-owned and foreign-owned research-based companies accounted for $112.0 billion of the total in 2000. Sales abroad by U.S.-owned companies accounted for the remaining $52.6 billion.

In 2000, manufacturers' net U.S. sales of human-use prescription pharmaceuticals amounted to $21.8 billion and were dominated by eight major product classes. In 1999, the largest class, representing 23.3 percent of manufacturers' U.S. sales, was pharmaceuticals affecting neoplasms (cancers), endocrine system, and other metabolic diseases. Over the same period, products acting on the digestive or genito-urinary system generated 4.2 percent of sales. Cardiovascular drugs accounted for 14.3 percent of sales. Sales of anti-infective drugs totaled 14.2 percent of the market. Sales of pharmaceuticals acting on the central nervous system amounted to 22.7 percent of the U.S. market. Vitamins and nutrients accounted for 0.6 percent of the market. Smaller classes included respiratory products with 4.4 percent of the market and dermatological products with 0.6 percent.

Pharmaceutical manufacturers' sales are mainly to large drug wholesalers. Wholesalers, in turn, distribute the products to retail pharmacies, hospitals, HMOs, clinics, mail-order companies, and other organizations that fill prescriptions. In 1999, 79.5 percent of sales of human-use ethical pharmaceuticals flowed through wholesalers, up from 78.4 percent in 1997, 71.8 percent in 1990, and 57.3 percent in 1980.

In 1999, the retail sector — including independent, chain, food store, and mass-merchandise pharmacies — dispensed more than 2.8 billion prescriptions, according to IMS Health. In terms of dollar sales, retail channels account for over 63.8 percent of dispensed prescription sales in the U.S. Sales by hospital pharmacies account for 11.5 percent of the market; mail-order pharmacies comprise 12.1 percent; clinics 7.0 percent; long-term care pharmacies 3.1 percent; home health-care 1.1 percent; and staff-model HMOs 1.0 percent.

Compliance with Medication Regimens

Unless patients take their medicines according to physicians' instructions and systems are in place to guard against adverse drug interactions, prescription drugs may not be used cost-effectively. It is estimated that only about half of prescribed medications are taken correctly.

Noncompliance is a costly problem — for employers, insurers, the health-care system, and, of course, patients. The National Pharmaceutical Council (NPC), an industry research organization, estimates that noncompliance costs more than $100 billion a year, due to increased hospital admissions, nursing-home admissions, lost productivity, and premature deaths.[31] Noncompliance results in more hospital admissions, emergency-room care, physician visits, and, occasionally, surgery. There are also serious personal consequences. For example, failure to take contraceptives can lead to unwanted pregnancies, failure to take

[31] National Pharmaceutical Council, *Noncompliance with Medication Regimens: An Economic Tragedy*, June 1992.

estrogen-replacement medication can cause osteoporosis, and failure to take hypertension medicine can result in heart attacks or strokes.

Compliance rates vary with the disease and setting of the patient group. According to data reported in the *Journal of Clinical Pharmacy and Therapeutics*, patients in homes for the aged had relatively high rates of compliance, as did patients in the first year of antihypertensive treatment. In contrast, patients taking penicillin for rheumatic fever had relatively low rates of compliance.

The National Council on Patient Information & Education (NCPIE) divides noncompliance into two categories: acts of omission and acts of commission. Acts of omission include never filling a prescription; taking less than a prescribed dosage; taking a medicine less frequently than prescribed; taking medicine "holidays"; and stopping a regimen too soon. Acts of commission include overuse; sharing medicines; and consuming food, drink, or other medicines that can interact with a prescribed drug.

One way to improve compliance is to provide patients with easy-to-understand information about their medicines. As a result of voluntary, private-sector programs, more than 60 percent of patients now receive written information about their medicines with their prescriptions. This percentage increases every year.

Chapter 17

The Growth of Managed Care*

Managed care had 165.4 million members in 2000.[1] Although the nature of drug coverage varies, generally 95 percent of people enrolled in HMOs receive prescription-drug benefits.[2]

Almost 80 percent of employed Americans are now covered by either an HMO, a preferred provider organization, or a point-of-service plan — all examples of managed health care. Point-of-service plans — in which enrollees can choose to receive services out of the managed-care network and still be reimbursed for a portion of the costs — are responsible for much of the growth in managed-care plans among employed Americans. In 1992, point-of-service plans covered only 5 percent of insured workers; their share had jumped to nearly 20 percent by 1996.

Managed-Care Cost-Containment Techniques

Managed-care organizations frequently use a variety of cost-containment techniques specifically for pharmaceutical expenditures. The resulting effects on total health-care costs and quality of patient care, however, are not always adequately assessed.

About 90 percent of HMOs now use formularies. A formulary is a list of prescription drugs approved for insurance coverage. Drugs are selected principally on the bases of therapeutic value, side effects, and cost. Formularies range in restrictiveness from "open," under which both listed and non-listed drugs are reimbursed, to "closed," under which only listed drugs are reimbursed. In 1998, an estimated 48.4 percent of HMOs used closed formularies, up from 38.1 percent in 1997.[3] Closed formularies may deny coverage for newer, more expensive, or experimental drugs regardless of their effectiveness.

A study published in the March 1996 issue of *The American Journal of Managed Care* found that overly restrictive formularies used by managed-care organizations often have unintended consequences. The researchers looked at six HMOs in various parts of the U.S., all of which used formularies with varying degrees of restrictiveness. The study focused on

---

* Excepted from Pharmaceutical Research Association and related websites.

1 Managed Care National Statistics, Managed Care Fact Sheets, www.mcareol.com.

2 American Association of Health Plans, 1999.

3 Hoechst Marion Roussel Managed Care Digest, *HMO-PPO/Medicaid Digest*, 1999.

patients with asthma, ear infections, arthritis, ulcers, and high blood pressure — diseases usually treated with prescription drugs. The researchers found that restrictive formularies increased patients' use of other medical services. In general, the greater the limitation on physicians' use of medicines, the more patients used physicians, emergency rooms, and hospitals — all of which cost more than prescription drugs.[4]

In addition to formularies, HMOs also use a number of other techniques to limit expenditures on prescription drugs.

- **Therapeutic Interchange:** This practice involves the dispensing of a different drug having a different chemical composition than the one prescribed — usually, but not always, in the same therapeutic class. In some circumstances, pharmacists make this substitution without the knowledge of the prescribing physician. About 40.2 percent of HMOs now use therapeutic interchange, up from 22 percent in 1990.
- **Step-Care Therapy:** Step-care therapy requires that physicians follow a sequence of treatments for a given condition, usually starting with the lowest-cost treatment and progressing to higher-cost treatments only if previous treatments are not effective. Patients may be denied immediate treatment with the most effective medicines and suffer a delayed recovery as a result. The percentage of HMOs using step-care therapy increased from 35 percent in 1996 to 68.5 percent in 1998.
- **Drug Utilization Review (DUR):** DUR programs involve retrospective monitoring of physicians' prescribing patterns. Historically, they have been used to ensure the appropriate, safe, and effective use of prescription drugs. More than 90 percent of HMOs now require DUR. Intense cost pressures in the managed-care environment, however, threaten to change the focus of DUR programs from quality and patient safety to cost savings.
- **Generic Substitution:** The percentage of HMOs requiring generic substitution, where a brand-name drug is replaced with a generic copy, increased from 63 percent in 1984 to 72.4 percent in 1998. Switching patients from a brand-name to a generic copy can cause problems, particularly with illnesses such as heart failure, cancer, diabetes, and seizure disorder that are treated with drugs that have a narrow therapeutic index. This means there is a narrow dosage range between an ineffective amount of a drug, a safe and effective amount, and an amount where the risks of the drug begin to exceed its benefits.

The more widespread use of cost-containment techniques in managed-care organizations is especially significant given their increasing share of total prescription-drug payments. According to IMS Health, third-party sources — including Medicaid, HMOs, and other insurance plans — paid for 82 percent of all retail outpatient prescription drugs in 1999, up from 37 percent in 1990. While the proportion of prescriptions paid by Medicaid has remained stable, the proportion paid by private third parties has more than doubled since 1990.

---

[4] Horn, S.D., Sharkey, P.D., Tracy, D.M., et al., "Intended and Unintended Consequences of HMO Cost-Containment Strategies: Results from the Managed Care Outcomes Project," *The American Journal of Managed Care*, Vol. II, No. 3, March 1996, pp. 253-264.

The increasing trend toward managing drug benefits has spawned specialized companies called pharmacy benefit managers (PBMs). Virtually nonexistent until the late 1980s, these companies evolved from insurance-claims processing and mail-order prescription companies. PBMs now provide managed-pharmacy benefits for approximately half of the insured population in the United States. PBMs manage pharmaceutical care only, marketing their services to employers, insurance companies, managed-care groups, and Medicaid. There are approximately 40 PBMs in the United States today, although the top five companies account for more than 75 percent of the market.[5]

Disease Management

Some managed-care organizations have found that disease-management programs are a good way to control costs while improving health outcomes. These programs attempt to improve care by integrating various treatment components. Most disease-management programs focus on chronic diseases, which account for 60 percent of U.S. medical costs.[6]

Under a typical program, a single health-care provider will be responsible for the entire range of services needed by a patient. Such a program will usually try to monitor and coordinate physician-office visits, hospitalization, emergency-room visits, medical tests, the use of supplies, and patient compliance through the use of an integrated information system.

Additional measures such as treatment guidelines, health-outcomes studies, and patient-education programs further systematize the provision of care.

Employers are also involved in disease-management programs. The use of chronic-disease-management programs jumped sharply in 1999, with 58 percent of the largest employers' health plans participating. This is up from 49 percent in 1998. In addition, growing numbers are adding coverage for alternative medicine.[7]

Early intervention and prevention techniques — including proper use of physician-education programs aimed at earlier identification and appropriate specialist referral — could save substantial health-care costs, according to an analysis by The Boston Consulting Group. Conditions that are the focus of disease-state-management programs include asthma, diabetes, gastrointestinal disorders, high cholesterol, allergies, hypertension, depression, and arthritis.[8]

Shorter Exclusivity Periods

The pharmaceutical market also is characterized by increasing competition between brand-name drugs, as demonstrated by the shrinking time during which the drug in a therapeutic class is the sole drug in that class. For example, Tagamet®, an ulcer drug introduced in 1977, had an exclusivity period of six years before another drug in the same class, Zantac®, was introduced. In contrast, Recombinate®, a genetically engineered clotting factor for hemophilia introduced in 1992, had less than one year of exclusivity before the

---

[5] Congress of the United States, General Accounting Office, *Pharmacy Benefit Managers: Early Results on Ventures with Drug Manufacturers*, November 1995.

[6] Peter T. Kilborn, "Managers of Care, Not of Costs," *The New York Times*, December 7, 1998.

[7] Mercer/Foster Higgins National Survey of Employer-Sponsored Health Plans, 1999.

introduction of a competitor product, Kogenate®. Invirase®, the first of a new class of anti-viral drugs known as protease inhibitors, was on the market only three months before a second protease inhibitor, Norvir®, was approved.

During the 1980s, the profitable lifetime for drugs — the time companies have to recoup development costs and build reserves for future drug development — was greatly shortened. This is due to passage of the Drug Price Competition and Patent Term Restoration Act of 1984, which allowed quick approval of generic copies of brand-name drugs. Although this law increased the time between FDA approval of a drug and patent expiration, it virtually eliminated the period between patent expiration and the entry of generic competitors into the market. The effect has been to reduce to less than 12 years the time available for research-based drug companies to recoup their R&D investments.[9] Increasing emphasis on generic substitution by managed-care organizations has led to more rapid market share erosion for originator products once their patents expire. For originator drugs first facing generic competition in the 1989-1990 period, generics gained 47 percent of the market after 18 months. For products whose patents expired in the 1991-1992 period, generic competition claimed 72 percent of prescriptions after 18 months.[10]

Competition from Generic Drugs

Over the past decade, generic drugs have more than doubled their share of the prescription market — from 18.6 percent at the end of 1984 to 47 percent in 2000. The large number of innovator products due to lose patent protection over the next 10 years will foster robust growth in the generics industry. Although some brand-name companies own and operate generic subsidiaries, the commodity nature of the generic-drug business does not sustain R&D programs. Funds available for R&D depend on the ability of companies to discover, patent, and bring to market a steady stream of innovative products.

Strategic Alliances

Companies have responded to shorter product-life cycles, cost-containment pressures, and research opportunities by increasingly forming strategic alliances. The total number of such alliances grew from 121 in 1986 to 712 in 1998. These alliances are diverse in nature and may involve domestic and foreign pharmaceutical companies, biotech firms, university research centers, contract research organizations, and other parties. Strategic alliances often allow pharmaceutical companies to draw upon others' research expertise, bring products to market more rapidly, and more effectively commercialize products after approval by FDA. For example, a biotech firm developing a new product may form a strategic alliance with a larger pharmaceutical company to gain venture capital, obtain regulatory expertise, or establish market presence.

---

[8] The Boston Consulting Group, *The Contribution of Pharmaceutical Companies: What's at Stake for America*, September 1993.

[9] The Boston Consulting Group, *Sustaining Innovation in U.S. Pharmaceuticals*, January 1996.

[10] Grabowski, H., and Vernon, J., "Longer Patents for Increased Generic Competition: The Waxman-Hatch Act After One Decade," working paper, June 1995.

MERGERS AND ACQUISITIONS

Since the mid-1980s, the pharmaceutical industry has been characterized by larger and more frequent acquisitions and mergers. These structural changes, combined with economic pressures, have dramatically slowed employment growth in the industry. According to the Bureau of Labor Statistics, annual employment growth in the industry averaged a healthy 2.9 percent during 1983-1993. Since 1993, when it peaked at 264,400, pharmaceutical employment declined to an estimated 260,300 in 1997.

INDEX

D

E

Q

R